Africa South of the Sahara
Continued Failure or Delayed Success?

Africa South of the Sahara

Continued Failure or Delayed Success?

by

Charles Pasternak

published on behalf of
Oxford International Biomedical Centre

ISBN: 978-1-909075-59-7

Typeset in Garamond
Printed and bound in the UK
by CPI Group (UK) Ltd, Croydon, CR0 4YY

Dedicated to the peoples of sub-Saharan Africa whose ancestors have suffered at the hands of slave traders, colonists and corrupt dictators. May they prosper in the years ahead.

Also by Charles Pasternak

Blinkers: Scientific Ignorance and Evasion (2012)
Quest: The Essence of Humanity (2003; paperback 2004)
The Molecules Within Us:
Our Body in Health and Disease (1998)
Introduction to Human Biochemistry (1979)
The Biochemistry of Differentiation (1970)

Books edited by Charles Pasternak include:
Access Not Excess: The Search for Better Nutrition (2011)
What Makes Us Human? (2007)

CONTENTS

Tables and Figures

Figure 3.1 adapted from from Herrnstein and Murray, *The Bell Curve. Intelligence and Class Structure in American Life* (1994) p 121 All other figures adapted from Oliver, Roland: *The African Experience* (Weidenfeld & Nicolson, London, 1991).

Acknowledgements

I am grateful to George Ayittey, Haruko Fukuda, John Iliffe, Tim Jeal, David King, GianLudovico de Martino, John Meakin, Len Newton, Aridea Fezzi Price, Terence Ryan, Tira Shubart, Eldred Smith-Gordon and Susan Williams for helpful comments. I am indebted to the staff of the London Library for their efficient service, to Kasia Lewis, Director of the Oxford International Biomedical Centre, for office facilities, to Camilla and GianLudovico de Martino di Montegiordano for tranquillity at their palazzo in Amantea, Calabria and to Tony Gray of WORDS BY DESIGN for bringing this book to fruition.

Prelude: A Taste of Africa

This book is about Africa south of the Sahara. It is this region of the continent – 'black Africa' – that people associate with failure. Several reasons have been advanced over the years. The first is that its indigenous inhabitants are somehow intellectually less able than those from North Africa or elsewhere. The purported evidence for this is flawed in all respects. The second is that the climate of tropical Africa has held the region back. This is undoubtedly true, especially in regard to agriculture and the health of the people. Nevertheless five hundred years ago kingdoms south of the Sahara were the match of some in the northern hemisphere. Only since then have they failed so conspicuously in comparison. The slave trade and ensuing colonization have obviously been critical, though I consider their significance to be less than often thought. Failure continued to beset sub-Saharan Africa: independence did not bring prosperity. Indeed there are those who consider continued failure to be the hall mark of the region. I do not agree and will show that at least *some* of the nations have begun to turn failure into success, as suggested in the second part of the title. This book, then, is a reality check on some widely-held beliefs.

My first visit to the African continent was not, in fact, to any country south of the Sahara, but merely across the Straits of Gibraltar. I had traversed these a few times during my military service on the Rock in 1954 (as if those stern words describe peace-time soldiering on the shores of the Mediterranean). Once I accompanied a British services rugby team playing a French one in Tangier and another time a group of us visited a colleague's father who was the British Consul-General there. But Tangier is not really Africa. It is no more typical of that continent than Gibraltar is of Europe. It was not until the following year that I first visited Africa proper, and then only the northern country of Morocco. But it proved to be an enthralling experience that in subsequent years would draw me to the very heart of Africa south of the Sahara. I had been truly hooked by the continent that gave birth to the human race.

Why did I cross the Straits of Gibraltar again in 1955? I was back at Oxford working on my doctorate. A group of Oxford students were embarking on an expedition to survey the fauna and flora of the Atlas mountains: to compare the varieties found on the northern slopes with those on the southern. The former may have been driven south by successive ice ages, the latter might have become established during the wet season in the Sahara that started around ten thousand years ago, before it began to revert to desert again some three thousand years later. I was invited to join them.[1] The fauna I was interested in were human. No one really knew the origin of the Berbers who inhabit these parts (they're still not sure). There are some similarities with the Basques in the Pyrenees, and some with Semitic people of Arabia. But though there has been much genetic mixing between Arab and Berber since the Muslim conquest of North Africa thirteen centuries before, the languages have remained distinct, and the Berber in the mountainous region of southern Morocco is fiercely defensive of his own heritage

At that time the presence in the blood of aberrant haemoglobins, such as haemoglobin S (sickle cell) instead of normal haemoglobin A, was proving to be characteristic of certain populations. Might some of the Berbers in Morocco harbour an abnormal haemoglobin? Only a pin-prick of blood would be required, and analysis could be carried out by a technique known as paper electrophoresis. This required a simple apparatus, together with a 12-volt battery, that could be transported relatively easily. Apart from such scientific preparations, I needed to organise access to as large a group of Berbers as possible, and the services of an interpreter. The first was arranged through diplomatic channels. The Pasha of Marrakech and friend of Winston Churchill, T'hami El Glaoui, Lord of the Atlas, owned several forts or *kasbahs* in the mountains. His Khalifa at the Kasbah of Telouet would ensure that a suitable number of his people were ready to volunteer their blood. An interpreter, fluent in Arabic, Berber and French, would be available for me to pick up in Fez on my way to the Atlas. The 'diplomatic channels' suggested that I might be able to help the British government to up-date its knowledge of roads and bridges in southern Spain (I was planning to spend a short time in Andalusia before crossing to Africa) and in Morocco. Thus began a second career of part-time spy. Since this was without remuneration, I set off by the cheapest route, travelling across France and Spain by train.

I had some difficulty at the Spanish border in Irun. The customs official was more than intrigued by my apparatus and the 12-volt battery. He was unconvinced that these were for medical research and would be used only in French Morocco (Spain at that time still controlled the north of Morocco as a protectorate). He also seemed to be concerned that I might be planning a potential anti-Franco attack in Spain itself. Eventually my protestations of good intentions and a brief summary of the benefits to mankind of medical knowledge about the ingredients of red blood cells started to bore him and he allowed me to continue my journey south. Clearly he was unaware of my new vocation. He need not have worried. Near every road bridge across which I travelled in a friend's car after reaching Algeciras stood a Guardia Civil, a rifle slung across his shoulder. In Morocco my mission was equally unsuccessful. No Guardias Civil, but it is difficult to judge the width and method of construction of a bridge when you are travelling in a crowded bus, wedged between a malodorous lady with a live chicken on her lap and an obese Arab gentleman counting his prayer beads.

In Fez I stayed in the cheapest hotel I could find (remember the unpaid nature of my assignment), where the only available water for one's ablutions was in a communal trough outside the back door. Never mind, at least I was savouring the true Africa. I found Mohammed, my interpreter, and we set off for Marrakesh. Sitting in the Jamaa el Fna at dusk, savouring a glass of wine with my supper, I could not understand his urging to return to our lodging because of a *couvre-feu* at 7 pm (which in my pitiful French I mistook for 'firework'). '*Comme c'est jolie*', I said, '*J'adore les couvres feu*'. Mohammed obviously thought he had acquired an unhinged patron, until the penny finally dropped and I realised it was time to leave the square. Suddenly French police with sub-machine guns were in evidence and we hurried off. It began to dawn on me that the indifference to French authority enjoyed by El Glaoui might be coming to an end. This was confirmed when we finally arrived at the Kasbah of Telouet.

'I have the agreement of Pasha El Glaoui to do my scientific work among his people' I announced, waving a piece of paper at the official who confronted us. 'The Pasha is no longer in charge. You must have the permission of the French authorities in Rabat' he replied. 'It is possible that they may allow you to do this work in a hospital, but certainly not here in the field'. Since there was evidently no need for an Arabic and Berber-speaking interpreter if I was to work in a French hospital, I reluctantly dismissed Mohammed and we went our separate ways: he back to Fez, and I to Rabat. On the way I stopped off at the mountain village of Idirh where the rest of the expedition was encamped. My recollection of events more than fifty years ago is hazy, but the account of the expedition says 'On 17 August, Charles Pasternak arrived at Idirh, with two mules carrying his equipment. He told us news of happenings in the north. The Nationalist party, it seemed, was increasing in strength, and there were more and more "events", shooting, bomb-throwing, and the burning of tobacconists' shops.'[2] What I do remember is lying on the ground outside a tent, body fluids issuing simultaneously from both ends, and wishing to die on the spot (my colleagues had recently hired a village lad to do the washing up, and all had suffered similarly). As soon as I recovered, I hitch-hiked to the Moroccan capital, Rabat, sleeping in a ditch *en route* (I was past assessing its dimensions: my role as agent of the intelligence service was long over). At the Ministry of Health an official agreed for me to work in the military hospital at Ouarzazate, a French outpost on the southern slopes of the Atlas.

Hitch-hiking back to Idirh to pick up my equipment, I was made aware of the extent to which even the French, never mind El Glaoui, were losing control to nationalists eager to see the foreigners depart their country. Again, I will let the expedition's leader, with events a mere three years earlier in his mind instead of half a century in mine, tell the story. '… Charles returned from Rabat. … He stayed with us only a brief time before continuing on his way to the desert, but he was able to give us a true account of the situation in the north. In two small French settlements, Oued Zem and Khouribga, a large part of the European population had been massacred. A whole tribe had swept down from the mountains to attack Oued Zem. The town had been taken completely unprepared. People were murdered in their homes. A doctor was cut down among his patients in the hospital. Charles hitch-hiked back from Rabat, and was picked up by a couple in a small car. The woman was weeping. She had just lost her daughter at Oued Zem. The girl had been preparing to go out, when a gang of men broke into the house, chopped off her head with a hatchet, and killed her children. Her husband returned to find them all horribly mutilated.'[3]

At the hospital in Ouarzazate, Dr Dulière, a charming French doctor who had served in the Free French Air Force during the war, welcomed me. His Berber patients were, with their agreement, at my disposal. I stayed in a small establishment adjacent to the Foreign Legion fort, where its commander graciously allowed me to use their swimming pool. He also offered me a trip to the desert town of Zagora, where the French army had another base. At the hospital I set up my equipment, which gratifyingly worked well. I began to pin-prick the Berber patients and analyse a spot of their blood by paper electrophoresis. I also kept a sample for closer examination on return to England.

While working in the hospital one morning, Dr Dulière approached me. 'Are you a Protestant?', he asked. I answered in the affirmative, unsure where this was leading. 'A Swiss of your denomination' (he was probably a Calvinist) 'has just died. Does he need to receive the last rites?' Religious dogma, particularly in the finer points of eschatology, is not within my armamentarium of knowledge. 'No', I replied, pretty much off the cuff. 'I will go and say a prayer for him at his side'. Even if I'd got it wrong, I didn't think I was laying myself open to censure by any ecclesiastical authority. He was the first dead person I had laid eyes on (both my parents were still alive and human anatomy had not been one of my subjects). He looked a little wizened, but remarkably peaceful. I hope his relatives would have approved my actions.

The time for my vacation was coming to an end. My experiences in Morocco had been memorable. Oh, and by the way, I found an abnormal haemoglobin (Hb C) in two of the Berber patients.[4] This is probably less characteristic of Berbers *per se*, than of intermixing with immigrants moving along the trans-Saharan trade route from West Africa, especially from Nigeria where the incidence of haemoglobin C is high. On return to Oxford, Sir Howard Florey, with whom my supervisor was collaborating, quizzed me about my trip. I mentioned, among other things, the unexpected rout of the French by Moroccan nationalists. 'It seems you should have taken a bucket, not a packet of needles, to do your work' he commented in his wry Australian drawl.

The introduction to Africa that I have described opened my eyes to Arab and Berber, to Fez and Marrakesh, to a mountain village and a military hospital, to the French administration and the first stages of its toppling by nationalists eager for independence. I well understood the sense of a writer who said 'Africa is a most fascinating wild mistress. She gets a tenacious hold on most persons; bewitching, magnetic, irresistible … and once experienced is never lulled into forgetfulness.'[5] When I next visited Africa – sub-Saharan Africa proper, namely Nigeria –

during the early 1980s, independence had been achieved by every country on the continent. Even South Africa had severed its ties with Britain, though 80% of the population was still disenfranchised. In contrast to Asian countries like Malaysia or Singapore, the new nations of Africa had not prospered. On the contrary some, including the north African countries, seem to have slid back to pre-colonial days. This is why the word *failure* in the first part of the title is justified. The second part – *delayed success?* – reflects the fact that over the last few decades democracy and an improved quality of life are beginning to emerge in certain countries. Assessing the extent to which my title is valid represents the aim of this book. I hope you enjoy it.

End Notes
[1] Clarke (1959)
[2] *ibid*, p 103
[3] *ibid*, p 105
[4] C A Pasternak & D F Roberts: Haemoglobin C in Berbers. *Man* **52** (1956)
[5] These words were written by May French Sheldon, a friend of the explorer Henry Morton Stanley: Jeal (2007) p 431

Chapter One
ANALYSIS: A VISIT TO THE PRESIDENT

Meeting people with blood on their hands does not deter me. It is true that I would not like to have discussed the merits of Protestantism with Queen Mary I of England, [1] taken a glass of wine with Catherine Deshayes,[2] or confessed to being a university professor in the presence of Jiang Qing.[3] But the President of the sub-Saharan African nation I am about to meet denies that he is of this mould (others disagree).

It is a warm spring day in Kigali. Beads of sweat shine on the faces of the gardeners hoeing the sparse flower beds in the President's compound. After a rigorous security check – remember this is Rwanda – I am sitting with my colleagues and a couple of senior civil servants in the cabinet room. Cool air silently permeates the room. Assistants come and go, adjusting the lighting and the air flow. Finally the President enters and we all stand. Paul Kagame is tall, lean and straight-backed. Hardly surprising for a former army officer. He wears a dark suit with a red tie over a crisp white shirt. I suppress from my sub-conscious the reports concerning his role in the 1994 genocide and the disappearance of some politicians during a recent election, and look him straight in the face. His eyes are bright and glint sharply behind his spectacles. He shakes us by the hand and welcomes us to his country. He speaks English with a slight French accent. The President lowers himself on a slightly raised chair – not quite a throne – and we all resume our seats. We discuss our project in some detail, and the President outlines the tremendous progress his country is making. Free schooling for all youngsters, with a commitment to extend this up to the age of 16. More than eighty percent coverage of childhood vaccination against hepatitis B and meningitis across the entire country. Bold plans for agriculture, industry and tourism (to the mountain gorillas of Volcanos National Park). Half an hour quickly passes, and Kagame stands up. We all follow suit, and I present him with a gift. He tears the wrapping apart and sees that it is a signed and dedicated copy of *Quest: The Essence of Humanity*. He smiles and says that it sounds interesting and he looks forward to reading it. Hands are shaken once more, and the President walks rapidly out of the room.

Rwanda is developing fast. This is due entirely to Paul Kagame's vision and drive. He models himself on leaders like Lee Kuan-Yew of Singapore or Syngman Rhee of South Korea: a European-style democracy is not appropriate for Rwanda. As a result, the streets of the capital Kigali are almost as clean and safe as those of Singapore. Rwanda is also one of the least corrupt countries in Africa. It is set to move from a least-developed country,[4] with a GDP per capita in 2016 of US$1,977, to a developing one like those listed in the middle of **Table 1**. The interpretation of GDP per capita as indicative of a nation's success in regard to the well-being of its citizens is fine for European countries like Denmark, Germany or Sweden where the difference between the richest and poorest is no more than around 6-fold, but less so for countries like the USA (14-fold) or Mexico (27-fold),[5] and certainly not for most countries in sub-Saharan Africa. Equatorial Guinea, with a GDP/capita of $38,639 and a President whose family and cronies squander the revenues from oil, is a particularly striking example. Moreover the accuracy of these numbers leaves much to be desired,[6] and GDP doesn't really measure a nation's actual performance [7] anyway. Nevertheless they do clearly indicate a trend. No sub-Saharan nation – nor any in northern Africa either, for that matter – has achieved the economic status of a developed country like some of those shown in Table 1; even the least prosperous European countries, like Latvia, Croatia or Romania, have a GDP/capita above $22,000.

If instead of GDP per capita we take a different gauge of a country's well-being, one finds a similar trend, though the difference between countries in Africa and those elsewhere is much less marked. A measure known as The Global Quality of Life Index is based on more than 50 separate sets of figures, taken from bodies such as the World Health Organisation, that have been converted into a single score, or 'social progress index', indicative of the average quality of life and success in a country. It takes into account measures such as health and education, housing and water quality. The ranking of some of the countries listed in Table 1 is shown in **Table 2.** Countries outside Africa again score higher, but not *that* much. Rwanda has moved up having developed well over the past decade. But all African countries are still lower than developed ones.

Another appraisal of success is the Human Development Index prepared by the United Nations Development Program (UNDP). This takes into account factors such as life expectancy, adult literacy, school enrolment and adjusted income per capita in purchasing power parity. The results, for 1999 and 2013, are shown in **Table 3**. Most African countries have improved over the 14 years (unlike some of the developed ones, or indeed the world average), with only South Africa and the Democratic Republic of Congo showing a fall. The main point to note is that the difference between countries in Africa and those in the rest of the world is similar to that illustrated in Tables 1 and 2. Why is that? Why has the continent in which *Homo sapiens* was born not produced a single nation comparable to those of Asia, Europe or North America?

The answer is that it has. First, of course, there is ancient Egypt, one of the oldest civilisations by several millennia. But even in sub-Saharan Africa, at a time when northern Europeans were but barbaric vassals of the Roman Empire, the idea of kingship and its power through administrators and armies, through art and architecture, had already taken root in several areas (though none survived into modern times). So if we had compared the 'success' (we don't of course have actual data for something like GDP per capita) for different nations in, say, 1,000 AD, there would be little difference between Africa and Europe. Before describing some of these early nations in detail, I will examine the essential ingredients of nationhood. What makes a nation successful in the first place, and what are the reasons for eventual failure (chapter 2)?

The idea that black Africans are less successful than others because of an inherent lack of ingenuity persists in some quarters. The debate about IQ and 'race' continues. The fallacy of this argument is exposed in chapter 3. It is extended to groups of people who were able to found successful nations in sub-Saharan Africa during the time that northern Europe was itself embracing nationhood (chapter 4).

The climate has long been regarded as a reason for the lack of progress of its nations. The heat of the tropics may have allowed the emergence of *Homo sapiens* a few hundred thousand years ago, but it has held back – according to some – the development of modern nations. Geographically, sub-Saharan Africa lies well below the temperate belt in which agriculture first appeared in the fertile crescent of Mesopotamia or the highlands of Central America, so the potential for the cultivation of crops is less than that outside equatorial Africa. Then there is disease. The tropics favour some of the most virulent microbes that affect both humans and farm animals: mosquitoes and the tsetse fly are prime examples (chapter 5).

Interference from outside has been a major brake on the development of sub-Saharan nations. First there was the promotion of slavery. Although servitude has been endemic since early times in Africa as in Europe or Asia, the widespread export of slaves from central and eastern Africa to the Middle East for over a millennium and from western Africa to the Americas for more than three centuries had a significant demographic effect on the native population (chapter 6).

While the arrival of Muslim scholars in West Africa following the Arab conquests along the northern shores of the continent had caused little friction, a succession of European traders backed by mercenaries who began to penetrate into the interior was another matter. The consequential partitioning of the entire continent between the major European nations at the end of the nineteenth century was surely responsible for holding back the innate potential of Africans to manage their own affairs (chapter 7).

During the latter half of the twentieth century every African nation gained its independence. Yet success continued to elude virtually every one. Were the politicians not up to the job? Partly it was their policies. On achieving independence, many leaders – some with the support of the Soviet Union – took a rather Marxist standpoint. This resulted in economic decline that military coups and dictatorships did nothing to reverse. Aping the developed nations in their styles of government did not necessarily work either. And the financial aid that the former colonial powers, together with the United States, now injected into every country has often not proved beneficial either. Indeed, it is aid that has actually been holding most sub-Saharan countries back (chapter 8).

Nevertheless the twenty-first century may see some of the negative influences discussed in chapters 5 to 8 reversed. The time for sub-Saharan Africa may finally have arrived. Many obstacles remain: the havoc caused by HIV / AIDS, the reluctance of western nations to offer a level playing field for African exports, continuing strife within Africa and interference by Islamic groups from without, are prime examples. But it is possible to point to several countries for which the future looks brighter. That is the reason for the second part of my sub-title, *delayed success?*[8] This phrase has latterly been used by school authorities in the UK to tell students they've flunked an exam, because 'delayed success' is less stressful than 'failure'. I now use it in its literal meaning because several African nations *have* succeeded in turning past failure into relative success. These include Botswana (chapter 9), Ghana (chapter 10), Rwanda (chapter 11) and – at least until recently – South Africa (chapter 12).Then there are countries like Senegal (chapter 13) and Nigeria (chapter 14) – as well as Ethiopia (within chapter 8) – that also have potential, but are not quite there yet. To sum up: Africa south of the Sahara has clearly been a failure relative to Europe, Asia or America for a number of reasons. But hope *is* on the horizon (chapter 15).

There are those who might consider the title *Africa South of the Sahara* to be misplaced. Columnist Simon Kuper, for example, notes that 'Despite certain shared drivers – Chinese investments, cheap mobile phones, the end of the cold war – countries have diverged sharply. Africa now has fast-growing democracies such as Ghana and Botswana, repressive mini-Chinas like Rwanda and Ethiopia, corrupt oil states like Angola and Gabon, failed states like Chad and Somalia; and post-Arab spring north Africa. Not much connects these experiences.'[9] But the perception of sub-Saharan Africa as one of general failure persists, and is supported by the data quoted in Tables 1 to 3. Around 200,000 years ago, as *Homo sapiens* emerged from the savannah of east Africa and started to move around,[10] it was definitely one continent. It continued to be so during Pharaonic times as Egyptian influence percolated south into Nubia (and back). From around a thousand years ago, as Arab merchants from north Africa moved south into the empires growing along the upper reaches of the Niger River, and traders from Arabia itself crossed the sea into east Africa, they brought with them two things: the civilising influence of Islam, and its predilection for slavery, both of which left their mark on much of the continent. So far as the substance of this book is concerned, I rest my case. However, as the later chapters show, Simon Kuper is correct in that since independence, countries have begun to diverge.

End Notes

[1] during her reign (1553-1558), in which she strove to restore Catholicism to England, some 300 clerics and others, including simple agricultural labourers and artisans, who continued to support the 'new religion' of the previous monarch, Mary's young half-brother Edward VI, were burnt at the stake; politically-motivated offenders had their heads chopped off at the Tower

[2] a 17th century supplier of poisons to aristocratic womenfolk who had tired of their husbands

[3] Mao ZheDong's fourth wife. After Mao's death, she became leader of the 'Gang of Four' who encouraged the Red Guards to terrorise the populace. Academics were hounded from their posts and sent to toil in the countryside away from their families. Children denounced their parents for such bourgeois crimes as being successful teachers, doctors or lawyers. US President Nixon merely thought her to be 'unpleasantly abrasive and aggressive', but her own husband considered her 'as deadly poisonous as a scorpion'. During the Cultural Revolution, more appropriately named the Great Purge, she had actively and willingly assisted in ruining the lives of tens of millions of people, not to mention the destruction of Chinese culture itself. See Jung Chang and Jon Halliday: *Mao. The Unknown Story* (Jonathan Cape, London, 2005), pp 627, 523 and 622, resp.

[4] as of 2017, according to the UN Committee for Development Policy; see https://www.un.org/development/desa/dpad/wp-content/uploads/sites/45/publication/ldc_list.pdf

[5] see http://en.wikipedia.org/wiki/Economic_inequality

[6] as economist Morten Jerven warns in regard to values of GDP in sub-Saharan nations: 'How good are these numbers? The short answer is that the numbers are poor. ... The arbitrariness of the quantification process produces observations with very large errors and levels of uncertainty'. [Morton Jerven: *Poor Numbers. How We Are Misled by African Development Statistics and What to Do about It* (Cornell U Press, Ithaca, 2013), p xi]

[7] Robert Costanza *et al*: Time to leave GDP behind. *Nature* **505**:283-285 (2014). For the history of GDP, see Ehsan Masood: *The Great Invention: The Story of GDP and the Making (and Unmaking) of the Modern World* (Pegasus, 2016), reviewed in *Nature* **534**: 472-4 (2016)

[8] there are those who consider that *THERE'S NO FAILURE: ONLY SUCCESS DELAYED*: see: http://bulanobserver.wordpress.com/2008/05/12/

there%E2%80%99s-no-failure-only-success-delayed/

[9] Simon Kuper: Africa? Why there's no such place (*FT – Financial Times* – November 2/3, 2013, p 7

[10] Ewen Callaway: Ancient genomes expose Africa's past. DNA analyses reveal extensive migration around continent. *Nature* **547**: 149 (2017)

Table 1: GDP per capita
The ten top developed countries, some developing countries in sub-Saharan Africa and some least developed countries in sub-Saharan Africa.

Country	US$
Qatar	127,660
Luxembourg	104,003
Singapore	87,855
Brunei	76,884
Kuwait	71,887
Norway	69,249
Ireland	69,231
UAE	67,871
Switzerland	59,561
San Marino	59,058
Mauritius	20,422
Gabon	19,965
Botswana	17,042
South Africa	13,225
Namibia	11,290
Angola	6,844
Congo (Republic of)	6,676
Nigeria	5,942
Ghana	4,412
Zambia	3,880
Côte d'Ivoire	3,609
Kenya	3,361
Tanzania	3,080
Senegal	2,577
Rwanda	1,977
Ethiopia	1,946
Sierra Leone	1,672
Liberia	855
Congo (Democratic Republic of)	773

IMF figures for 2016 see: https://en.wikipedia.org/wiki/List_of_countries_by_GDP_(PPP)_per_capita

Note that some of the figures are inflated due to particular causes such as the discovery of oil (Gabon) or a high rate of HIV infection resulting in low population growth (Botswana)

Table 2
Quality of Life in the ten top countries and in some African countries

Country	Rank	Social progress index
New Zealand	1	88.24
Switzerland	2	88.19
Iceland	3	88.07
Netherlands	4	87.37
Norway	5	87.12
Sweden	6	87.08
Canada	7	86.95
Finland	8	86.91
Denmark	9	86.55
Australia	10	86.10
Mauritius	34	73.68
Botswana	57	65.60
South Africa	69	62.96
Namibia	78	61.19
Ghana	96	55.96
Senegal	97	53.52
Kenya	103	50.20
Zambia	104	49.88
Rwanda	105	49.46
Congo (Republic of)	110	47.99
Tanzania	114	46.06
Nigeria	123	42.65
Angola	127	39.93

Figures (for 2014) taken from:
http://www.telegraph.co.uk/news/politics/
10740555/Britain-still-great-but-distinctly-overweight-global-
quality-of-life-index-shows.html

**Table 3: Human Development Index for the top ten countries
and for some in sub-Saharan Africa**

Country	HDI in 1999	Country	HDI in 2013
'High'		**'Very high'**	
Norway	0.939	Norway	0.944
Australia	0.936	Australia	0.933
Canada	0.936	Switzerland	0.917
Sweden	0.936	Netherlands	0.915
Belgium	0.935	United States	0.914
United States	0.934	Germany	0.911
Iceland	0.932	New Zealand	0.910
Netherlands	0.931	Canada	0.902
Japan	0.928	Singapore	0.901
Finland	0.925	Denmark	0.900
'Medium'		**'High'**	
Mauritius	0.765	Mauritius	0.771
South África	0.702	Gabon	0.617
Namibia	0.601	Botswana	0.683
Botswana	0.577	Gabon	0.670
Ghana	0.542	South Africa	0.658
Kenya	0.514	Namibia	0.624
Congo	0.502	Ghana	0.573
		Congo	0.564
'Low'		**'Low'**	
Nigeria	0.455	Kenya	0.535
Tanzania	0.436	Angola	0.526
D R Congo	0.429	Rwanda	0.506
Zambia	0.427	Nigeria	0.504
Côte d'Ivoire	0.426	Tanzania	0.488
Senegal	0.423	Senegal	0.485
Angola	0.422	Côte d'Ivoire	0.452
Rwanda	0.395	D R Congo	0.338
sub-Saharan Africa	0.467	sub-Saharan Africa	0.502
world	0.716	world	0.702

Figures taken from the UNDP Human Development Report 2001 [http://hdr.undp.org/sites/default/files/reports/262/hdr_2001_en.pdf] and that for 2015 [https://data.undp.org/dataset/Table-1-Human-Development-Index-and-its-components/myer-egms?] respectively. Countries assessed as 'high', 'medium' and 'low' in 1999 and 'very high', high' and 'low' in 2013 according to UNDP criteria.

Chapter Two
NATIONHOOD: FAILURE AND SUCCESS

A t a time when much of Europe was populated by illiterate savages, kingdoms and empires had already appeared in sub-Saharan Africa. I shall describe some of them in chapter 4. None survived as such into modern times. The same is true elsewhere. 'Much of the central floodplain of the ancient Euphrates now lies beyond the frontiers of cultivation, a region of empty desolation. Tangled dunes, long disused canal levees, and the rubble-strewn mounds of former settlement contribute only low, featureless relief. Vegetation is sparse, and in many areas it is wholly absent. Rough, wind-eroded land surfaces and periodically flooded depressions form an irregular patchwork in all directions, discouraging any but the most committed traveller. To suggest the immediate impact of human life there is only a rare tent … Yet at one time here lay the core, the heartland, the oldest urban, literate civilization in the world.'[1] Further east, the Indus Valley civilisation (in present day Pakistan) and the Mauryan Empire in India both died out. The great temple complex at Angkor Wat still stands, but the Khmer empire of which it was the focus, is no more. The cultures of the Olmec and the Maya in Central America, and that of the Huari and Tiahuanaco in present day Peru, all collapsed long before the arrival of invading Spaniards. In Europe itself, the Roman Empire fell apart after no more than four centuries of supremacy in its western half. Elaborate stone structures erected at Callanish in the Outer Hebrides during the third millennium BC indicate a once vibrant society. A few crofters are all that remain. And so on. No nation, it seems, stays at its peak forever. To social scientists, the demise of nations is more interesting than their birth: 'It goes without saying that the collapse of ancient civilization is the most outstanding event in its history ....'[2]

Ingredients of Failure

What, then, are the ingredients of failure? Wars don't necessarily destroy civilisations. True, it was the Spanish *conquistadores* whose zeal wiped out the Aztecs in Mexico and the Incas in Peru. Genghis Khan did much the same to the remnants of former empires that lay in the way of his Mongol hordes sweeping westwards during the first decades of the thirteenth century. But the Roman Empire had collapsed as much from internal decay as from northern invasions. Conversely the nations of Europe that had been defeated by Napoleon regained their integrity within a few decades after 1815. Hitler's conquests of 1940 were equally short-lived: the defeated nations bounced back after 1945 and Germany itself, although reduced to smithereens at that time, soon became Europe's leading nation in economic terms.

Climatic changes, though, can be decisive. To return to the example of Mesopotamia quoted at the start of this chapter. A major drought around 2100 BC caused the collapse of the Akkadian Empire. Surviving Akkadians abandoned their settlements in the north (where farming had been dependent on rain) and moved south (where irrigation from the Euphrates and Tigris was able to maintain agriculture). The elements of Sumerian culture, that had preceded Akkadian influence by a thousand years, survived. Urban life continued for almost three more millennia, despite constant wars and conflicts between Assyrians, Babylonians, Kassites, Hittites, Persians, Seleucids (after Alexander's campaign), Parthians, Romans and Muslim Arabs. It was a gradual but catastrophic environmental change in the alluvial nature of the ground that began around 700 AD, a few centuries before the time that Europe was experiencing its medieval warm period, which appears to have changed everything. Agriculture declined rapidly, and with it the entire population: by the eleventh century it was at its lowest in five thousand years. Taxable income dropped precipitously and the state could no longer cope. Urban life became impossible and rebellions ensued. Mesopotamia was essentially ungovernable, and nomads took over the land. Einstein's view about the demise of civilisations is telling: 'I do not know with what weapons World War III will be fought, but World War IV will be fought with sticks and stones.'[3]

Earlier I mentioned the demise of the Indus Valley civilisation in Asia and that of four cultures in America. The first of these is also known as Harappan on account of one of its major centres at Harappa, now an insignificant village in the Indian Punjab. During the Bronze Age, though, Harappa was a busy trading centre on the Ravi River, a tributary of the Indus. Another large settlement was further south at Mohenjo-Daro, in Sindh province. A third, more recently discovered, centre was at Ganweriwala in Pakistani Punjab, half-way between the other two. Some five million people may have lived in these and other towns along the Indus Valley between 2600 and 1900 BC when this culture was at the height of its activity. By 1700 BC a decline in the fortunes of these people began. The cause is likely to have been climatic. A series of droughts is believed to have occurred throughout the region at this time. This led to a realignment of rivers like the Ravi and the Indus, with a dramatic deterioration in agriculture. Unable to feed itself, the population shrank. A few centuries later the Mycenian kingdom in the Aegean and the territories occupied by the Egyptian New Kingdom in the eastern Mediterranean also collapsed.

The Olmec culture – the oldest in Central America – spanned roughly a thousand years, from around 1500 to 400 BC. They built huge stone statues, similar to those constructed millennia later on Easter Island. Their territory covered the coast line of south eastern Mexico in the present states of Veracruz and Tabasco. It is possible that a volcanic eruption, or climatic deterioration, caused the abandonment of Olmec sites and the disappearance of Olmec culture from the historical record. The reason for the collapse of the Mayan civilisation – the only one in pre-Columbian America to have developed a written script – may also have been climatic. Mayan cities reached their zenith around 250 AD. They began to be abandoned during the eighth and ninth centuries, at a time of frequent droughts. But the loss of agricultural produce may have been due to the opposite effect: over-cultivation by Mayan farmers. Another man-made cause of decline may have been excessive hunting, leading to the disappearance of game.

It was just such an effect that was the likely cause for the collapse of the Rapa Nui civilisation on Easter Island. Their forebears were clever enough to have navigated more than ten thousand miles against the prevailing wind across the Pacific and to have constructed the most amazing statues, but their resourcefulness left them when they resorted to disproportionate deforestation in order to make boats for fishing. The forest could not respond, and it is thought that eventually the Easter Islanders were left without the means to feed themselves. Recent evidence, however, suggests that they may have derived half their food from farming, perhaps introducing fertilizers along the way.[4] The Huari, who occupied the coastal area of northern Peru from around 500 to 1000 AD, suffered centuries of drought which may have caused their downfall. The Tiahuanaco civilisation – that produced statues similar to those of the Olmec and the Rapa Nui – was spread around the shores of Lake Titicaca, which lies in the high Andes between Bolivia and Peru. A hundred thousand people, perhaps as many as 1.5 million, inhabited the area before its decline around 1000 AD. The reason for this is pretty much unknown.

Infectious disease is another factor responsible for population decline. The Black Death of the fourteenth century may not have brought any empire to its knees, but it is estimated to have killed 30% – if not double that number – of Europe's population. Likewise the famine caused by potato blight (*Phytophthora infestans*) in mid-nineteenth century Ireland led to the death by starvation of a million people, while another million emigrated to the USA, which together accounted for a 20 – 25% decline in its population. The country (under British occupation), however, rumbled on. In Central America, though, an outbreak of *Salmonella enterica* during the sixteenth century is thought to have compounded the demise of the Aztec empire brought on by the Spanish conquistadors.[5]

Another aspect of failure, that contributed to the fall of the Roman Empire, has been analysed by the historian (and former commander of the Arab League between the two world wars) John Glubb: 'Apart from the casualties caused by wars, pioneering and emigration, national decadence is probably largely attributable to too long a duration of wealth and power. The nation gradually, but unconsciously, assumes that pre-eminence is automatically its due, without any obligation to toil or struggle. … Eight or nine generations seem to be sufficient to change the hardy and enterprising pioneers into the idle and querulous citizens of the welfare state. … In brief, the life of a dynasty, the rise of which was due to the outstanding personality of its founder – not to a national expansion – is in the vicinity of a hundred years, or four generations.'[6]

The collapse of the Mauryan Empire falls into this category. Founded by Chandragupta Maurya, the empire reached its height between 322 and 185 BC. The stimulus was the military ability of the grandson of the founder, namely Ashok Vardhan Maurya also known as Ashoka the Great. It was as a result of his conquests that the empire reached from Afghanistan in the west to Assam in the east, from the Himalayas in the north to almost the tip of India in the south. The population at this time was in excess of 50 million – the largest empire in the world. Although there are few architectural remains to attest to the success of this dynasty, it is clear that a centralised government with trade links stretching well beyond the empire made it economically extremely effective and stable. But it was not to last. The very concentration of authority at the centre eventually proved its undoing and the empire split in half. Invasions by Greeks from the west, and revolts within the empire could not be resisted. Most important, though, was the fact that Ashoka's heirs were weak and not up to the job. In the case of Rome, four centuries of rule by (partly) hereditary emperors petered out as administrative control began to fail: Germanic incursions from the north, Christian dogma and imperial weakness in the centre, malarial mosquitoes from the south, all contributed.

In truth, then, there are many reasons why civilisations decline. Sometimes the cause is climatic change and a precipitous drop in the population. Other times the reason is man's own folly. Other times again, it is a wane in the drive of a nation's leadership. We tend to think of continuity in the case of China and Egypt simply because the name of the country has not changed. This is deceptive. The ingenuity of the Han has not been supported by the state for several of the past centuries (though this may be changing even as I write). The brilliance of the New Kingdom has been missing in Egypt for three millennia. Conversely the creative legacy of Cyrus the Great can be detected in the lives of some of Teheran's citizens today, even though the name of the country has changed several times and the economy faltered in concert. While the quality of life in Europe remains high, the ambitions of its nations are being strangled by unelected bureaucrats of the European Union who allow political dogma to trump economic expediency.

For most of the cultures I have described, the exact reasons for failure are still being debated. As an example of active research in this area. I draw the reader's attention to the plight of the Pueblo people living in an area that now covers the south east of Utah, the south west of Colorado, the north west of New Mexico and the north east of Arizona. From 600 AD onwards, farming communities began to move into this region and to build spectacular dwellings clinging to the sides of deep canyons. Those in the Mesa Verde Highlands of Colorado and the Chaco Canyon of New Mexico are typical. By 1200 more than 25,000 people inhabited this area. Within less than a century all had left, many settling several hundred kilometres to the south east. Yes, there were droughts around this time, but sophisticated archaeology together with high-performance computing is pointing also to a combination of political instability and social upheaval, the details of which are only now emerging.[7]

Another example, again in the USA, where high-tech methods are being employed concerns the Mississippi valley, home to the Sioux Indians for more than a thousand years. In this case the questions relate more to the emergence of a civilisation than to its decline. Ancient Cahokia, at the juncture of the Missouri with the Mississippi, lies buried below large mounds of earth and vegetation. Around 1050 it appears to have been the administrative centre of a burgeoning state that stretched from present-day Wisconsin all the way down to Louisiana. The inhabitants may not have built their monuments in stone, but the sophistication of the structures led some to believe that this was the original home of the Aztecs, subsequently driven south by warring tribes. This view is no longer held. Instead it is thought that Siouan-speaking North American Indians *were* smart enough to have embarked on nationhood. Unfortunately for them, their efforts failed on account of three of the common factors underlying failure: climate (the warm and moist global Medieval Warm Period of 800 to 1300 was replaced by a series of droughts around 1200), strife among the people (class distinctions, that generally reflect the growth of empires, in this instance had the opposite effect), and external pressures (the arrival of Hernando de Soto's men in the sixteenth century brought any chance of nationhood to an end).[8]

Ingredients of Success

It probably goes without saying that for any community to grow and to succeed, a sprinkling of bright individuals – those whose innate qualities of curiosity, intellect and drive are above average – is a necessary, or at least beneficial, prerequisite. I return to this point in the next chapter.

In terms of culture, social anthropologist Edmund Leach considered that 'During the hundred years of their existence academic anthropologists have not discovered a single universally valid truth concerning either human culture or human society other than those which are treated as axioms: eg that all men have language.'[9] So far as the title of this book is concerned, the only African society mentioned by Tainter (apart from the Old Kingdom of Pharaohnic times) is a sub-Saharan one: that of the Ik in northern Uganda. In his description of failure he actually gives an insight into one of the factors necessary for complex societies to succeed. 'The Ik … are a morbidly fascinating case of collapse in which a former, low level of complexity has disappeared. Due to drought and disruption by national boundaries of the traditional cycle of movement, the Ik live in such a food- and water-scarce environment that there is absolutely no advantage to reciprocity and social sharing. The Ik, in consequence, display almost nothing of what could be considered societal organization. They are so highly fragmented that most activities, especially subsistence, are pursued individually. … Although little is known about how the Ik got to their present situation, there are some indications of former organizational patterns. They possess clan names, although today these have no structural significance. They live in villages, but these no longer have any political meaning. The traditional authority structure of family, lineage, and clan leaders has been progressively weakened. It appears that a former level of organization has simply been abandoned by the Ik as being unprofitable and unsuitable in their present distress.'[10]

Social cohesion, then, is a prerequisite for success. What other criteria can be identified? We tend to assess ancient civilisations in terms of royalty and religion, agriculture and astronomy, art and architecture, language and literacy. Some of the most innovative civilisations I have mentioned, namely Sumer, Pharaohnic Egypt, China from the time of the Shang Dynasty, Athens and other Greek city states (royalty replaced by elected rulers), and the Maya of central America, had all the ingredients. But is this really the right way to gauge success? The rulers, the priests, the officials and others in the ancient states lived well. All menial work was carried out by slaves. This is not incompatible with the concept of civilisation, since this is derived from the Latin word for citizen (*civis*). Slaves were not citizens, whether in Athens, the Roman Republic, or anywhere else, so there is no reason why the term 'civilisation' should not also be applied as a measure of success of the early African nations which will be mentioned in chapter 4.

Slavery in Europe was replaced by feudalism during the Middle Ages, but a large part of the population continued to live in poverty well past the industrial revolution. Even as recently as the middle of the nineteenth century, by which time Britain's economy was emerging as the most successful in Europe, children as young as twelve were put to work in factories and mines. In the Yorkshire coal mines, women and girls were 'chained, belted, harnessed like dogs in a go-cart, black, saturated with wet and more than half-naked, crawling on their hands and knees and dragging heavy loads behind them.'[11] By the end of the century, more than a quarter of the British people were living at or below subsistence levels in filthy slums; a tenth could not afford the food necessary for survival. Two thirds of the nation's wealth was owned by just one percent of the population. In the United States in mid-nineteenth century, a seventh of the population was enslaved (teaching black Americans literacy was an indictable offence). Is the success of a nation to be judged by the accomplishments of the few, or by the misery of the many? Nowadays we tend to combine the two, which is why in chapter 1 I used an economic criterion that encompasses the mass of the population, namely the GDP per capita, as a rough measure of success. I did, though, point out its limitations and referred to alternatives such as 'quality of life' and 'human development' indices.

Another index is that Economic Freedom, compiled annually by the Heritage Foundation and *The Wall Street Journal*. Economic freedom is defined as 'the fundamental right of every human to control his or her own labor and property. In an economically free society, individuals are free to work, produce, consume, and invest in any way they please. In economically free societies, governments allow labor, capital, and goods to move freely, and refrain from coercion or constraint of liberty beyond the extent necessary to protect and maintain liberty itself'. The index ranks a country's performance in regard to Rule of Law (Property Rights and Freedom from Corruption), Limited Government (Government Spending and Fiscal Freedom), Regulatory Efficiency (Business Freedom, Labor Freedom and Monetary Freedom) and Open Markets (Trade Freedom, Investment Freedom.[12] **Table 4** lists the ten top nations for 2015, as well as some of the sub-Saharan countries listed in Tables 1 – 3. Most of these fall into the category of 'Mostly unfree' or 'Repressed'. Only four (plus Morocco) make it into 'Moderately free', apart from Mauritius which is in the top ten. Those four nations support my thesis of 'delayed success'. Their performance is therefore assessed in greater detail towards the end of this book. Of the index in 2001 it has been said that sub-Saharan Africa 'remains the most economically unfree – and the poorest – area in the world.'[13] Little – apart from the four countries that have become 'Moderately free' – has changed since then.

The economists Daren Acemoglu and James Robinson follow up on the idea of an individual's economic freedom and put it like this: '… while economic institutions are critical for determining whether a country is poor or prosperous, it is politics and political institutions that determine what economic institutions a country has.'[14] This implies that countries in which people's aspirations are met may be considered successful. Where they are not, the country has failed. They talk not in terms of democracy or its lack, but of economically 'inclusive' versus 'extractive' communities. In an inclusive society, a country's wealth is shared among all (according to merit). In an extractive society, much of the wealth is retained by a few. The former leads to prosperity: because the people see the fruits of their labours rewarded and therefore strive for more. This, through taxation, enriches the government, which is able to distribute yet more wealth. An extractive society leads to poverty: the people feel alienated and do not exert themselves beyond their minimal requirements. Revenue to the government is curtailed, and its assets decline. The prime example of failure by an extractive state is that of Russia and the Soviet Union. There had been little inclusiveness in Russia during Tsarist times, none in the Soviet Union under the Bolsheviks, and Gorbachev's attempts to introduce some into Russia weren't properly followed up by Yeltsin or Putin.

Acemoglu and Robinson dismiss arguments about the ignorance of populations, about geography and climate, as being determining factors for success or failure. They point to two instances in which success and failure sit side by side. The first is the town of Nogales that lies astride the Rio Grande. The southern half is in Sonoma, Mexico; the northern half is in Arizona, USA. The southern half is poor, the northern half is rich. The ethnic make-up of the two populations is identical. There is no difference in geography or climate. The only difference is that the economic institutions in Mexico are extractive, whereas those in the USA are inclusive.[15] The second example, which is even more telling, is that of South Korea and North Korea, which were a single nation for centuries prior to 1945. Again, no difference in ethnicity, geography or climate. South Korea is rich, one of the Asian tiger economies. North Korea is poor, one of the most impoverished in the world. The institutions of South Korea are inclusive (despite a somewhat authoritarian regime, elections are entirely democratic). The institutions of North Korea are totally extractive.[16] While these instances illustrate the importance of economic institutions, Acemoglu and Robinson's dismissal of arguments based on ignorance, geography or climate cannot be used in relation to the difference in wealth between African and European nations. I shall discuss the 'ignorance' hypothesis in the next two chapters, and the role of geography and climate in chapter 5.

A key element that has denied African nations success is that of law and order. (I appreciate that North Korea has a surfeit of law and order, but such elements are merely contributory to success, not in themselves sufficient). 'At the dawn of the nineteenth century, many parts of the world, especially in Africa, lacked a state that could provide even a minimal degree of law and order, which is a prerequisite for having a modern economy. ... Without some degree of political centralization, even if the elites of African polities had wished to greet industrialization with open arms, there wouldn't have been much they could have done.'[17] The only African country that Acemoglu and Robinson consider as successful is Botswana (see also Tables 1 – 4), which is considered in chapter 9.

Destructive events like earthquakes kill people and destroy their livelihoods. But they may be beneficial in the long-term. American geologist Eric R Force points out that 'High tectonic activity has accompanied the birth and growth of many ancient civilizations in the Middle East, Greece and Italy and, to a lesser extent, the Indus Valley and China. During the second and first millennia BC around the Mediterranean Sea, the Minoan, Mycenaean, Greek, Etruscan and Roman civilizations arose during eras of major seismic activity in their regions. No comparable cultures developed on the relatively inactive coasts of Spain, France and Libya'. He suggests that 'frequent tectonic activity was a "long-term cultural stimulant,"' – shades of Arnold Toynbee's 'challenge of adversity' hypothesis [18] – 'forging ancient communities that were resilient, cooperative, innovative and outgoing, and where "elders would be passing on an expectation of change to younger generations".'[19]

None of the early empires in sub-Saharan Africa that will be described in chapter 4 ever achieved the success of ancient Egypt, China or Persia, but they clearly show that black Africans had the ability to found nations as successfully as did their contemporaries in Europe. The latter began to flourish after the industrial revolution of the eighteenth century. No such advancement occurred in Africa: its nations, especially those within tropical Africa, remained stagnant. Will the present countries of sub-Saharan Africa now be able to catch up and achieve the living standards of Europe, North America and far-east Asia? That is the question that this book strives to answer.

Conclusion

Nations come and go. Few last intact forever. The ingredients for success comprise social cohesion, inclusive policies in so far as its citizens are concerned, and sometimes the challenge of adversity. Failure is due to many causes: war, severe climatic change, population decline (that often results from the first two), the folly of the people, and a weakening of resolve among hereditary rulers.

End Notes

[1] Robert McC Adams: *Heartland of Cities* (Aldine, Chicago, 1981), p xvii

[2] James Paton Isaac, quoted in Tainter (1988) p 2.

[3] Suddendorf (2013) p 280

[4] Resourcefulness of Rapa Nui: *Nature* **547**: 141 (2017)

[5] Ewen Callaway: Salmonella suspected in Aztec decline. *Nature* **542**: 404 (2017)

[6] Glubb (1969) p 296

[7] Richard Monastersky: And then there were none. *Nature* **527**: 26-29 (2015) and Kohler, T A and Varian, M D (eds): *Emergence and Collapse of Early Villages: Models of Central Mesa Verde Archaeology* (University of California, Berkeley Press, 2012) quoted therein

[8] Pauketat (2004)

[9] Leach (1982) p 52

[10] Tainter (1988) p 17

[11] Bailey (2008) p 68

[12] http://www.heritage.org/index/about

[13] Ayittey (2005) p 16

[14] Acemoglu and Robinson (2012) p 43

[15] *ibid*, p 7

[16] *ibid*, p 73

[17] *ibid*, p 238

[18] see Pasternak (2003) p 140

[19] Andrew Robinson *Nature* **528**: 36 (2015), reviewing Eric R Force: *Impact of Tectonic Activity on Ancient Civilizations: Recurrent Shake-ups, Tenacity, Resilience, and Change* (Lexington Books, 2015)

(Opposite: Figures for 2016, taken from http://www.heritage.org/index/ranking)

Table 4: Index of Economic Freedom in the ten top countries and in some African countries

Country	Rank	Overall economic freedom
Free		
Hong Kong	1	89.6
Singapore	2	89.4
New Zealand	3	82.1
Australia	4	81.4
Switzerland	5	80.5
Mostly free		
Canada	6	79.1
Chile	7	78.5
Estonia	8	76.8
Ireland	9	76.6
Mauritius	10	76.4
Moderately free		
Botswana	36	69.8
Rwanda	65	64.8
Ghana	71	63.0
South Africa	72	62.6
Morocco	89	60.1
Mostly unfree		
Uganda	92	59.7
Namibia	93	59.6
Zambia	100	58.7
Côte d'Ivoire	103	58.5
Gabon	104	58.3
Senegal	106	57.8
Tunisia	107	57.7
Tanzania	109	57.5
Nigeria	120	55.6
Kenya	122	55.6
Egypt	124	55.2
Repressed		
Angola	158	47.9
DR Congo	168	45.0
Equatorial Guinea	173	40.4
Zimbabwe	175	37.6

Chapter Three
ABILITY: GENES AND INGENUITY

Well into the twentieth century, the belief that negroid Africans are less intelligent, less able to cope, than people of European descent, continued to find adherents. A typical mid-nineteenth century stance is illustrative: 'I will say then that I am not, nor ever have been in favor of bringing about in anyway the social and political equality of the white and black races – that I am not nor ever have been in favor of making voters or jurors of negroes, nor of qualifying them to hold office, nor to intermarry with white people; and I will say in addition to this that there is a physical difference between the white and black races which I believe will forever forbid the two races living together on terms of social and political equality. And inasmuch as they cannot so live, while they do remain together there must be the position of superior and inferior, and I as much as any other man am in favor of having the superior position assigned to the white race. I say upon this occasion I do not perceive that because the white man is to have the superior position the negro should be denied everything.' Not everything. Well, that's something. The interesting thing about this quote is that five years later, the speaker – now 16th President of the United States – in his Emancipation Proclamation as Commander in Chief during the Civil War, freed some 3.1 million out of the 4 million slaves then living in the United States. Perhaps I'm being harsh on Lincoln. His 1858 discourse was, after all, a political speech [1] that would help him to gain the presidency.

On the other hand enlightened thinkers like Charles-Louis de Secondat, Baron de Montesquieu [1689-1755], Francis Hutcheson

[1694-1746], Adam Smith [1723-1790], Edmund Burke [1729–1797] and James Beattie [1735-1803] had all expressed rather different views already a century earlier. I will let the latter speak for himself: 'We have therefore every reason, that the case admits of, to believe, that all the men upon earth, whatever be their colour, are our brethren, and neighbours: and if so, both reason and Scripture declare, that it is our duty to love them, and to do unto them as we would that they should do unto us. And if natural peculiarities of *shape* and *stature* as well as *colour*, may be accounted for, as I think they may, from the foregoing principles; it follows that Laplanders, Samoeydes, Esquimaux, the Hurons, the Chinese, and the American and Asiatic, as well as Africans, Indians, and, in a word, all the inhabitants of this globe, who have reason, speech, and erect figure, must be considered as one great family, and as informed with souls of the same order, whatever slight variations may appear in their bodies.'[2] A century later the Abbé Boilat, admittedly a rather lone voice in 1853, considered black Africans not to be biologically inferior or lacking in culture in comparison with Frenchmen. Endorsing Beattie's conclusions, he pointed out that 'these men are children of Adam, created in the image of God.'[3] But such views would remain the minority stand point for more than a hundred years.

Debate about *g* and *IQ*

The idea that you could measure a person's intelligence, in the way that we define someone's height or weight, goes back more than a century to the studies of the English psychologist Charles Spearman. He realised that children who do well in one subject, say English, also excel in apparently unrelated subjects such as maths or French. In other words traits like verbal fluency correlate with others like mathematical skills in any one child. Spearman called this quality *general intelligence* or *g*. Since then, the idea of defining a person's intelligence by a mathematical number has gained ground, and led to the concept of an individual's *intelligence quotient* or *IQ*. This was first proposed by a German psychologist, William Stern, who defined IQ as one's mental age – determined on the basis of a number of different 'intelligence tests' – divided by one's chronological age, times 100. So if one's mental age is less than one's chronological age, one has an IQ of less than 100; if greater, one's IQ is greater than 100. Such a definition of IQ really works well only with children. So instead, psychologists now use the ratio between a person's overall score on a number of tests and the mean of all those sampled taken as 100. Again, if one's IQ score is less than 100, a person's intelligence is said to be below average, if greater than 100, above. G is defined in roughly the same way: it is 'a quantitative trait that varies from a low end of mild mental retardation to a high end of gifted individuals ... although intelligence means different things to different people, g has a more precise definition: g is what diverse cognitive abilities have in common. ... including tests as different as reasoning, spatial ability, verbal ability, and memory.'[4] For the purpose of this book – far removed from a psychometric treatise – g and IQ can be considered more or less interchangeable. Both rely on tests that depend on the ability to reason rationally. At this point I had better remind the reader of Bertrand Russell's remark that 'Man is a rational animal – so at least I have been told. Throughout a long life, I have looked diligently for evidence in favour of this statement ....'[5]

It has long been recognised that if you take a large sample of people and measure each one's height, or weight, or IQ/g, and record the frequency with which any particular number is found, the result is a bell-shaped curve (or Gaussian distribution in mathematical terms). This was first shown in 1846 by L A J Quetelet, a Belgian statistician and astronomer. He arranged a large group of French soldiers in a line according to height (the abscissa), with all those of similar height standing one behind the other (the ordinate). Most people are (by definition) of average height or weight or intelligence, with the numbers that are below or above gradually getting less and less (see **Fig 3.1**). So what determines someone's IQ or g: is it nature or nurture? A huge amount of data collected over the past half-century, largely on identical and non-identical twins, brought up in their parents'

The Distribution of IQ

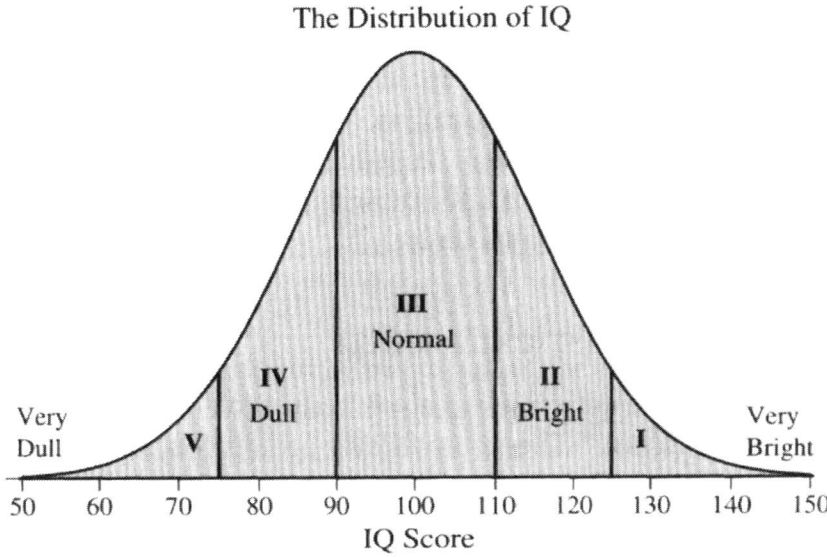

Figure 3.1. Defining the Cognitive Classes

environment or in that of foster parents, point to the fact that it is both.

The nature part is one's genetic make-up (the genes inherited from one's forebears). The nurture part is environmental influences like upbringing (whether your parents read to you – indeed, whether were there any books in the house at all; whether your parents lived comfortably or whether your father worked in a South African gold mine for a pittance), nutrition (whether you suffered from caloric deficiency or lack of animal protein early in life), pollution (whether you live in Beijing or Bermuda), infectious disease (whether you have chronic malaria or tuberculosis), and so on. I have given just some examples, but the list could continue for several pages. Just to complicate matters, we now know that environmental effects may themselves lead to genetic changes in an individual as a result of 'epigenetic' mechanisms.[6] Environmental influences also include the effect that some of the factors just mentioned have on foetal development: offspring of severely malnourished mothers are born smaller and with impaired IQ; and because IQ doesn't change much with age, such children never catch up. Exactly how much of one's IQ depends on nature, and how much on nurture, varies from one person to another. 40 – 80% of one's IQ can be due to nature, with 20 – 60% due to nurture. For the purpose of this discussion, we'll assume an approximately 50% – 50% *average* derivation.

If roughly half of one's IQ is inherited, can we identify an 'IQ' gene? The answer is no, for the same reason that there is no 'size' or 'weight' or 'cancer' or 'diabetes' or 'depression' gene. The hereditary component of all these conditions depends on a subtle interplay between many different genes, each of which may be slightly altered. Height, for example, is said to be affected by as many as 700 different genes.[7] The existence of 'single-gene' diseases like cystic fibrosis or muscular dystrophy are the exception, not the norm. Nevertheless a recent study [8] of a group of adolescents has identified a particular gene that influences both intelligence and the number of gray cells in the cortex (the layer at the top of the brain) measured by its thickness. As the lead author says 'It's important to point out that intelligence is influenced by many genetic and environmental factors. The gene we identified only explains a tiny proportion of the differences in intellectual ability'.

Let me now return to the opening paragraph of this chapter. Is there any evidence to support nineteenth century opinions about the intelligence of sub-Saharan Africans? Despite the views of a handful of enlightened philosophers of the seventeenth, eighteenth and nineteenth centuries whom I mentioned at the beginning of this chapter, most theorists since then have taken a different view. Typically, at the end of the nineteenth century Léopold de Saussure insisted that differences between French and colonial people were the result of 'fixed and hereditary' differences in their mental make-up.[9] The abolition of slavery in the USA (proclaimed by Abraham Lincoln in January 1863 and ratified by the 13th amendment to the Constitution in December

1865) implied to two Englishmen that 'fixed and hereditary' differences were no longer being recognised. They were horrified. (So far as the USA was concerned, they need not have worried: equality of opportunity didn't happen for another hundred years). One was Dr James Hunt, a speech therapist whose stuttering patients included the writers Charles Kingsley and Lewis Carroll (Charles Lutwidge Dodgson). The other was the maverick explorer, linguist and orientalist Richard Burton (who should have known better). Together they founded the Anthropological Society, the aim of which was 'to prove him [the black African] unimprovable, therefore unimproved since the beginning, and, consequently, fitted only to remain a hewer of wood and drawer of water for the members of that select society.'[10] The shorter Larousse dictionary of 1905 defines 'nègre' as an inhabitant of certain countries in Africa 'who form a race of black men inferior in intelligence to the white race, called Caucasian' (the much respected Francis Galton, half-cousin of Charles Darwin, used similar terminology to refer to the destitute lower classes of white England). The purported difference between 'primitive people' and Europeans was voiced as recently as 1923 by the psychologist Lucien Lévy-Bruhl.[9] Even more recently, the American educational psychologist Arthur Jensen expressed such views, albeit in a more toned down version.

Jensen spent much of his life comparing the IQ of American Blacks with that of American Whites, and came to the conclusion that there is indeed a small but consistent difference: 'The key point I want to make is that full siblings within the same family, on average, differ in IQ by about as much (around 12 IQ points) as the average difference between Blacks and Whites of the same social class.'[11] Naturally this racist assertion has been vigorously challenged. The fact that other investigators find that 'East Asians (eg Chinese, Japanese), whether in America or in Asia, typically earn higher scores on intelligence and achievement tests than white Americans' [12] may have given white Americans an inferiority complex, but did little to ameliorate criticism of Jensen's views

One objection by some academics to Jensen's views is that IQ has nothing to do with heredity. This, however, is unsustainable as shown above. Another objection, that comparing individuals 'of the same social class' is extremely difficult, has more merit. Furthermore, aren't there different kinds of intelligence, and some people may display more of one than another? At least five types – not all of which are revealed by the usual sorts of psychometric tests – have been identified. These include Linguistic Intelligence, Musical Intelligence, Logical-Mathematical Intelligence, Spatial Intelligence and Bodily-Kinesthetic Intelligence.[13] This 'raises the possibility that just as individuals differ in cognitive abilities, populations that evolved in somewhat different environments' – tropical Africa versus Eurasia, for example, some 10,000 years ago – 'may have developed correspondingly different cognitive abilities.'[14] Indeed, 250 years ago the French philosopher Helvetius already pointed out that 'education makes us all what we are ... mental inequalities are the results of differences in education' [9] (as a result of which his books were publicly burned in Paris).

. Interpretation of differences in mean IQ in terms of race are flawed for another reason. If some 50% of IQ is due to non-genetic causes like upbringing, then any difference in the value of the mean for two particular groups of people is as likely to reflect nurture as nature. Moreover there is no reason to believe that skin colour is in any way linked to intelligence, or height or appetite or facial nuances for that matter. Indeed some southern Indians are as black as any African Negro, but the two are no more related than a Korean to a Mexican. In fact the acquisition of dark skin, to which I will return towards the end of this chapter, is – I suspect – an example of convergent evolution. Just as eyes have developed independently in cephalopods (like octopus), cnidaria (like jellyfish) and vertebrates (like humans), so dark skin has probably developed independently in southern Asians and tropical Africans. Neither is in a direct line of descent from the other.

My interpretation of all this in regard to the achievements of Africans and their cultures is as follows. Whether small differences in average IQ or *g* between various groups exist or not is irrelevant. What matters is that there are enough clever people, enough of those endowed with exceptional curiosity and drive,[15] in any one society to lead it to thriving nationhood: those who have the qualities for potential leadership.[16] In other words, it is those to the right of any bell curve of IQ (see Fig 1), or of other innate attribute like curiosity or drive, as much as those around the mean, that matter. Where a society lacked such a nucleus it did not grow beyond 150 or so [17] individuals. Such isolated tribes in, for example, South America or New Guinea – there were said to be as many as a hundred throughout the world in 2013 [18] – have essentially been frozen in time for millennia. However elsewhere, every group that expanded into an extended community, whether in Asia, Europe or Africa, had more than enough bright individuals. Detractors of sub-Saharan Africa may point to the fact that no Pericles or Charlemagne, no Ashok Maurya (Ashoka the Great) or Xuanye Kangxi (fourth emperor of the Qing Dynasty), has emerged to lead any of its nations to undisputed success. They may also remind us that no Isaac Newton or Marie Curie, no Confucius or Rabindranath Tagore, has materialized as part of a sub-Saharan country's elite. Persons with such talents have undoubtedly existed over the centuries, but they are likely to have been impoverished peasants restricted by the nature of the society in which they lived. The same is true today. Individuals of exceptional talent exist, but the opportunity to realise their potential is absent. To put it another way, 'I am, somehow, less interested in the weight and convolutions of Einstein's brain than in the near certainty that people of equal talent have lived and died in cotton fields and sweatshops.'[19]

George Saitoti (1945-2012) may not have been Einstein's equal, but this poor Kenyan-born Maasai, who spent his childhood herding cattle, was fortunate to have received an elementary education that revealed a brilliant mind. He was able to go to England where he obtained an MSc in mathematics (Sussex

University), followed by a PhD in the same subject (Warwick University). On return to Kenya he taught mathematics at Nairobi University and played a major part in founding the African Mathematical Union. His mathematical flair led him to economics and thence into politics. The latter probably resulted in his untimely death in a helicopter crash in 2012, the year his *The Challenges of Economic and Institutional Reform in Africa* was published. I mention him merely as one of thousands of Africans whose intellect has been proved to be second to none.

The thirteenth century Islamic scholar Ibn Khallikan is said to have described a Negro who reigned as Caliph in Baghdad during the ninth century as 'a man of great merit and a perfect scholar.' A contemporary poet commented on that gentleman's ability in the following terms: 'Blackness of skin cannot degrade an ingenious mind, or lessen the worth of the scholar or the wit,'[20] words that many a racist should bear in mind. In terms of more martial pursuits, Amr ibn al-As, the man who commanded the Arab army that successfully invaded Egypt in 639, was of black African descent.[21] In India, also, the racial tolerance of Islam allowed black Africans, most of whom arrived as slaves, to fulfil their potential. Malik Sarwar, an Ethiopian eunuch, was appointed a provincial governor by the Sultan of Delhi in 1394. He was succeeded in that role by his adoptive son, another former black slave, who took the name of Mubarak Shah. The governorship passed to Mubarak's brother Ibrahim in 1402. Ibrahim ruled successfully over what had become an independent province for almost forty years. 'He was no mere militarist, however. Ibrahim Shah became as renowned for the art and scholarship he encouraged at his court as for the many impressive new buildings that distinguished his reign.[22]

Another Ethiopian slave who showed himself to be the equivalent of any Asian notable was Shambu, born around 1550. Sold on from owner to owner, one of whom named him Ambar, he found himself in the employ of the Sultan of Bijapur (in southwest India). The sultan was so impressed by Ambar that he called him Malik (King-like) and gave him a high position in the army. Ambar deserted in about 1590 and set himself up as a mercenary with more than 1500 men. In 1595 the Sultan of Ahmadnagar's prime minister asked Ambar to join him in the Deccan's opposition to Mughal rule in the north. He proved to be so successful a leader that he was able to take the Sultan prisoner and appoint himself Regent. His army now encompassed 60,000 horsemen and proved effective in preventing the Moghul Emperor Akbar, and later his successor Jahangir, from wresting control of the Deccan. Only after Ambar's death in 1626 would the Mughals be able to claim control of the Deccan. Jahangir subsequently wrote that 'In the art of soldiering Ambar was unique in his age'. Ambar was also an innovator: he initiated a postal service, promoted trade, developed agriculture with novel irrigation systems, and introduced taxation rules that were ahead of their time. He invited writers and academics from Arabia and Persia, as well as from within India, to join him in his new capital at Kirkee (near Pune). 'With a passion for planned civic development and embellishment, he furnished his capital with wide roads, canals, drains, public gardens, and buildings. ... Ambar was certainly not the last Habshi [Abyssinian] to leave a mark on Indian history, though he remained the most notable.[23]

Of course it wasn't just the odd slave who showed what an Ethiopian of intellect and drive could achieve. Rulers like Tewodros II who unified the country in 1855, or his successor Menelik II, who halted an Italian invasion in 1896 and averted colonial rule, show that Africans in power are as capable as any European of political or military success. The following chapters will provide more examples of outstanding men from all parts of sub-Saharan Africa. These personages were presumably all to the right of a bell curve like that of Fig. 1. But that is precisely my point. Such people have existed throughout the world and at all times – though no more frequently today than in the past: as Tennyson wrote, 'Knowledge comes, but wisdom lingers.'[24]

So there is a Guido somewhere in sub-Saharan Africa. Readers of an older generation will remember the short story by Aldous

Huxley, in which the narrator and his wife have rented a Tuscan villa for the summer. Their four-year-old son Robin's playmate Guido is a somewhat older peasant boy – at six or so years of age too young to work in the fields just yet.

"Kneeling on the floor, he was drawing with the point of his blackened stick on the flagstones. And Robin, kneeling imitatively beside him, was growing, I could see, rather impatient with this very slow game.

'Guido,' he said. But Guido paid no attention. Pensively frowning, he went on with his diagram. 'Guido!' The younger child bent down and then craned round his neck so as to look up into Guido's face. 'Why don't you draw a train?'

'Afterwards,' said Guido, 'but I just want to show you this first. It's *so* beautiful,' he added cajolingly.

'But I want a train,' Robin persisted.

'In a moment. Do just wait a moment.' The tone was almost imploring. Robin armed himself with renewed patience. A minute later Guido had finished both his diagrams.

'There!' he said triumphantly, and straightened himself up to look at them. 'Now I'll explain.'

And he proceeded to prove the theorem of Pythagoras – not in Euclid's way, but by the simpler and more satisfying method which was, in all probability, employed by Pythagoras himself. He had drawn a square and dissected it, by a pair of crossed perpendiculars, into two squares and two equal rectangles ... ...

'Guido!' I called. The two children turned and looked up. 'Who taught you to draw those squares?' It was conceivable, of course, that somebody might have taught him.

'Nobody.' He shook his head. Then, rather anxiously, as though he was afraid there might be something wrong about drawing squares, he went on to apologise and explain. 'You see,' he said, 'it seemed to me so beautiful. Because those squares' – he pointed at the two small squares in the first figure – 'are just as big as this one.' And, indicating the square on the hypotenuse in the second diagram, he looked up at me with a deprecating smile.

I nodded. 'Yes, it's very beautiful,' I said – 'it's very beautiful indeed.'

An expression of delighted relief appeared on his face; he laughed with pleasure. 'You see, it's like this,' he went on, eager to initiate me into the glorious secret he had discovered ....''[25]

Many factors, of course, contribute to success or failure of a nation, as discussed in the previous chapter. For now, let me remind the reader of where we all came from. Then in the next chapter I will refer briefly to one of the world's oldest nations – one that emerged on African soil. I'll also show that sub-Saharan Africa was home to thriving kingdoms long before any European entered that continent.

The Earliest Africans

We are all Africans. Ancestral *Homo* species emerged along the Rift Valley in eastern Africa around 2 million years ago. By 200,000 to 160,000 years ago [26] our own species, *H sapiens*, had appeared. Recent re-dating of skulls found in Morocco has pushed back the arrival of *H sapiens*, or at least of a *H sapiens*-like precursor, to some 300,000 years ago.[27] By this time, some of our most recent ancestors (*H heidelbergensis*) had moved westward into West, Northwest and Central Africa;[28] such a subset of *H heidelbergensis* descendants, who appear to have lived around 14^0 N latitude, 12^0 E longitude, near the present border between Niger, Nigeria and Chad [29] could be our direct ancestors. Gradually *H sapiens'* habitat expanded. I will occasionally use the word 'his' in referring to *H sapiens* for convenience in this book, but mean, of course, 'his and hers': everywhere *H sapiens* went, it was in groups containing females. By 100,000 years ago they were in South Africa. By 70,000 years ago they had begun to move into Eurasia (across the land bridge at the eastern end of the Mediterranean and across the Red Sea). Around 40,000 years ago they had reached Australia by way of south-east Asia. The earth was still in the grips of its most recent ice age and sea levels were lower than today. Many of the Indonesian islands were a single land mass ('Sunda Land'), as were New Guinea, Australia and Tasmania ('Sahul'). But to get from Sunda Land to Sahul meant crossing a considerable amount of open water, a remarkable achievement. By 40,000 years ago *H sapiens* were also settling in Europe. Here they met other humans (*H Neanderthalis;* Neanderthal Man) whose ancestors had left Africa at a much earlier time. Neanderthals were gradually displaced over the next 10,000 years or so. Whether the newcomers were actually responsible for driving their predecessors to extinction is not clear. That human populations are constantly on the move is indicated also by evidence that some of those who ventured *out* of Africa subsequently returned: it appears that modern humans who had lived in the Middle East returned to settle in the Horn of Africa some 23,000 years ago.[30] A more recent migration of Eurasians back to Africa may have occurred around 10,500 to 7,500 years ago,[31] a period, incidentally, that also saw the 'greening' of the Sahara due to heavy rains. The fact that skeletal remains found in Israel and Morocco have recently been reassessed as older than previously-thought 'are a reminder that corridors on the African periphery 300,000 years ago might have periodically linked northern Africa and western Asia.'[31a]

Much earlier, around 1.9 – 1.6 million years ago, as the ancestors of *H sapiens* moved from dense forest into open savannah, they began to lose their body hair.[32] Loss of body hair aided dissipation of heat through sweating, and enabled them to roam far and wide in bright sunlight. But being light-skinned made them vulnerable to the damaging effects of ultra-violet (UV) radiation in sunlight. A high concentration of the black compound melanin in one's skin protects against the damaging effects of UV radiation (as does thick body hair which other primates, whose skin underneath is light, have retained to this day). The possession of black skin therefore became advantageous to humans living in tropical Africa. The same is true of those who migrated from south-east Asia to Australia 40,000 years ago. They are more closely related to Eurasians than to Africans, and developed dark skin *after* they arrived in

Australia. This is an example of 'convergent evolution': the appearance of similar features in populations that have quite distinct ancestry. A prime example of convergent evolution in animals concerns the wings of insects and birds: these share many features, including the ability to fly, though they developed from quite different ancestors. Dark skin is actually a very poor genetic marker. Most black Ethiopians are more closely related to light-skinned Armenians, Jews and (surprisingly) Norwegians than to dark skinned Bantu speakers,[33] while black Somali people are more closely related to Arabs than to other Africans.[34]

The emergence of black skin occurs relatively rapidly in evolutionary terms, possibly over as little as a hundred generations (approximately 2,500 years). Other evolutionary changes are much slower: for example it took 2 million years for our ancestors' brain to double in size. North or south of the equator solar radiation is less intense, and so those who moved out of tropical Africa would gradually lose some of the melanin in their skin (or who never possessed it in the first place), through selection of lighter-coloured individuals.[35] An advantage of lighter skin is that it allows the generation of vitamin D through UV radiation. The vitamin aids the absorption of calcium, which is required for the growth of bones and other processes. As humans settled further north, lighter-skinned ones held sway, though some scientists think this happened long *after* our ancestors reached Europe and began agricultural practices.[36] Whatever else, the idea that skin colour is in any way related to a characteristic like intelligence is absurd. As mentioned, non-human apes like chimpanzees have lighter skin but no member – even of the Ku Klux Klan –has suggested that chimpanzees outperform American blacks.

An equally rapid rate of evolution concerns another genetic variant that became selected and rapidly spread among northerners. This is the ability to degrade lactose, the sugar in milk. All mammals have this capacity as babies, of course, since they feed on their mothers' milk. But at weaning, the gene that is responsible for the enzyme lactase – that splits indigestible lactose into nutritious glucose and galactose – becomes inactivated. No more lactase enzyme is made and any lactose that enters the gut cannot be digested (passage of lactose into the blood stream and its breakdown into glucose and galactose occur simultaneously). Drinking milk then makes one sick – a condition known as lactose intolerance. Until the domestication of animals like sheep, goats and later, cows, the problem did not exist. Farming of sheep and goats began to spread out of the Middle East some ten thousand years ago, reaching northern Europe around four thousand years later. Initially the lactose-intolerant inhabitants would have used milk mainly to make butter and cheese. The meat, of course, they cooked. Only as lactose tolerance gradually spread among them, were they able to drink milk. This ability emerged during the early Bronze Age, concomitantly with the spread of Indo-European languages, by migrations out of a region between the Black Sea and the Caspian, long after the appearance of light skin.[37] As for cattle, we now believe that their domestication began not only in the Middle East, but independently in India and Africa – the eastern Sahara – as well.[38] So it is not surprising that lactase persistence is higher in eastern Africa than in the west.[39] What is clear is that Africans of seven thousand years ago had the perspicacity to invent a new way of life: taming wild animals in order to be able to feed off their meat on demand. Not bad for an 'inferior' people of 'lesser intelligence'.

Conclusion

Intelligence (*g* or IQ) is around 50% inherited, with the rest due to environmental influences. These include the mother's health during development of her offspring *in utero*, upbringing, infectious episodes, and so forth. It is senseless to make comparisons between different ethnic groupings. There are bright individuals in any cluster of *Homo sapiens*. Whether they are able to realise their innate potential or not depends on the society in which they live. A group's ability to innovate and form civilisations does not depend on the average *g* or IQ of its members either.

End Notes

[1] Fourth Debate with Stephen A. Douglas at Charleston, Illinois, September 18, 1858 (The Collected Works of Abraham Lincoln edited by Roy P. Basler, Volume III, pp. 145-146.)

[2] James Beattie: *Elements of Moral Science*, 3rd ed (Edinburgh 1817 – published after his death) III 65; quoted in Anstey (1975) p 112

[3] quoted by Vaillant (1990) p 50

[4] Robert Plomin: *General Cognitive Ability* in Plomin *et al* (2002) p 183

[5] quoted by Suddendorf (2013) p 139

[6] Carey (2011)

[7] *Nature* **514**:142 (2014)

[8] Sylvane Desrivières *et al*: Single nucleotide polymorphism in the neuroplastin locus associates with cortical thickness and intellectual ability in adolescents. *Molecular Psychiatry* (2014) 1-12

[9] quoted by Vaillant (1990) p 51

[10] Horton (1868) p i

[11] Miele (2002) p 180

[12] Herrnstein and Murray (1994) p 269

[13] Gardner (1984)

[14] Edgerton (1992) p 68

[15] Pasternak (2007)

[16] van Vugt and Anjana (2010)

[17] Dunbar (2010)

[18] *New Scientist* 31 August 2013

[19] Science aid. Donors and African governments must invest in advanced science and maths education. *Nature* **491**: 159-160, 2012

[20] Blyden (1967) p 16

[21] Segal (2001) p 46

[22] *ibid* p 72

[23] *ibid* p 75 *et seq*

[24] Alfred, Lord Tennyson: *Locksley Hall* 1, 143

[25] Huxley (1928) p 317 *et seq*

[26] see for example Tattersall (2012) p 186. Note that a partly 'out of Asia' hypothesis has re-emerged recently; see Jane Qiu: The forgotten continent *Nature* **535**: 218-220 (2016)

[27] Chris Stringer and Julia Galway-Witham: On the origin of our species. *Nature*: **546**: 212-214 (2017)

[28] Cruciani, Fulfil; Trombetta, Beniamino; Massaia, Andrea; Destro-Bisol, Giovanni; Sellitto, Daniele; Scozzari, Rosaria: A Revised Root for the Human Y Chromosomal Phylogenetic Tree: The Origin of Patrilineal Diversity in Africa. *The American Journal of Human Genetics* **88** (6): 814–8 (2011)

[29] Dunbar (2016) p 220

[30] *Nature* **510**: 447 (2014)

[31] *Nature* **517**: 276 (2015)

[31a] A more recent return, a mere 3,000 years ago, has also been suggested by M Gallego Llorente *et al*: *Science* http://doi.org/78d 2015, referred to in *Nature* **526**: 296 (2015)

[32] Tattersall (2012) p 110

[33] Wilson, James F *et al*: Population genetic structure of variable drug response. *Nature Genetics* **29**: 265-9 (2001)

[34] Mohamoud, A M: P52 characteristics of HLA Class I and Class II antigens of the Somali population. *Transfusion Medicine* **16** (supplement s1): 47 (2006)

[35] Gregory S Barsh: What controls variation in human skin color? *PLOS Biology* Oct 13, 2003; DOI: 10.1371/journal.pbio0000027

[36] see https://en.wikipedia.org/wiki/Human_skin_color

[37] DNA deluge reveals Bronze Age secrets. *Nature* **522**: 140-141; John Novembre: Ancient DNA steps into the language debate. *Nature* **522**: 164-165; Morten E Allentoft *et al*: Population genomics of Bronze Age Eurasia. *Nature* **522**: 167-172 (2015)

[38] Zeder MA. Domestication and early agriculture in the Mediterranean Basin: Origins, diffusion, and impact. *Proc Nat Acad Sci* **105**:11597-11604 (2008); see also Stephen Mithen, *Phil Trans R Soc B* **362**: 705-718, 2007, quoted in Wilson (2012), p 16, for a list of where and when different agricultural products were first raised

[39] Erika Check. Human evolution: How Africa learned to love the cow. *Nature* **444**: 994-996 (2006)

Chapter Four
ABILITY: GOVERNMENT AND CULTURE

Ancient Egypt

Derogatory views about African intelligence during the nineteenth and early twentieth century were rarely extended to the lighter-skinned inhabitants of North Africa. It could hardly be otherwise. Did not the ancient Egyptians precede, by more than two thousand years, the ingenuity of the Athenians – whom Europeans regard as their forefathers – in astronomy, architecture and sculpture? There are even those who regard Egypt as the very inspiration for Greek civilisation. Solon of Athens is said to have visited Egypt 'in order to draw inspiration from the laws of that country' [1] and '… it was said that the ancient Greeks represented their favourite goddess of Wisdom – Minerva – as an African princess.'[2] Moreover 'At least in principle, studying the influence of Egyptian vocabulary on the language spoken by the proto-Greeks in the second millennium BC can tell you more about classical Greek culture than studying Sophocles and Plato.'[3] To really complicate matters, two historians, Martin Bernal [4] and Cheikh Anta Diop [5] have suggested that the ancient Egyptians were actually black, which would turn the Eurocentric view of civilisation on its back.

While surviving sculptures cannot tell us anything about skin colour, cranial shape has led anthropologists to suggest one or other ethnicity. But this is dangerous ground. First, as in portrait painting, the artist or the subject – especially if he's a Pharaoh – can choose to hide certain traits. Second, features of quite unrelated groups often show a resemblance. For example you may say that the black granite statue of Amenemhat III [6] that is in the Hermitage in St Petersburg, displays rather negroid traits with a broad nose, a feature that is also apparent – though to a lesser extent – in the lighter statuette of him in the Louvre. I could then point you in the direction of the statue of the clearly non-African neo-Sumerian king Gudea of Lagash [7] in the Metropolitan Museum of Art in New York that shows the subject with a similarly broad nose. It is precisely this sort of ambiguity (as well as much cultural information) that has led some historians to propose a Mesopotamian origin of the Pharaohs. Nevertheless, Cheikh Anta Diop's assertion that the early Pharaohs were black is not easily dismissed. That certain later ones, such as the Nubian king Piye and his successors of the twenty-fifth dynasty (see below), were negroid is not in dispute, any more than that the Hyksos invaders of the 15th Dynasty and their successors of the 16th Dynasty were of Asiatic (Semitic) origin.

The point is that no one knows exactly where the ancient Egyptians came from. The likeliest origin of the first settlers in the Nile valley is from the Libyan desert to the west, that began to be occupied by pastoralists 12,000 – 10,000 years ago during the Sahara's wet period as desert turned to savannah, before reverting to its desiccated state again some three thousand years later. In this region animal husbandry preceded the raising of crops, in contrast to the situation in the Fertile Crescent of Mesopotamia. Rock paintings found in the Saharan highlands dating back to around 6,000 years ago confirm the presence of sheep and goats, with no evidence of agriculture. Three distinct groups of humans appeared to occupy the region: negroid people, black but non-negroid people and lighter-skinned people.[8] As noted in the preceding chapter, some of these may have been Eurasians who migrated *back* to Africa at this time. Once some of these desert inhabitants were settled along the banks of the great river, they found the opportunities for agriculture astounding. The annual floods brought nutrients to the land, and once the water had receded, the earth was so fertile you could simply drop grains of wheat or barley on to it, and the cereals would prosper: no need for hoeing or ploughing.

The first villages began to appear around 7,000 years ago. As mentioned, the generally-held view, that the domestication of both plants and animals started in the Fertile Crescent around 9,500 years ago, may need revision.[9] Undoubtedly there was contact between Egypt and the Arabian peninsula from this time onwards, and the possibility that the ancient Egyptians learned the art of kingship and its attendant ideas from the Sumerians persists. Nevertheless 'Egypt's emergence as a true nation state … is well charted. Her roots lay deep in the earth of the Valley on which her splendid temples, palaces, and tombs were to be built; but she was also profoundly African….'[10] Whatever theory you care to espouse, it is likely that most of the people in North Africa or the Arabian peninsula were not dark-skinned.

What of Martin Bernal and his *Black Athena*, then? There was certainly contact between those living along the Nile delta, and those occupying the upper reaches of the Nile, in Nubia (present day Sudan). These were probably then, as now, of negroid stock, many of whom might have been imported into ancient Egypt as slaves. So far as the ruling and priestly classes are concerned, sculptural remains exist, but as remarked earlier, it is difficult to discern the subject's exact origin. Much more research needs to be carried out on Pharaohnic mummies to establish their exact ethnic origin. So far, what has been reported for ancient DNA by one team is hotly disputed by another.[11]

Sub-Saharan states
Nubia (the region also known as *Kush*)
While succeeding dynasties were ruling Egypt with pomp and splendour, beyond its southern border along the upper Nile, a number of village settlements were growing into states of their own. One of the earliest was based on Kerma, a city around the third cataract up the Nile that had risen to prominence during the second millennium BC. It has been dubbed 'black Africa's first identifiable state' [12] and 'the earliest city in Africa outside of

Egypt.'[13] The burial of their kings, for example, predates any Egyptian influence.[14] After Kerma was taken over by warring Egyptians during the expansionist New Kingdom (1540-1070 BC), Nubian culture moved further south. A kingdom known as Napata emerged just below the fourth cataract during the ninth century BC. A hundred years into its history, Napata reversed the situation: its king Piye conquered his northern neighbours, and Egypt's twenty-fifth dynasty was effectively ruled by a succession of Nubians. Moreover Piye did so from his original power base in Napata.[15] Gradually the dominance of Napata declined, and around 400 BC, a settlement yet further up the Nile developed statehood. This was Meroë, considered by some to be part of a continuing Napatan society. It was situated between the fifth and sixth cataract, some 200 km below the present city of Khartoum. 'Meroë was an African civilization, firmly based on African soil, and developed by an African population.'[16] Moreover 'Nubian burials, pottery, and pictographs confirm the cultural independence of African Nubia from African Egypt.'[17] All these states have left impressive architectural remains, but how independent of Egyptian influence were they really? According to archaeologist Graham Connah, 'Rather than continuing to see the development of social complexity in Nubia as secondary to that of Egypt, we should perhaps begin to regard them as parallel and interacting African achievements. It is no longer Egypt that can claim Nubia but Africa that should reclaim Egypt.'[18]

Aksum (Axum)

There is evidence that a few hundred miles away from the Nile valley, in the mountainous region of present day northern Ethiopia, Cushitic-speaking people were raising cereals and vegetables some 5,000 years ago [19] – long before any Semitic-speaking immigrants from southern Arabia arrived on the scene.[20] Indeed, there is a view that the parent language – Afro-Asiatic (Hamitic-Semitic) – actually split into Proto-Cushitic and Proto-Semitic 'in the Sudan-Ethiopian borderlands' [21] Pastoralism, a prerequisite for the establishment of villages and a communal form of life, led over the next three millennia to the emergence of a city state that would rival the achievements taking place in Nubia. One of the reasons for success is the climate. At a height of 6,000 to 10,000 feet, despite being near the equator, the temperature is mild enough to prevent the heat-loving tsetse fly (see Fig 5.1) and other transmitters of disease from breeding. Domestic animals could therefore thrive and invigorate the economy.

As a result Aksum 'boasted urban centres; its own form of writing; coinage in gold, silver and bronze; masonry buildings of distinctive architectural style ... the technological achievements of the Acuity period ... must rank amongst the most sophisticated to be found in pre-colonial Africa. ...To quarry and transport and attempt to erect such a monolith as the largest of the stelae at Aksum, nearly 33 m long and about 517 tonnes in weight, must have involved theoretical knowledge, practical skill and good organisation. ... The dam at Kohaito and the Mai Shum reservoir at Aksum ... suggest that engineering expertise was applied to the task of water storage.'[22] Aksum, close to the Red Sea below it to the east, was not an isolated state. In its heyday it traded not just with Nubia and Egypt, but also with South Arabia, the Persian Gulf, and as far away as India and Sri Lanka. Its inhabitants were early converts to Christianity, a religion that was not displaced here by the arrival of Islam. Indeed, like Egypt but unlike Nubia, Aksum-Ethiopia can be said to have maintained its national identity in one form or another from ancient to modern times (see chapter 8). Its importance, though, began to decline after the Muslim Arab invasions of the seventh century, coupled with the loss of trade with Rome as that empire began to collapse. Cities like Baghdad, to the north of the Arabian Peninsula, now took pride of place.

Ancient Ghana, Mali and Songhay

Trade across the Red Sea may have stimulated the economy of Aksum, but in the states that were growing up in the savannah region of West Africa, sea trade was not an option. The winds along the Atlantic coast are from the north at all times of year, and until the arrival of the Portuguese with their lateen sail in the fifteenth century, it would have been foolish to leave a coastal area and sail south, as there was no way of returning. In contrast, along the Nile valley trade was easy. Northern winds facilitated upstream traffic, while to return north the current alone could do the job. What trade there was in West Africa centred on the camel not the boat. The ancestor of today's camels evolved millions of years ago, in North America as it happens. By 12,000 years ago modern versions of the camel had wandered across the ice-bound Bering Straits into Asia (in the direction opposite to that taken by the humans who would populate the Americas). The single-humped camel or dromedary was domesticated in the Arabian Peninsula around nine thousand years later, whence it was subsequently imported into Africa. The wild camels that had roamed across that continent had become extinct around 5,000 years ago.[23]

During the Late Stone Age, at the time the now-domesticated camel reappeared in Africa, the human population on the continent was between three and four million people. At least half of these were living in West Africa, south of the Sahara.[24] The latter had become desert a thousand years earlier and had consequently driven its inhabitants east into the Nile Valley and south into West Africa. It was in the region of fertile savannah around the bend of the upper Niger, where its flow in a north-eastern direction gradually swings to the south-east (with Timbuktu roughly in the middle) that stable settlements took hold. Gradually these became kingdoms. One of the earliest, founded around 300 AD, was Wagadu or Ghana (not to be confused with the modern country of that name 500 miles to the south east on the coast of the Bay of Guinea). The word *ghana* was one of the king's titles that translates to 'war chief'. Few records remain, and our knowledge of this and other kingdoms is based largely on Muslim scholars who visited in later times, or wrote about it based on other travellers' knowledge, in far away Cordoba. Islam provided a cohesive force with a strong basis for empire-building.

The wealth of Ghana depended on trade: gold, ivory and slaves were exported north across the Sahara in exchange for salt and cloth. By the twelfth century slaves had appeared in Muslim-controlled southern Spain, and by the fourteenth century (by which time Ghana had been supplanted by Mali as the dominant kingdom) in Christian states like Valencia and Mallorca, as well as in Montpellier and Marseilles.[25] Since the king kept most of the profits (as favoured by some African rulers to this day), he became extremely rich and was able to raise large armies when required: two hundred thousand warriors are said to have been at his behest. His administrative capital (Koumbi Saleh, also called Ghana) numbered as many as 15,000 inhabitants by the eleventh century. Its exact location is not known: it was probably situated in the south eastern corner of what is now Mauretania. The king's chief advisers were literate Muslims who occupied their own town close by. Although the main trade routes were north across the Sahara, there was also likely contact with Nubia and Egypt to the east (that brought bilharzia as well as novel goods to tropical Africa).

Trade across the Sahara may have been the source of Ghana's prosperity, but other trans-Saharan excursions brought the empire to its knees. By 1054 the Almoravid rulers of Morocco decided that instead of paying for their imports from Ghana, they would take the country over. Superior in weaponry, they were in the capital within ten years. Ghana's prestige declined rapidly, with rivalry between chieftains contributing to its demise, and by about 1240, Mande-speaking groups had supplanted the Soninke in Ghana to form the kingdom of Mali. Whereas Ghana had ruled only the lands to the north of the Niger, Mali occupied the southern banks as well, and as far west as the Atlantic, encompassing present-day Senegal as well as the modern country by that name. Trade across the Sahara continued. And not only trade. In the early fourteenth century a charismatic ruler called Mansa Musa who, unlike the kings of Ghana, was a Muslim, established embassies in Morocco and Egypt and himself went on the *hadj* to Mecca. Musa was as generous as he was devout. He distributed so much gold in Cairo on his way to Mecca, that the price of bullion actually fell.[26]

Two major cities on the Niger, Timbuktu to the west and Gao to the south east of the middle of the Niger bend, stand out. Houses were made of brick, and palaces and mosques, designed by the premier architect of Granada, appeared. Both towns have remained important trading centres on this great river right up to the present time. Mali's army, made up of infantry (free bowmen) reinforced by cavalry after the introduction of war-horses during the fourteenth century, fought several successful skirmishes. Around 1450 however, Mali's domination began to wane when the Songhay people of Gao gradually took over the empire. Songhay kings, like their Mali predecessors, were Muslim. One of their most successful rulers, Muhammad I Askia, repeated in style the extravagant *hadj* that Mansa Musa had undertaken nearly two hundred years earlier. 1,500 soldiers accompanied the caravan to protect the 300,000 pieces of gold carried by the king. Muhammad was more scholar than warrior: 'It may well be that he was the greatest ruler that West Africa ever saw, and that is saying a good deal. That greatness did not depend on warfare and massacre and the large scale misery of thousands of innocent people: it was due to the spirit and the intellect of this man.'[27]

At no time, however, was the religion of Islam forced upon the rest of the population, the bulk of whom continued their observance of African beliefs. The structure of nationhood was conducive to cultural innovation. According to one of its own sons 'Throughout the whole of the Middle Ages, West Africa had a more solid politico-social organisation, attained a greater degree of internal cohesion and was more conscious of the social function of science than Europe.'[28] Much of this was due to Islamic influence. 'It was no accident that the Islamic empires, such as Ghana and Kanuri (comprising parts of today's Nigeria, Chad and Cameroon), lasted the longest in Africa's history.'[29] A sixteenth century account about the 'Kingdom of Melli', which probably refers to the area south west of Timbuktu, is illustrative of life at that time: 'The region itself yieldeth great abundance of corn, flesh and cotton. Here are many artificers and merchants in all places; and yet the king honourably entertaineth all strangers. The inhabitants are rich, and have plenty of wares. Here are great store of temples, priests and professors, which professors read their lectures in the temples. The people of this region excel all other Negroes in wit, civility, and industry.'[30] The Dogon tribe who live in this area are said to be particularly knowledgeable due to a postulated descent from the ancient Egyptians. They have apparently been aware that the bright star Sirius A, in the constellation of Canis Major, is orbited by another star Sirius B that is too small to see with the naked eye.[31] Maverick author Robert Temple puts this down to the possibility that the Dogon developed the telescope centuries before anyone else.[32]

All empires encompass a heterogeneous mix of people who identify themselves with smaller enclaves. The Roman Empire at the beginning of Hadrian's reign ranged from Hispania in the west to Babylonia in the east, from Britannia in the north to Egypt in the south; each community spoke its own language. The same was true of the empires of Ghana, Mali and Songhay: The latter, at its height under Sonni (Sunni) Ali in the late fifteenth century, was the largest of the three. Its lands stretched from the Atlantic coast in the west to Hausaland (present-day north eastern Nigeria, around its capital Kano) in the east, from present-day Mauretania in the north to present-day Guinea and Benin in the south. Its vassal states were home to Berbers in the north, Wolof in the west, Ewe in the south east, Fulani in the north east, Mande and Songhai throughout.

It may be thought that without the contribution of Islamic scholars and traders, the empires of Ghana, Mali and Songhay would not have come into being. This is not true, though Arab influence certainly contributed toward their political development and the introduction of literacy. 'So it came about that important centres of book learning arose in West Africa, the first of their kind: after 1300 at Niani, the capital of the Mali Empire; after 1400 at Timbuktu, which became a city of the Songhay Empire, and elsewhere. The Muslim schools of

Timbuktu became especially famous: they formed an early kind of university.'[33] But according to Graham Connah, '…archaeology has confirmed the historical evidence that … the inhabitants of the earliest cities and states of the West African savannah were definitely not Muslims … urban development at Jenné-jeno', another city on the upper reaches of the Niger, 'by early in the first millennium would appear to confirm the impression that the origins of urbanization and state formation in the West African savanna *were* pre-Islamic.'[34]

Long before the arrival of Arabs during the seventh century, indigenous African crafts had already begun to emerge. The mining industry, for example, encompassed not just gold, but also iron. The metal was being smelted in West Africa by 650 BC (some put it even earlier, as part of Nok culture around 800 BC [35]), at the same time as the practice was being introduced into northern Europe. And it did not derive from the clever Egyptians, who lacked this crucial technology (though they did fashion magnetic, iron-containing meteorites into precious objects that have been found in pharaonic tombs.[36] Iron *was* being worked in Meroë at this time, but as mentioned above, these Nubians were distinctly of sub-Saharan descent. Moreover 'the beehive and cylindrical furnaces of West Africa were quite different from those in North Africa and Mesopotamia and were indicative of innovations in, if not the invention of, iron-smelting technology that were unique to (sub-Saharan) Africa.'[37]

Nor did these people lack commercial capabilities. They developed 'economies which made agricultural produce available in amounts large enough to be sold in rural and urban markets; craft specialization often organized along the line of craft guilds, whose members manufactured goods to be sold in these markets; different kinds of currencies which were nearly always convertible one to another and, later, to European denominations of values; and elaborate trading systems, external as well as internal. Goods produced in even the smallest West African societies were circulated in local market centers, and ultimately by porters, caravans, and boats, to the large Sudanese emporiums from which they could be shipped to Mediterranean areas in exchange for foreign products.'[38]

Novelty was not restricted to commercial enterprise. West African art is as distinctive as that from Aksum,[39] Nubia [40] or Great Zimbabwe (iron-age pottery found by a schoolboy in 1962 near Lydenburg in South Africa [41]). Most of the artefacts relate to cultures that developed close to the Niger River: from the savannah region of the lower Niger valley in present-day Niger,[42] from further downstream near Nok in present-day Nigeria [43] and from the forest region between Ife and Benin.[44] The people of sub-Saharan Africa were just as interested in producing novel works of art as those in contemporary European, Asian, or American cultures. Some of the artefacts that were produced inspire artists to this day. American author Adam Hochschild speculates that Picasso and his contemporaries developed Cubism only after they had seen primitive figurines from the Congo brought to the African art exhibition in Paris of 1907.[45] It is interesting to note that some rock art, which flourished particularly in Southern Africa,[46] is claimed to be as old (28,000 to 26,000 years ago in a cave in Namibia) as that found in Europe (32,000 to 30,000 in the Chauvet cave in southern France, for example). But a more realistic estimate puts rock paintings such as those found South Africa's Eastern Cape Province at around 5,700 years ago.[47] A recent finding of non-figurative art in the Southern Cape, said to be 100,000 years old,[48] would predate even the time that *H sapiens* first migrated out of Africa into Eurasia.

My point is simple. Complex societies emerged in western Africa independently of outside influences. They had the ingenuity and drive to make it happen. So why did they all decline? As pointed out in chapter 2, at least four reasons for failure can be identified: wars, climate change (both of which can lead to unsustainable demographic changes), human error, and decadence due to too long a duration of wealth and power in any one dynasty. In the case of the early West African nations, the first reason was probably predominant: partly through wars amongst themselves and partly through subjugation by Berber and Tuareg invaders from North Africa. But as Ghana, Mali and Songhay declined, a new kingdom in the rain forest that stretched as far as the Gulf of Guinea to the south, in the land of the Akan people, came into being. This would grow into the empire known as Asante or Ashanti (chapter 10). And in the case of Aksum, the gradual development into modern Ethiopia (chapter 8) was fairly continuous.

Great Zimbabwe

In the south eastern highlands of Zimbabwe there is a small town called Masvingo. If you were to visit it, you would be astonished to find the ruins of what was once the largest stone structure in the whole of sub-Saharan Africa. From late in the thirteenth century, for the next two hundred years, the people of this region were building elaborate edifices made of local granite that are indicative of a structured and hierarchical society. Gold and iron, tin and copper were in use. The people traded not just with coastal cities like Kilwa to the north, but with countries as far away as Persia and China. A glazed Persian bowl and objects made of Chinese porcelain that have been found among the ruins attest to the Zimbabweans taste for exotic artefacts. Farming was extensive, cattle were abundant, and the people could afford to live off meat. But by the sixteenth century, before the arrival of Europeans, Great Zimbabwe and its surrounding towns and villages were abandoned. The main reason for this was over-use of their resources – just like the Maya in Central America or the Rapa on Easter Island – though disease and climatic change may have played a part. It is no surprise that when Bishop Abel Muzorewa, head of the United African National Council, was searching for a name to replace that of Southern Rhodesia in 1979, he chose the illustrious name of Zimbabwe (originally Zimbabwe Rhodesia).

Conclusion

The four examples I have given – and there are others,[49][50] – show that in several areas of sub-Saharan Africa that were relatively isolated from each other, civilised societies with different ethnic roots emerged at a time when northern Europeans were barely beginning to disseminate Celtic culture. Whether the people were Noba (in Nubia), Ge'ez speakers (in Aksum), Soninke (in Ghana, Mali and Songhay), or Shona (in Zimbabwe), all were distinctly African. As the German anthropologist Leo Frobenius pointed out a century ago, European and African cultures are each unique. To place them in a kind of hierarchy makes no sense. Africans may not have developed the wheel (any more than did the sophisticated pre-Columbian cultures of the Americas), the plough, or a written language (except in Aksum), but they initiated agriculture, and their own versions of kingship and nationhood, as well as buildings of stone and painted pottery.

Most historians of Africa ascribe the demise of these empires to the ravages of war and some of the other reasons mentioned earlier. But another, more specific, hypothesis is that 'The conformance to tradition arose from a pervading fear of the of the spirits who were believed to frown on innovation: their unceasing influence bred mental discipline, fortitude, and self-denial, as well as lack of initiative or ambition. … Of necessity so much of their time was spent in acquiring food or propitiating the ancestral spirits that little was left for intellectual pursuits. Few questions were asked, few doubts raised, and curiosity was discouraged by the tribal elders lest it challenged their authority. And so, because the inhabitants of Old Africa sustained a culture of acceptance and encountered the minimum of novel experiences, the already conservative pressures of society tended to be perpetuated and made them highly resistant to change.'[51] As I have pointed out elsewhere, it is curiosity that drives humanity forwards.[52]

Certain cultural practices of Pharaohnic Egypt may have been transmitted southwards into Nubia and possibly westwards across the desert into ancient Ghana, but they were adapted and refashioned by the inhabitants of those areas in the same way that Graeco-Roman ideas filtered into the barbarian lands of northern

Europe. If Europeans pride themselves on their Athenian heritage, there is no reason why their African counterparts should not look back on ancient Egypt with equal satisfaction. But they don't really need to.

End Notes

[1] Diop (1987) p 27

[2] Horton (1868) p 66

[3] North (2003) p 38

[4] Bernal (2003) pp 23-30

[5] Cheikh Anta Diop: *The African Origin of Civilization: Myth or Reality* quoted in Collins and Burns (2014) p 28

[6] Egyptian Middle Kingdom; 12th dynasty; late nineteenth/early eighteenth century BC

[7] twenty-first century BC

[8] Iliffe (1995) p 14

[9] Wendorf and Schild (1980) p 398

[10] Rice (1990) p 24

[11] Ancient DNA: Curse of the Pharaoh's DNA, *Nature* **472**: 404-406 (2011)

[12] Connah (2001) p 34

[13] O'Connor (1993) p 50

[14] Collins and Burns (2014) p 30

[15] Fuller (2003) p 169

[16] Shinnie (1967) p 169

[17] Collins and Burns (2014) p 35

[18] Connah (2001) p 64

[19] Oliver (1991) p 44

[20] Iliffe (1995) p 15

[21] Marcus (1994) p 3

[22] Connah (2001) pp 66 and 93

[23] Bulliet (1975) p 34

[24] Davidson (1998) p 6

[25] Levtzion (1973) p 177

[26] Mackintosh-Smith (2002) p 325, footnote 17

[27] Niven (1964) pp 104-115

[28] Armattoe (1946) p 34

[29] Ayittey (1992) p 72 *et seq*

[30] from *The history and description of Africa and of the notable things therein contained / written by al-Hassan ibn Mohammed al-Wezaz al-Fasi, a Moor, baptized as Giovanni Leone, but better known as Leo Africanus; done into English in the year 1600 by John Pory; and now edited, with an introduction and notes, by Robert Brown* (Hakluyt Society, London, 1896); quoted by Blyden (1967) p 195

[31] see, for example, Temple (1976)

[32] Temple (2000) p 17

[33] Davidson (1998) p 154

[34] Connah (2001) p 138

[35] Collins and Burns (2014) map 4.1 on p 60

[36] Temple (2000) p 285

[37] Collins and Burns (2014) p 62

[38] Skinner (1964) p 205; quoted by Ayittey (2005) p 337.

[39] seated figure; 5th or 4th century BC: Garlake (2002) p 77

[40] winged standing figure; between the 4th and 6th century AD: *ibid* p 65

[41] hollow mask-shaped head; probably 9th – 10th century AD: *ibid* p 145

[42] terracotta Bura sculpture heads; between 3rd and 13th century AD: *ibid* p 109

[43] terracotta Nok sculpture of kneeling man; between 1000 BC and 300 AD: *ibid* p 112

[44] brass head of a Yoruba man; between 1300 and 1550 AD: *ibid* p 125

[45] Hochshild (1999) p 73

[46] Garlake (2002) pp 29-49

[47] Sarah Wild: Dreams of the Stone Age dates in southern Africa breakthrough. *Nature* **545**: 14-15 (2017)

[48] see http://www.bradshawfoundation.com/africa/oldest_art/

[49] Davidson (1998)

[50] Connah (2001)

[51] Ransford (1983) p 19.

[52] Pasternak (2003)

Chapter Five
GEOGRAPHY: AGRICULTURE AND DISEASE

The previous two chapters have shown that sub-Saharan Africa's failure, viewed from today's perspective, cannot be ascribed to a lack of ingenuity among its people. What might explain its lack of progress? Charles de Secondat, baron de Montesquieu thought that those who live in a tropical climate are lazy and lack inquisitiveness: 'The heat of the climate can be so excessive that the body there will be absolutely without strength. So, prostration will pass even to the spirit; no curiosity, no noble enterprise, no generous sentiment; inclinations will all be passive there; laziness there will be happiness....'[1] Can this really be true? Just look at the success of Singapore, situated right on the equator. If ever a nation took the advice of William Falconer, eighteenth century Scottish poet and sailor, to heart, it was Singapore. 'A commercial life may, in several respects, be accounted favourable to the intellectual faculties. Thus it tends to exercise, and consequently to improve, the memory it introduces a methodic arrangement into the business of life, which facilitates greatly, by instructing us to apply our abilities separately to their proper purposes. Commerce also enlarges the ideas, teaches nations their true interests, and is a cure for the most pernicious prejudices.'[2] Within a few years of liberation from colonial rule, Singapore's GDP per capita began to exceed that of the USA. Having only a small population (of hard-working people), of course, helps to inflate the figure. But that's the point. Why were they all hard-working in such a hot climate? The answer is to be found in the argument of Acemoglu and Robinson [3] that was presented in chapter 2. Post colonial administrations in Singapore may have been somewhat dictatorial, but they were essentially inclusive, not extractive. Practically all the early sub-Saharan African nations have been extractive, with little incentive for individuals to prosper. Moreover a key aspect of Singapore's success is that 'Lacking natural resources, the country was forced from the outset to adopt a long-term view that involved investing in human capital and imparting a strong work ethic. These are critical sources of economic transformation that continue to elude African countries.'[4]

Why Tropical Countries are Under-Developed

The American economist Jeffrey Sachs agrees with Montesquieu up to a point. Tropical countries don't do as well as temperate ones, but the reason is not torpor among the people. Rather it is a matter of deficient agriculture and poor health. Singapore (like Hong Kong) is a special case, in that its economy does not depend on agriculture. It has a highly educated work force that specialises in electronics, banking and other services. It is a seaport, and coastal nations in the tropics are said to outperform internal ones (though land-locked Botswana clearly bucks this generalisation). Early in the nineteenth century, when the economic benefits of the industrial revolution in Europe were only just beginning to take effect, the difference between the success of tropical and temperate regions was less marked. 'In 1820, GNP [5] per capita in the tropical regions was roughly 70 percent of GNP in the temperate-zone. By 1992, GNP per capita in the tropical regions was 25 percent of that in the temperate-zone.' [6] In short, the economies of nations in temperate zones grew steadily (more than 12-fold) throughout the nineteenth and twentieth centuries while those of tropical nations expanded only sluggishly (less than 5-fold).

The main point that Sachs [7] and others make is that climate is the main reason for sub-Saharan Africa's poor performance. Acemoglu and Robinson put it all down to the extractive nature of its societies. Who's right? That African nations prior to the arrival of Europeans were extractive cannot be denied. European nations themselves were extractive well into the eighteenth century. Most African nations remained extractive throughout the sixteenth, seventeenth, eighteenth, nineteenth and first half of the twentieth century, largely as a result of interlopers from abroad (chapters 6 and 7). Surprisingly, the situation did not change dramatically after independence (chapter 8). So both hypotheses have merit. The rest of this chapter will focus on the parts that agriculture, disease (the flip side of health), and natural resources play in holding back African nations. Let us not forget that today 'Africa is still an agricultural and pastoral continent. … More than 70 percent of Africans still toil the soil as subsistence farmers or tend their herds of sheep, goats, cattle and camels.'[8]

Agriculture

Domestication of crops and animals has arisen independently at least eight times in different regions of the world. In some areas cultivation of crops preceded animal husbandry, in others it was the reverse: 9,000 years ago, wheat and barley in Mesopotamia; 8,000 years ago, rice in middle China; 7,500 years ago, millet in northern China; 8 – 5,000 years ago, maize, beans and squash in central America; 7,000 years ago, cattle in Sahel (the belt of savannah between the Sahara to the north and the tropical forest to the south); also 7,000 years ago, llama and alpaca in Peru; 6,500 years ago, Taro and bananas in New Guinea; and 4,000 years ago, sunflowers and marsh elder in south east USA.[9] So by seven thousand years ago, farming communities along the lower Nile in the region of Faiyum, south west of Cairo, were grazing cattle and beginning to grow wheat and barley. The impetus appears to have come as much from the western desert as from Asia.[10] But then the climate changed, and today the Saharan desert supports little agriculture.

In southern Africa the situation is the reverse. The climate is sub-tropical, the soil is rich. That is why the immigrant Dutch became farmers (Boers) when they arrived at Cape Town in the eighteenth century, and why they followed this practice when they moved further inland, to the Orange Free State and the

Transvaal, in the nineteenth. Cecil Rhodes well recognised the agricultural potential of Matabeleland and Mashonaland to the north (Rhodesia became the bread basket of Africa) though the mineral resources (including diamonds and gold) excited him considerably more.

The earliest documented evidence of agricultural practices in sub-Saharan Africa is to be found in the savannah region of West Africa, where three thousand years ago cereals like millet and rice were domesticated and cattle, sheep and goats raised;[11] as mentioned above and in the previous chapter, cattle had already been domesticated thousands of years earlier. Within the bend of the upper Niger River the soil is particularly fertile because of the many lakes and tributaries that allow the land to be extensively irrigated. This has caused the region to be known as the Inner or Island Niger Delta. It is one of the areas where farming communities grew into urban centres. One of the earliest of these was Djenné-Djenno, in Mali, that by 800 AD was an established city *before* the arrival of knowledgeable Muslim traders from North Africa. So the progression from successful agriculture to city life in sub-Saharan Africa was achieved by the indigenous population not much later than it was in northern Europe.

Major crops

The most important crop in Africa today is maize (corn), with cassava (a root vegetable also known as yucca) a close second. Neither is indigenous. Maize derives from Central America, where it was domesticated more than five thousand years ago. Edible cassava is twice as old and probably originated in South America (around present day Brazil). Both crops were introduced to West Africa by Portuguese traders during the sixteenth century (in part to feed the African slaves who were being exported across the Atlantic) and are now cultivated throughout Africa. Cassava is rich in carbohydrate but low in protein: 7.4 mg protein per calorie, compared to 26 mg protein/cal for maize. It is also deficient in trace elements and vitamins (a situation that is being remedied, as described below).

Rice is the third most important crop in Africa. Although it was first domesticated eight thousand years ago in China,[12] the African variety (*Oryza glaberrima*) is indigenous to the Island Niger Delta, where it was being cultivated three thousand years ago. In other words, the antecedents of the Soninke people, who would go on to found the empires of Ghana, Mali and Songhay, had the ingenuity to domesticate rice, independently of influences from Egypt (who did not have rice) or the Arabian Peninsula. Only thousands of years later did variants of the original wild Chinese variety (*Oryza rufipogon*) find its way westwards across Asia and into Africa, where its descendants are now the main species of rice that is grown. These contain almost as much protein as maize.

Reasons for failure

One of the consequences of farming in a tropical climate compared to a temperate one is that the yields are much lower. For example, the average yield for cereal crops (rice, maize and wheat) in a tropical zone such as that in sub-Saharan Africa is 18,051 kg (18 tonnes)/hectare; in a temperate zone such as that in North America it is twice as high (37,288 kg/ha).[13] Partly this is economic: poor subsistence farmers can't afford the nitrogen- and phosphorus-based fertilisers that enrich depleted soil. Partly it is geographic: a lack of steady rain. But aren't the topics the very regions of regular monsoons? True, but at other times there is a shortage of rainfall. One of the main reasons for droughts (that are often accompanied by invasions of locusts) is that only 4 percent of land in sub-Saharan Africa is irrigated (compared to nearly 40% in South Asia for example). Yet some improvements are under way. In Mali, for example, the Alatona Irrigation Project aims to increase 'drought-proof' cropland by 20%.[14] However there is a problem with conventional irrigation in hot climates: surface water quickly evaporates. That is why in Tamil Nadu (India), sugar cane plantations are now irrigated by the 'drop' technique. This delivers water directly to the roots of the cane, rather than to the crop above ground, by means of a series of pipes below the surface. An added advantage is that the growth of weeds above ground is avoided. It is more expensive to set up than surface irrigation, but the increased yield that is obtained means that farmers can pay off the initial costs –without subsidy – within a single year. The introduction of such 'drop' techniques should surely be applicable to tropical Africa.[15]

Conversely there is soil erosion across the rain belt of sub-Saharan Africa when the rains do arrive: the downpour leaches out essential plant nutrients, which are not replaced because the farmers can't afford fertilisers. Moreover 50-70% of rainfall evaporates before it reaches thirsty crops.[16] In addition, over 50% of crops are also lost every year because of overgrowth by weeds and attack by viruses, moulds and insect pests. Then there are wars. In the south of the Sudan alone, 4 – 5 million people were displaced between 1955 and 2005. 'Tribal animosities, proliferation of fire arms, perceptions of insecurity, cattle rustling, breakdown of cultural norms and values, and limited economic opportunities continue to build pressures and often erupt into tribal conflict and violence.'[17] And that's *after* the conflict ended. While it was on, with warring soldiers trampling over farmlands, normal agriculture virtually ceased. However 'On a continental scale, violence was less destructive than famine. Throughout the tropical African savanna, the favourable rains of the mid-nineteenth century faltered during the 1880s, inaugurating 40 years relative aridity before rainfall recovered during the 1920s.'[18]

The way that produce is marketed is another reason for poor results. In most countries prior to independence and continuing thereafter, prices of agricultural products were set by marketing boards. They remove 'any incentives for the farmers to invest, use fertilizers, or preserve the soil. The reason that the policies of the marketing boards were so unfavourable to rural interests to tax farmers was that these interests had no political power.'[19] In Europe the situation is the reverse: the farmers have political power and are supported by the Common Agricultural Policy of the European Union: it is the population that suffers because of high prices.

All in all, 'Africa is … the only continent in the world unable to feed itself. And yet … one third of the remaining untilled arable land left on earth is also in Africa. … Africa should be able to feed itself. Africa should be a net supplier of food to the rest of the world … Many African nations blessed with arable land are also burdened by unreliable and ever-changing regimes, making for ineffective and sporadic enforcement of legal rights. No reasonable long-term investor is willing to invest in a place that lacks necessary infrastructure or enforceable property regimes'.[20]

A problem related to low agricultural yields is deforestation. At first sight logging of the sub-Saharan rain forest would seem beneficial in the short term, since it increases the land area available for subsistence and commercial farming. Moreover some 90% of Africans burn firewood for cooking and heating: half their total energy demands are met in this way, according to the *African Technology Forum* of 1998.[21] But apart from the impact on climate change (a reduction of the arboreal carbon 'sink'), loss of the natural forest means that many products, such as antiseptic soaps derived from the bark of certain trees, will be lost.

Future hopes

The situation in sub-Saharan Africa is slowly improving, and there are grounds for optimism. The extent of cassava cultivation doubled during the first three decades following independence, with Ghana and Nigeria being the main producers. During this period the yield also increased: from 5 – 10 tonnes/ha to 10 – 15 tonnes/ha.[22] The cultivation of sweet potato, a staple diet for many Africans, is another case in point. Senegal managed to achieve a yield of 33.3 tonnes per hectare in 2010, compared with a world average of 13.2 tonnes/ha.[23] In Malawi (former Nyasaland), where by 2005 nutrient-depleted soil and failed privatization of agriculture had combined to leave five million people requiring food aid, President wasee Mutharika made agricultural reform his priority: 'Enough is enough. I am not going to go on my knees to beg for food. Let us grow the food ourselves.'[24] Ignoring the counsel of the International Monetary Fund (IMF) and the United States Agency for International Aid (USAID), he decided to use aid money to buy better seeds and fertilisers and to distribute these to farmers at subsidised prices. It worked. Within a year the production of maize, the country's staple food, had doubled, prices had fallen, and the following year Malawi began exporting maize to its neighbours. Simply growing more indigenous, nutritionally-rich green vegetables can also benefit the hungry.[25]

Another improvement is 'Biofortification'. This is the introduction into food crops, by novel fertilisers, by breeding programmes, and especially by genetic engineering, of essential nutrients such as iron, zinc and vitamin A in which they are deficient. In the case of genetic modification (GM), crops can also be rendered resistant to viruses and pests, and tolerant to drought or heat. One current project is BioCassava Plus that puts iron, zinc and pro-vitamin A (converted into vitamin A in the body), into new varieties of cassava.[26] A similar approach is to fortify maize and sweet potato with provitamin A, and beans with zinc.[27] Both projects are ongoing and are introducing such crops into various sub-Saharan countries, as outlined by HarvestPlus, an organisation whose mission is 'to improve nutrition and public health by developing and promoting biofortified food crops that are rich in vitamins and minerals, and providing global leadership on biofortification evidence and technology.'[28] So far as rice is concerned, there is the possibility of a 50 percent increase in yield through changing the way that current strains of rice use photosynthesis for growth: 'Supercharging photosynthesis is the only way to improve yield potential substantially in rice while not increasing the demand for water and nitrogen.'[29]

Then there is AGRA (Alliance for a Green Revolution in Africa), a non-governmental organisation launched in 2006 with support from the Bill & Melinda Gates Foundation and The

Rockefeller Foundation. Depleted soil costs African farmers US$4 billion a year. AGRA seeks to redress this. Over the past five years it has helped 1.7 million African farmers to rejuvenate 1.6 million hectares of land and to increase crop yields two to three-fold. This has been achieved through a number of measures, like improving soil fertility and sponsoring poor farmers to buy chemical fertilisers.[30] In regard to rice, the reader interested in this topic is encouraged to look at a number of articles that appeared recently under the title *New thinking about an old grain*.[31]

Much of the research mentioned above is carried out in the USA and other countries outside Africa. Expanding the research base within the continent, by training more Africans in dedicated institutions, is obviously the next step.[32] Equally important, if sub-Saharan Africa is going to compete on the world stage, is improving the infrastructure: roads, telecommunications, energy supply, irrigation and so forth. This comes at a price. It has been estimated that almost US$500 billion,[33] raised through private, governmental (national and regional) and international investment will be required over the next decade. Is Africa capable of integrating and achieving such a huge project? It's quite a challenge for any continent.

And if that weren't enough, there's the prospect of climate change, which is likely to have deleterious effects on sub-Saharan Africa: 'food security will be the overarching challenge, with dangers from droughts, flooding, and shifts in rainfall.'[34] On the other hand, some successful adaptations have already been noted.[35] Moreover research into the bacteria and fungi that live in the soil, and that feed the plants growing above them, is also under way through funding from the US Agency for International Development (USAID). This soil ecosystem or microbiome – relatively unexplored in the past – is particularly important as its viability may help to ameliorate climate change in the future.[36]

Disease

Poor agriculture is but one reason for sub-Saharan Africa's past failure. Equally important, if not more so, is disease. The global warming of around 8⁰C that terminated the last ice age between 20,000 and 12,000 years ago may have enabled *H sapiens* to settle in northern Europe, and probably helped to initiate agriculture around the world, but its effect in middle Africa was disastrous. The tropical belt that stretches across Africa from 15⁰ N, across Senegal, Mauretania, Mali, Niger, Chad, Sudan and Eritrea, to 15⁰ S, across Angola, Zambia, Malawi and Mozambique, is home to some of the world's most virulent microbes. The link between the burden of disease and economic performance is clear to see. Some of the poorest countries in Africa fall within this region: from Central African Republic, Democratic Republic of Congo, Burundi, Liberia, Niger, Malawi, Mozambique, Guinea, Togo, South Sudan, The Gambia, Sierra Leone, Guinea-Bissau, Burkina Faso, Ethiopia, Rwanda, Uganda, Benin, Mali, Chad, Senegal, Tanzania, Cameroon, Kenya, Côte d'Ivoire, Zambia, Mauretania, Ghana, Sudan to Nigeria (in ascending order of GDP/capita).[37] These sub-Saharan countries, harbouring over 700 million people or two thirds of the entire population of Africa, are also all at the bottom of rankings like 'Quality of Life', 'Human Development' and 'Economic Freedom' (see Tables 2, 3 and 4).

The diseases are not trivial: dengue fever, dysentery (amoebic and bacterial), Ebola hemorrhagic fever, HIV/AIDS (though this is not related to geography), leishmaniasis, lymphatic filariasis, malaria, onchocerciasis (River Blindness), trypanosomiasis (African sleeping sickness), tuberculosis (not related to geography either) and yellow fever. Other infections that are world-wide include diarrhoea, pneumonia, measles and meningitis. Children are particularly at risk, but in countries like Rwanda (chapter 10) effective vaccination programmes are proving remarkably effective.

On top of that, of course, is malnutrition: an under-nourished person – especially a child – is less able to fight off infections because their immune system is compromised. Of almost three million children under the age of five who die annually in the tropics, more than a million deaths can be attributed to malnutrition. The rate of childhood mortality in sub-Saharan Africa is the highest in the world. Not surprisingly, Africa is the only region in the world (compared with North America, Central America, Caribbean, South America, Europe, Asia and Oceania) where the percentage of those who are undernourished (almost 20% of the population) exceeds those (about 10% of the population) who are classified as obese.[38] Yet malnutrition is related as much to patterns of caloric and nutrient consumption as to lack of food production.[39] Moreover, it is Kofi Annan's aspiration to 'ensure a future in which all children get the food they need to thrive, not just to survive.'[39a]

So far as infectious diseases are concerned, it was not always so. Until the arrival of Europeans, especially during the latter half of the nineteenth century when Africa was carved up between Belgium, Britain, France, Germany and Portugal, isolated communities had developed a good deal of resistance against some of the infections I have mentioned. On the contrary, it was the Europeans venturing into the coastal regions of West Africa who finished up in the 'white man's grave'. They died mainly of yellow fever and malaria, to which the local population had developed some immunity. In the case of malaria, a genetic disorder (see below) also provided resistance. For their part, the newcomers introduced new germs against which the indigenous population had no resistance: cholera (bacterial dysentery), influenza, measles and pneumonia, as well as syphilis and gonorrhoea, being the most common. Some of the interlopers were themselves African. For example, a warrior tribe of Angoni (Ngoni) Zulus who had been ousted from their homeland in Natal by Shaka Zulu (whose half-nephew King Cetshwayo would, at Isandlwana in 1879, inflict one of the greatest defeats ever suffered by the British army) set forth in 1819 across the Zambesi to settle on the shores of Lake Malawi (then Lake Nyasa). They were very fit and healthy when they arrived in 1834. But by the late 1930s they had became a sickly people, unfit for military service. They had been debilitated by microbes to which the resident villagers had long ago developed immunity.[40] It was the same elsewhere. The German missionary Rev S W Koelle, writing in 1854, notes that 'The natives of dry and arid countries, as eg Bornou, Hausa (today Chad and northern Nigeria respectively), the Sahara, etc, die very fast in Sierra Leone; their acclimatization there seems to be almost as difficult as that of Europeans.'[41]

As regards the tropical infections mentioned earlier, most are transmitted through an animal that is itself infected. Exceptions are cholera (caused by drinking water infected with the bacterium *Vibrio cholerae*), Ebola (caused by contact with animals or humans infected with Ebola virus), HIV/AIDS (caused by entry of human immune deficiency virus into the blood stream – through blood transfusion, dirty needles or anal sex) and tuberculosis (caused by contact with humans infected with the bacterium *Mycobacterium tuberculosis*). The rest are all are caused by microbes growing in an animal host which introduces the parasite through a bite. The most common of these are mosquitoes and tsetse flies that proliferate in the humid atmosphere of the tropical rain forest.

Mosquitoes

In 1631, the wife of the Spanish Viceroy of Peru – the Countess Chinchon – lay ill in the Viceroy's residence in Lima with a fever. Her husband was despairing: she seemed on the verge of death when a Jesuit monk came along and said he could cure her. He gave her an extract of the bark of the quina tree, which had been known to the Incas to be effective in curing 'tertian fever', subsequently called malaria in the mistaken belief that the malady was caused by foul air. We now know that the active ingredient in the bark is quinine, which has saved countless lives over the centuries (because the Countess was so miraculously cured, the eighteenth century naturalist Carl Linnaeus renamed the tree 'cinchona'). Some derivatives synthesised during the last century – like chloroquine and primaquine – have proved even more effective at preventing the effects of the causative organisms.

These are protozoa: mainly *Plasmodium falciparum* and *P vivax*. They enter humans through the bite of a female, parasite-harbouring, *Anopheles* (generally *A gambiae*) mosquito. At the same time the mosquito ingests some nutritious human blood (the main reason for the bite in the first place). If the blood happens to contain the parasite from a previous encounter, the disease is transmitted to the next victim, and so on. Other plant-based drugs, such as artemesinin and related compounds from *Artemesia annua*, are also proving efficacious against malaria. As I write, the first Chinese scientist to win a Nobel Prize has just been announced. Youyou Tu has been awarded a share in the 2015 prize in Physiology or Medicine for her development of artemesinin. One of the best and cheapest treatments, however, is to prevent the mosquito ever making contact. Because this happens mainly at night, bed nets soaked with insecticide are widely used. Nevertheless almost a million people, mainly sub-Saharan children who succumb to malaria, die of cerebral fever every year. Many more, of course, are able to survive the fever, but the debilitated state of millions underlies the poor economic performance within tropical Africa.

I mentioned that, over long periods, some of the indigenous inhabitants of mosquito-infested areas have developed a measure of immunity against the disease. There is another reason for resistance. Some 10 – 40% of the population in tropical Africa carry an aberrant haemoglobin (haemoglobin S). Their red blood cells contain 50% haemoglobin S and 50% of the normal haemoglobin A. The presence of haemoglobin S makes it difficult for the protozoan parasite to reproduce within the red blood cells. As a result, these people are less susceptible to suffer from malaria. The reason for this fortunate situation is that they have inherited the gene for making haemoglobin S from one of their parents. But if they inherit the gene from both parents (100% of their haemoglobin being S), they suffer from 'sickle cell disease' [42] – a severe form of anaemia that results from the fact the red cells adopt a sickle-like shape, making them likely to get stuck in blood capillaries. Then it's a toss-up whether they succumb to malaria or anaemia (or both). The 10 – 40% who have both S and A are known as 'carriers' (heterozygotes) of the disease. The much smaller percentage of the population who have only S are known as homozygotes. The beneficial effect of haemoglobin S in carriers is the reason why sickle cell disease remains prevalent in malarial regions.

There are good reasons for both pessimism and optimism in the future. On the one hand, resistance by *P falciparum* and *P vivax* to anti-malarial drugs has been reported to occur in south-east Asia. Once such resistant organisms develop (in patients from whom the parasite has not been totally cleared by drugs), they are transmitted across the population by mosquitoes. The situation is similar to the world-wide surge of infectious bacteria that have become resistant to antibiotics. The good news is that a new, potentially active, drug has recently been synthesised, and may offer hope to those who are infected with artemesinin-resistant *Plasmodium*.[43] Even better news is that an effective vaccine against malaria, which has been sought for decades, may finally reach fruition.

Malaria is not the only disease carried by *Anopheles* mosquitoes. They also transmit the disease known as lymphatic filariasis. This is caused by the larvae of worms (mainly *Wucherenia bancrofti*) that affect the flow of lymph. As a result water is retained and parts of the body, especially legs and genitalia, swell up. So great is the increase in size that the deformity has been termed elephantiasis. It is not fatal but the disfiguration and gradual loss of movement have consequences almost as severe. The scrotum can increase up to 20 kg in weight and there are accounts of sufferers pushing their genitalia in front of them in a wheelbarrow. So great is the social impact of the disorder that preventative chemotherapy is administered to whole populations in particularly affected areas. The drugs do not kill the worms, but prevent the consequences: if maintained for a number of years, the worms gradually die off, and transmission to a new victim is halted. The use of insecticide-impregnated bed nets is another preventative tactic. Once an infection has taken hold, there are few effective medicaments, and as yet no vaccine.

Mosquitoes of the genus *Aedes*, especially *A aegypti*, transmit other types of infection: namely those caused by dengue virus and by yellow fever virus. The microbes are injected into humans by blood-sucking mosquitoes, just as in the transmission of malaria and lymphatic filariasis. The symptoms of dengue are relatively mild: fever, headaches, muscle and joint pain. But a small proportion of victims goes on to develop haemorrhagic fever, which is a lot worse. Yellow fever is more dangerous: fever, chills, loss of appetite and liver damage (causing yellow skin, as in jaundice, as well as renal impairment). Patients begin to vomit, and half will die simply from uncontrolled vomiting. As with malaria and other infectious diseases, indigenous Africans have built up considerable immunity to dengue and yellow fever over hundreds, if not thousands, of years. But visitors, whether Europeans, Asians or Afro-Americans, all succumb. As with most virus infections, there are no drugs to eliminate the parasite and prevent the ensuing illness. No vaccine against either virus currently exists.

Eliminating mosquito-borne diseases is in principle achievable by destroying the insects' breeding grounds through drainage, fumigation and other measures. The initial success of DDT proved elusive as the rapidly breeding *Anopheles* developed resistance to the drug. Drainage of infested swamps was more successful. You might think that this was achieved in Europe centuries ago (by 1859 London was free of it, but it lingered elsewhere in England for another twenty years), but you would be wrong. The incidence of malaria – admittedly very low – in Georgia and Greece, together with that in Azerbaijan, Tajikistan and Turkey, actually *increased* between 2011 and 2012.[44] But elsewhere eradication has proved successful. This is also true of yellow fever-carrying mosquitoes in Central America: the Panama Canal would not have opened in August 1914 (the month that war broke out in Europe) had yellow fever not been largely eradicated in the region. Wiping out *Anopheles* and *Aedes* throughout tropical Africa, however, remains as great a challenge as persuading warring leaders to desist from their murderous aims. At present, we don't even know where mosquitoes go during the dry season.[45] Better surveillance data should help in these regards.[46]

Tsetse Fly

The tsetse fly is endemic across the whole of tropical Africa – from the Sahara in the north to the Kalahari in the south **(Fig 5.1)**. It has been around for millions of years, infecting wild game even before the emergence of *Homo*. Only after the introduction of farming, did humans begin to suffer. The tsetse fly's bite transmits protozoa known as trypanosomes (mainly *Trypanosoma brucei*). The initial symptoms are fever, headache and joint pains. It is the second stage, during which the parasite enters the central nervous system, which has given rise to the name African sleeping sickness. The sleep patterns and other neurological functions of patients are so badly disrupted that – if untreated – they will die within months or years. Unlike malaria, no oral medicines are available. Intravenous injections of various drugs are the only palliative. No vaccine exists.

Humans are not the only victims. Most vertebrate animals – cattle, water buffalo, camels, horses, donkeys, sheep and goats – are vulnerable, with symptoms similar to those in humans. The economic consequences are obvious. Animal husbandry,

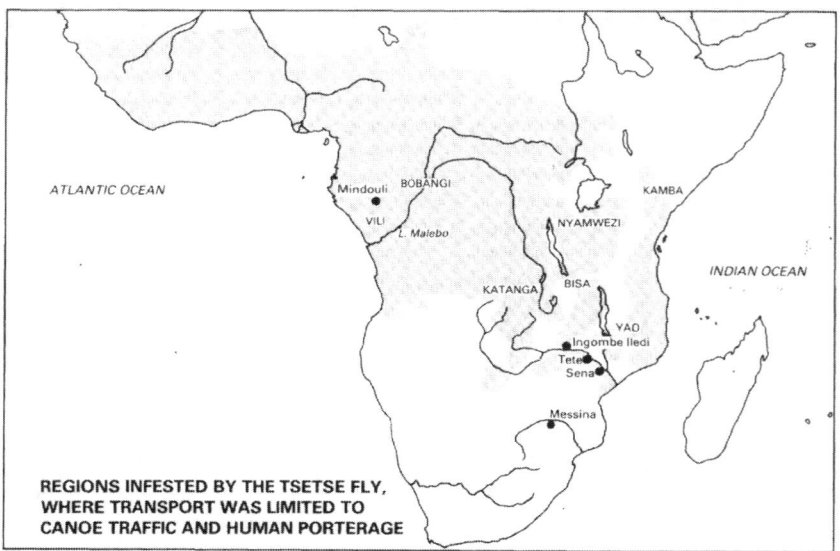

Figure 5.1.

specifically the raising of animals for food or transport, is severely compromised in tsetse-infected regions. It is one of the reasons why, until recent times, much of the trade within tropical Africa has been by human porters. Wheeled transport never developed, in contrast to the situation in southern Africa, where tsetse flies are absent.

Programmes to eradicate the tsetse fly through land clearing, use of pesticides, trapping and introduction of irradiated and hence sterile males are all being tried, with some success. This, at present, is more than can be said of similar attempts to destroy *Anopheles* and *Aedes* mosquitoes.

Sand Flies

Another insect that transmits a microbial parasite is the sand fly. Those that harbour a protozoan called *Leishmania* are prevalent not only in tropical Africa, but in the dry Sahara as well. The disease of leishmaniasis is triggered by the bite of a blood sucking sand fly, in the way that mosquitoes and tsetse flies spread the maladies associated with their respective parasites. Symptoms range from ulcers of skin, mouth and nose to more serious disorders involving red blood cells, liver and spleen. Around one percent of infections are fatal. There are few effective medicaments, and no vaccine. As with malaria, insecticide-impregnated bed nets offer the best protection.

Blackflies

A particular insect (genus *Simulium*) that lives along the streams of tropical Africa causes onchocerciasis or River Blindness. The disease is caused by a parasitic worm (*Onchocerca volvulus*) that is introduced through the bite of an infected blackfly. As with *Anopheles*-induced malaria, it is the females that carry the microbe, but unlike *Anopheles*, *Simulium* females bite only during the day, not at night. The worms breed in an infected host and gradually cause skin rashes and nodules under the skin. The larvae, even when dead, cause lesions in the cornea that can lead to blindness. 18 million people across sub-Saharan Africa are affected. There is no vaccine, but a number of medications such as ivermectin, taken over a long time, eventually kill the larvae but not the adults. Insect repellents and covering the skin are the only antidotes.

I have mentioned the most virulent infectious diseases that affect the peoples of tropical Africa. Another reason for their countries' poor economic performance is the continued presence of shamans or village doctors in rural areas. Traditional medicine has given us some wonderful remedies, such as quinine and artemisin against malaria (see above), aspirin from the bark of the willow tree against pain, fever and inflammation, digitalis from foxgloves against cardiac disorders, and so on. Traditional medicine should not be dismissed out of hand.[47] But shamanic practices can't compete with modern medicine. The problem is that in many countries across tropical Africa – Mali is a good example – villagers prefer to visit a shaman rather than attend a nearby health centre. Why? Not because they don't trust modern treatments, but because they can't afford them. A shaman's advice is free. A prescription from a health centre needs to be paid for, however modest the sum may be. The answer to this lies in education. As a former Director-General of UNESCO, Federico Mayor, once remarked to me 'We don't need an H (for Health) in UNESCO: quite apart from the creation of the WHO, the E (for Education) is sufficient. For from education about hygiene and sanitation, health emerges.'[48]

Natural Resources

Another aspect of geography concerns a region's natural reserves. Tropical Africa lacks the one resource that fuelled the Industrial Revolution in Europe: coal. Ninety percent of this energy-yielding material is found in deposits within temperate zones (one of which is in South Africa). Other reasons, of course, underlie the failure of Africa to industrialise. The relatively low population density, and the conservative nature of African society mentioned in the previous chapter, are but two of them.

The gold mines of West Africa that fuelled the ascendancy of ancient empires like Ghana, Mali and Songhay, continue to produce the precious metal but they contribute only marginally to the economy these days. 'Instead of being exploited for the benefit of the people, Africa's mineral resources have been so mismanaged and plundered that they are now the source of our misery' according to former UN Secretary-General Kofi Annan, speaking in 2000.[49] The discovery of diamonds and gold within southern Africa over the last 150 years transformed the economy of that region, but had little effect on tropical Africa. Within the last few decades, this has changed. Deposits of cobalt (57% of the world's resources; largely in the Democratic Republic of Congo and in Zambia), chromite (a mixed oxide of iron and chromium that accounts for 44% of that in the world, largely in South Africa, but also some in Zimbabwe) are actively being exploited by Chinese entrepreneurs who have brought a measure of prosperity to sub-Saharan Africa (and considerably more to China). Africa also contains important minerals like manganese, palladium, uranium, vanadium and tantalite (an oxide of iron, manganese, niobium and tantalum, used to strengthen alloys).

The discovery and extraction of oil has transformed the economies of countries like Angola, Gabon (see Table 1) and Equatorial Africa, with exports throughout the world. Fifteen of Africa's twenty top oil-producing nations are in sub-Saharan Africa. Were it not for endemic corruption, Nigeria – the largest oil producer in Africa and thirteenth in the world – would enjoy a much healthier economy than it does (chapter 14). But not just because of its oil. The country has the eighth largest amount of arable land in the world: 37% of its land area is usable for agriculture, compared with less than 8% across the whole of the continent.

Provision of suitable forms of energy to carry out sub-Saharan Africa's future programmes is an important topic. Preferably, of course, these should be 'green', in other words 'renewable'. Countries in North Africa, like Morocco, are making good progress with wind turbines and solar panels. Tropical Africa's weather – with extensive monsoon seasons – is less conducive to the use of solar panels, but countries like Zambia and Ghana have already begun to take steps in such a direction.[50]

Conclusion

It is pretty clear that geography has indeed played a part in holding back the economic potential of sub-Saharan Africa. This is particularly true in regard to agriculture and health. The productive potential of any person is seriously impaired if beset by malnutrition and chronic disease.

Of course there have been bouts of malnutrition and disease in Asia and Europe over the ages. During the nineteenth century the spread of potato blight, caused by the microbe *Phytophthora infestans*, destroyed the staple food of the Irish poor and caused a million deaths by starvation. A further million emigrated, reducing the population by a quarter. The Black Death that during the fourteenth century spread westward from central Asia into Europe, killing up to 25% of the world's population, was, like many tropical diseases in Africa, caused by a microbe living in an animal host. The microbe was probably *Yersinia pestis*, the causative agent of plague that was transmitted by the bite of fleas resident in the fur of rats. Africa suffered too, but the desert prevented the disease penetrating into sub-Saharan Africa. Terrible though the potato famine and the Black Death were, each eventually petered out, allowing the population to recover. In tropical Africa, on the other hand, the failure of crops and the transmission of disease have been on-going, year on year, without respite.

Economists have compared the success of sub-Saharan countries with those in other tropical regions. Take Ghana and Malaysia as an example.[51] Both lie just north of the equator. Each is covered largely by rain forest. They are of similar size (Ghana 240,000 sq km; Malaysia 320,000 sq km) and population (Ghana 27 million; Malaysia 30 million), each made up of one predominant ethnic group (Ghana: 48% Akan; Malaysia: 50% Malay with no other group contributing more than 20% to the population). Both were British during colonial times and received independence in the same year (1957). Both now have democratically elected governments. Yet the GDP per capita of Malaysia is six times higher than that of Ghana. Why? Geography, I believe, has played a major role. In terms of agriculture, Malaysia benefitted from the 'Green Revolution' of the 1970s. This introduced novel, high-yielding hybrids of wheat and rice into many Asian countries (as a result of which the health of 42 million pre-school children is said to have improved [52]). It had virtually no impact on tropical Africa. In Malaysia double cropping became feasible: land-owners and tenant farmers benefited and the economy boomed. In terms of communicable disease, malaria is rife in only a part of the country (Sabah and Sarawak on the island of Borneo), whereas it is endemic throughout Ghana. But the major difference is the tsetse fly, which is absent in Malaysia. As mentioned above, this insect transmits both human disease (African sleeping sickness) and a similar disability in cattle, both of which adversely affect the economy of the country.

Geography has indeed been a brake on the economic growth of tropical Africa. But advances in biomedical technology have the potential to change the situation, as has the exploitation of its oil and mineral resources. So sub-Saharan Africa has a future after all. That is what I wish to imply by the title of this book.

End Notes

[1] de Secondat (1989) p 234

[2] Curtin (1965) p 69

[3] Acemoglu and Robinson (2012)

[4] Calestous Juma: Africa can still learn important lessons from Lee Kuan Yew's work in Singapore. *The Daily Nation*, March 24, 2015.

[5] Gross National Product, slightly different from Gross Domestic Product; see http://www.economicshelp.org/blog/3491/economics/difference-between-gnp-gdp-and-gni/

[6] see http://www.nber.org/digest/jun01/w8119.html

[7] Sachs (2001)

[8] Collins and Burns (2014) p 41

[9] Stephen Mithen, *Phil Trans R Soc B* **362**: 705-718, 2007; quoted in Wilson (2012) p 16

[10] Iliffe (1995) p 12

[11] Connah (2001) p 131.

[12] Ewen Callaway: The birth of rice. *Nature* **514**: S58-59 (2014)

[13] see http://www.nber.org/papers/w8119

[14] Juma (2011) p 91

[15] *ibid* p 92

[16] Johan Rockström and Martin Falkenmark: Increase water harvesting in Africa. *Nature* **519**: 283-285 (2015)

[17] Clesensio Tizikara and Loro George Leju Logo: *Post-conflict development of agriculture in South Sudan: Perspectives on approaches to capacity strengthening.* http://www.erails.net/images/fara/secretariat/kigali-movement/file/Kigali%20Movement/Post-Coflict%20Agriculture_South%20 Sudan.pdf

[18] Iliffe (1995) p 209

[19] Acemoglu and Robinson (2012) p 339

[20] Moyo (2012) p 183

[21] http://web.mit.edu/africantech/www/articles/Deforestation.htm

[22] Felix I Nweke: *The Cassava transformation in Africa*: see http://www.fao.org/docrep/009/a0154e/A0154E02.htm

[23] Food and Agriculture Organization of the United Nations (FAOSTAT) 2011

[24] Juma (2011) p 3

[25] Rachel Cernansky: Super vegetables *Nature* **522**: 146-8 (2015)

[26] Richard T Sayre: *Biofortification of cassava for Africa: the BioCassava Plus program*; in Pasternak (2011) pp 113-120.

[27] J T Winkler: *Biofortification: improving the nutritional quality of staple crops*; in Pasternak (2011) pp 100-112

[28]. see http://www.harvestplus.org/.

[29] John E Sheehy and P L Mitchell: *Rice and global food security: the race between scientific discovery and catastrophe*; in Pasternak (2011) pp 81-90. See also Julian M Hibberd and Robert T Furbank: Fifty years of C-4 photosynthesis. *Nature* **538**: 177-179

(2016) and Katherine Bourzac: Solar upgrade. *Nature* **544**: S11 – S13 (2017)

[30] see http://agra-alliance.org/ and *Nature*: **512**, 353 (2014)

[31] Leigh Dayton: Blue-sky rice. *Nature* **514**: S52-54; Felix Cheung: The search for the rice of the future. *Nature* **514**: S60-61; and Karen Ravn: The next frontier. *Nature* **514**: S64-65 (2014)

[32] Calestous Juma: *Building New Agricultural Universities in Africa*. HKS Faculty Research Working Paper Series RWP12-026, John F. Kennedy School of Government, Harvard University, 2012.

[33] Juma (2011) p 113

[34] http://www.worldbank.org/en/news/feature/2013/06/19/what-climate-change-means-africa-asia-coastal-poor

[35] African trees cope with warming *Nature* **534**: 593 (2016)

[36] Sarah Wild: Mapping Africa's soil microbiome. Sub-Saharan project could one day help ecosystems resist climate change and improve agriculture. *Nature* **539**: 152 (2016)

[37] IMF figures for 2016

[38] Mohamed Ashour: A world of insecurity. *Nature* **544**: S6 – S7 (2017)

[39] John Ingram: Look beyond production. *Nature* **544**: S17 (2017)

[39a] *Nature* **555**: 7 (2018)

[40] Ransford (1983) p 26

[41] Quoted by Blyden (1967) p 54

[42] *Nature* **515**: S1-S16 (2014)

[43] David A Fidock: Chemical diversity targets malaria. *Nature* **538**: 323-325 (2016)

[44] see http://www.euro.who.int/en/health-topics/communicable-diseases/vector-borne-and-parasitic-diseases/news/news/2013/04/greater-effort-needed-to-eliminate-malaria-from-europe-by-2015

[45] Emily Sohn: The great mosquito hunt *Nature* **511**: 144-146 (2014)

[46] Scott F Dowell, David Blazes and Susan Desmond-Hellman: Four steps to precision public health. *Nature* **540**: 189-191 (2016)

[47] see, for example, Pasternak (2012) pp 89-91

[48] Pasternak (2003) p 212.

[49] Ayittey (2005) p 1

[50] Erica Gies: Can wind and solar fuel Africa's future? *Nature* **539**: 20-22 (2016)

[51] Gocking (2005) p 280

[52] R Evenson and D Collin: Assessing the impact of the Green Revolution, 1960-2000. *Science*: **300**, 758-62 (2003)

Chapter Six
INTERLOPERS:
SLAVERS FROM EAST AND WEST

O ne of the first foreigners on African soil were the Romans (though Assyrians, Persians and Greeks had earlier invaded Egypt). The Romans destroyed one city (Carthage; today's Tunis), built others (Sabratha and Leptis Magna; in today's Libya) and commandeered Egypt's grain for use in Rome. By the time the followers of Muhammad arrived in the seventh century, Roman influence had largely fizzled out. It would be another thousand years before they returned. Meanwhile the Arabs conquered the whole of North Africa along the Mediterranean coast, assimilating and marrying the indigenous Berbers. The Arabs' Semitic ethnicity did not conflict too much with that of the African Berbers. Together they would build great cities, mosques and madrassas from Marrakesh and Fez in the west to Cairo in the east. The oldest university in the world is said to be Cairo's Al-Azhar. Muslim culture would infuse the whole of North Africa down to the Niger and the Sahel. Their hegemony would be shattered only by the arrival of European colonists in the nineteenth century: French in the west, British in the east. Suddenly the indigenous Africans and their Arab successors became second-class citizens. To the far south of the tropical belt the arrival of Dutch and British colonists in the seventeenth century meant the expropriation from the native residents of any land suitable for farming. Africans were deemed savage and would be excluded from any participation in government until the final decade of the twentieth century. Charles Darwin is said to have remarked that 'Wherever the European had trod, death seemed to pursue the aboriginal'.

The stimulus for what Darwin had in mind was West African trade. Not by camel and not with other African nations. It was a fifteenth century Portuguese nobleman, Infante Dom Henrique de Avis, Duke of Viseu and better known as Henry the Navigator, whose curiosity for what lay in Africa, coupled with superb seamanship (by others: he went no further than the estuary of the Tagus), sowed the seeds of west Africa's decline even before Columbus crossed the seas. For what subsequent Portuguese explorers found was that African kings whom they encountered were happy to exchange their people for European goods. The Atlantic slave trade – originally only back to Portugal with Pope Nicholas V's blessing – had begun.

Europeans

The views of James Beattie regarding Africans that were mentioned in chapter 3 echoed in many ways those of Jean-Jacques Rousseau, who didn't mince his words either. In 1762 he wrote: 'So, from whatever aspect we regard the question, the right of slavery is null and void, not only as being illegitimate, but also because it is absurd and meaningless. The words *slave* and *right* contradict each other, and are mutually exclusive. It will always be equally foolish for a man to say to a man or to a people: "I make with you a convention wholly at your expense and wholly to my advantage; I shall keep it as long as I like, and you will keep it as long as I like".'[1]

In 1769 an American customs officer named Charles Stewart sailed for Britain with his slave, James Somersett, whom he had bought in Boston, Province of Massachusetts Bay. Once in England, Somersett managed to escape but was soon recaptured. He was now destined to be transported to Jamaica, where Stewart intended selling his captive. Three people, claiming that Somersett had recently been baptised and that they were his godparents, applied for a writ of *habeas corpus* before the Court of the King's Bench, arguing that slavery in England had never been approved by law (irrespective of the fact that over the previous two centuries half of the world's slaves had been transported on

British ships). The case was heard before the Lord Chief Justice, Lord Mansfield (formerly William Murray) in 1772. The trial lasted four months. At the conclusion, Mansfield ruled that chattel slavery was unsupported by common law and that Somersett must be released: 'The state of slavery is of such a nature that it is incapable of being introduced on any reasons, moral or political, but only by positive law which preserves its force long after the reasons, occasions, and time itself from whence it was created, is erased from memory. It is so odious, that nothing can be suffered to support it, but positive law. Whatever inconveniences, therefore, may follow from the decision, I cannot say this case is allowed or approved by the law of England; and therefore the black must be discharged'.

It was a landmark decision. More than 14,000 slaves who were being held illegally in England were officially freed. The law would be extended to the whole of the British Empire only in 1834 (by which time, of course, America was no longer under its jurisdiction). William Murray was a humanist as well as an outstanding lawyer. His great niece, Dido Elizabeth Belle, the offspring of a slave woman and Murray's nephew John Lindsay, was brought to England by her father at the age of four. She was educated alongside Murray's niece as a member of the family and remained at Kenwood, their country residence in Hampstead, north London, for the next thirty years.

Despite the opinions of enlightened men like Rousseau and Murray, the fifty years between 1761 and 1810 saw 3.6 million slaves transported out of Africa: of these, 3.2 million were carried on British, Portuguese and French vessels. Up to 10% died on board in terrible conditions, and the death rate among the crew was often even higher.[2] The Slave Trade Act, for which William Wilberforce ('Never can so much misery be found condensed into so small a space as in a slave-ship' [3]) had lobbied for more than two decades, was passed by the British parliament in 1807. It outlawed the trade as far as Britain was concerned, and henceforth the Royal Navy would attack any slave ship it could find. Some 24,000 slaves rescued from transports bound for Brazil finished up on St Helena. A grateful beneficiary was a Yoruba slave on a Portuguese ship bound for Brazil in 1821. Freed thanks to the Royal Navy, he was taken to the recently-founded colony for freed or escaped slaves at Freetown in Sierra Leone. Here he was baptised by British missionaries and forty years later William Ajayi Crowther became the first Anglican Bishop in West Africa.[4] Others were not so fortunate.

Of the 24,000 rescued from Rio de Janeiro-bound transports who finished up on St Helena, most remained on the island where they eventually died.[5] As mentioned, it took another 26 years for the Slavery Abolition Act to be passed by the British Parliament, again as a result of constant lobbying by Wilberforce, opposed by equally determined slave owners (of whom a prominent personage was the future Liberal prime minister W E Gladstone's father). Three days later the inveterate campaigner died, having spent his entire adult life fighting on behalf of African slaves. In the meantime the British Preventative Squadron was supported by vessels from France and the United Sates. The problem with impounding slave ships was that if one vessel in four made a successful journey, the owner's costs were repaid. So far as the trade across the Red Sea and the Indian Ocean was concerned, it was not until 1890 that the European nations (Belgium, Britain, France, Italy, Netherlands and Spain) agreed on abolishing the export of slaves from Africa entirely.

The slave trade is said to have fuelled the Industrial Revolution that occurred in Britain at about the same time that the French were having *their* revolution that began with the storming of the Bastille in 1789. Not quite so. The owners of plantations in Jamaica (sugar), and the American south (cotton) prior to independence, undoubtedly grew very wealthy, especially after slavery was abolished on British territories in 1834. For the slave owners (of whom there were more than 40,000 domiciled in Britain) were paid handsomely by the government for every freed slave (who of course received nothing). An owner of 415 slaves, for example, received £20,511, equivalent to nearly £17 million in today's money.[6] The total cost of emancipating the slaves was put at £20 million,[7] (nearly £17 billion today) which made a considerable dent in the British government's exchequer. Some of the slave owners' wealth was indeed invested in railways and industrial projects. A portion reached the home country through taxation (mainly the window tax; income tax was not levied in Britain until 1799, and thereafter only sporadically), though such revenue hardly matched the compensation paid out. So far as the owners of the slave transporters were concerned, they made a return of barely 10% of their investment, '…derisory enough for the myth of the vital importance of the slave trade to financing the Industrial Revolution to be demolished'.[8] What *is* true is that one of the uses to which new technology was applied was the manufacture of cotton goods. Their sale in Britain and abroad made the mill owners rich and, yes, the raw product on which the industry depended was indeed picked by the hands of ill-treated captives in the southern states of America (some came from India in the form of calicoe). By 1840 almost half as many cotton goods manufactured in Britain finished up in Africa as in the rest of Europe.[9]

In 1849 a sea captain plying the Niger wrote a pamphlet entitled *A plan for the immediate extinction of the slave trade … … and for the diffusion of civilisation and Christianity in Africa, by the cooperation of mammon with philanthropy*. An excellent idea, you might think. What the captain actually proposed was that the British government should enter into a convention with other governments to make it mandatory for slaves to be declared 'bond-servants' and that after a certain time on a plantation they would become free men. While waiting for transportation 'their labour shall be turned to immediate account … by employing them to build better accommodation for themselves and their successors, and in cultivating portions of land which will ensure to them a sufficiency of food'. Fine for keeping them fit for the ensuing sea journey across the Atlantic to the sugar and cotton plantations in the New World. They should not be shackled, but in order to 'ensure that they are recognised as serving only so long for free, they should be tattooed on their breasts….'[10] So they would no longer be chained like elephants, but branded like cattle. That's progress. Allen's 'philanthropic proposal' was not taken up by the British government.

Another proposal, that bore some resemblance to Allen's, fared better. In 1850 a French entrepreneur named Victor Régis submitted a scheme whereby he would recruit 'free labourers' and 'free emigrants' to his factory in the old slaving fort of Whydah in Dahomey (today's Benin), at which slaves had waited for transportation to Martinique and Guadeloupe. The fort now made palm oil for export, The 'free labourers' would work for ten years in the factory, after which they would become completely free. The men themselves were slaves whom he would buy from the king of Dahomey. The French government felt Victor Régis' distinction between slave labour and 'free' labour to be rather subtle, but nevertheless agreed to the plan.[11] In the Asante Empire (spanning what is today much of Ghana, Côte d'Ivoire and Benin), the abolition of the transatlantic slave trade by Britain in 1808 created a surplus of slaves who had been captured earlier. They were now employed as porters (the kingdom lacked wheeled traffic) and for the cultivation of kola nuts,[12] which became, together with gold, the chief export.[13] I cite these instances to show that slavery was not replaced by legitimate trade at a stroke, but continued alongside it for several decades.

The African Perspective

Slavery has been endemic in Africa, as everywhere else, since early times. It was an acceptable part of democratic Athens and the Roman Republic, and two thousand years earlier the Egyptians were already turning captured warriors into slaves who were then bartered as a commodity. Indeed, the rulers of the early empires of western Africa and their successors obtained slaves as a kind of taxation [14] and used the income from their sale to fund the state's expenditure on their armies and on altruistic projects. The use of slaves to pay taxes prevailed throughout the nineteenth century in parts of sub-Saharan Africa. The life and prospects of a slave could be a lot better than that of his equivalent (serf) in medieval Europe, not to mention that of a slave in the Americas. In the kingdom of Cayor (1549-1879; today's Senegal), for example, 'The slaves of the king formed the greater part of his forces and in consequence their condition was greatly improved. They were now slaves in name only. … they shared in the booty after an expedition; under protection of the king, during periods of social unrest, they could even indulge in discreet pillage within the national territory, against the poor peasants … The slaves were commanded by one of their own, the infantry general, who was a pseudo-prince in that he might rule over a fief inhabited by freemen.'[15] So while 'Slavery is certainly the great chink in African social organization … the African slaves who were not deported in general enjoyed living conditions incomparably superior to those of white slaves in Europe'.[16] Indeed the very emperor of Mali at the end of the thirteenth century, Mansa Sakura, was a freed slave. Outside Africa, many former slaves also prospered. I gave some examples of those who did so in the Middle East and India in chapter 3.

So far as the export of slaves is concerned, this was originally only from sub-Saharan Africa across the Sahara to the Mediterranean, across the Red Sea to Arabia, and from East Africa across the Indian Ocean. The trade, which began during the seventh century, was controlled largely by Arab and Indian merchants and the ill-fated cargo generally finished up in Muslim communities. To what extent they benefitted from the strictures of the Koran, that 'the master was advised not to show contempt for his slave, to share his food with him and provide clothing similar to his own; to set him no more than moderate work; not to punish him excessively if he did wrong, but to forgive him 'seventy times a day'; and, if they could not get on well together, to sell him to another master' [17] is debatable. Nevertheless Lady Mary Eleanor Sheil, writing from the perspective of the British Embassy in Tehran about African slaves in mid-nineteenth century Iran, pointed out that 'They are not treated with contempt as in America; there are no special laws to keep them in a state of degradation; they are frequently restored to freedom, and when this happens, they take their station in society without any reference to colour or descent.'[18]

From the sixteenth century onwards the traffic shifted westwards **(Fig 6.1)** and expanded enormously in order to quench the ever-increasing thirst for manpower by plantation owners in Brazil, the Caribbean Islands and the American south. The voyage across the Atlantic became known as the 'Middle Passage', the first leg of the slaving ships being from Europe to Africa, the third from the Americas back to Europe. Approximately two males were exported for every female [19] since their role was essentially that of beasts of burden. In contrast the Arabian trade involved roughly two females for every male, since in this instance their role was usually that of domestic chattels.

The idea that European slavers wandered into the interior to capture slaves is nonsense (apart from a few instances where the Portuguese came close to this). Generally the captain and his crew anchored off the coast and waited for the slaves to be delivered by local chiefs in exchange for guns, beads, various commodities or cash. A healthy young Nigerian man might fetch the equivalent of $4. When auctioned in the Americas a slave trader could make as much $130 off the same man.[20] So there is a question here. Should the chiefs have held out for much more? If so, might they have invested the proceeds back into their domains to improve infrastructure? It seems unlikely, but that they under-sold their human possessions is clear. European traders found it useful to build forts along the coast of the Gulf of Guinea to hold their goods – slaves and gold – awaiting transport. For this they paid rent to the local chiefs. Several of these grisly structures in present-day Ghana have survived and were designated World Heritage sites by UNESCO in 1979. By enriching the rulers, the slave trade made their nations even more extractive, according to Acemoglu and Robinson's definition. Europeans may well apologise for the way that slaves were transported so inhumanely and then so brutally exploited, but it is surely for African leaders

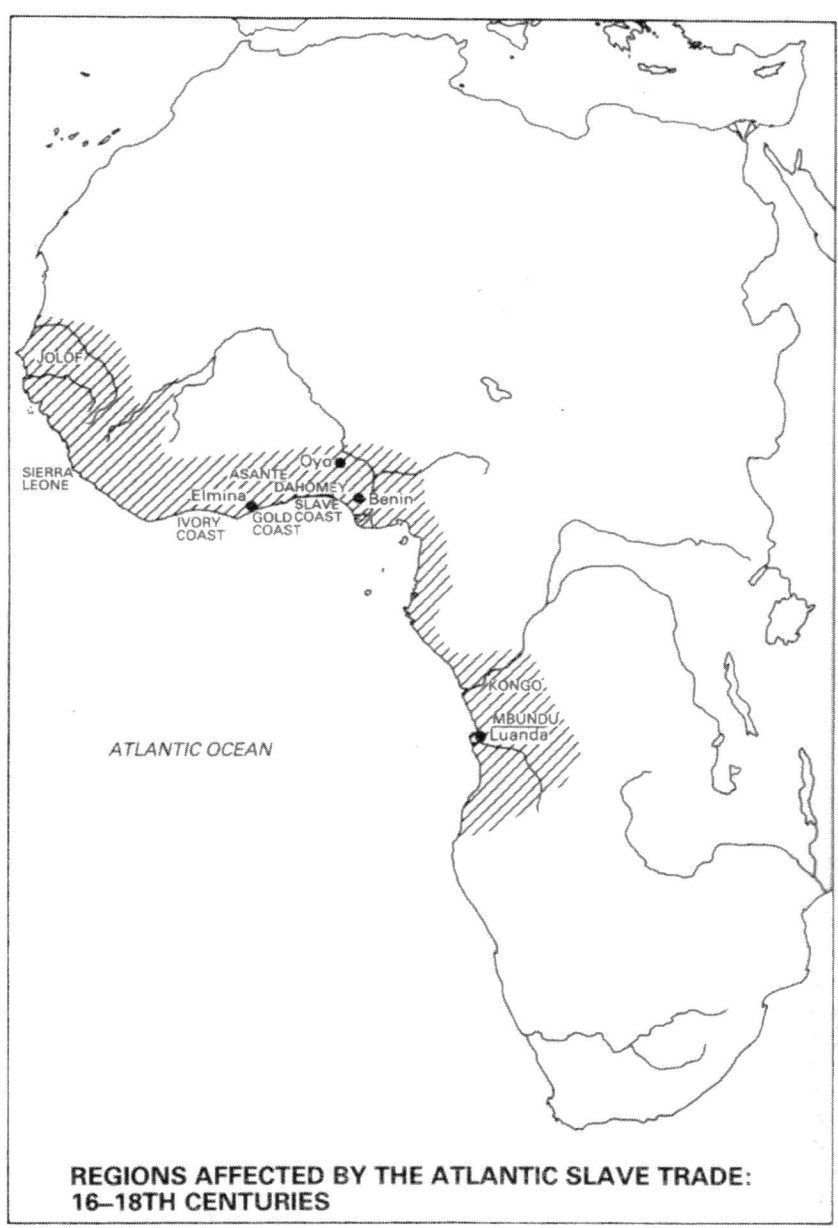

**REGIONS AFFECTED BY THE ATLANTIC SLAVE TRADE:
16–18TH CENTURIES**

Figure 6.1.

to apologise to their people for enslaving them.in the first place. In the case of Ghana they have done just that.[21]

King Agaja of Dahomey (now Benin) deserves a mention for his suggestion in 1726 that instead of exporting slaves, Europeans should establish plantations in his kingdom for which he would supply slaves.[22] Another consequence of the Atlantic slave trade was that West Africans, in particular, did not bother to develop trade in goods. Slaves were not only exported *out* of Africa, but in one instance, at least, re-exported *into* Africa. During the seventeenth century, the Dutch in the South African Cape Colony imported slaves from Dahomey in order to carry out arduous farm work that neither they, nor the resident Khoi, were prepared to do.[23]

So far as the traffic out of central and east Africa is concerned, the Arab slavers did indeed often round up their own booty, and at great cost to the unfortunate victims. The situation in Libya in 1818, described by naval Captain G F Lyon, is typical: 'A force is … annually sent, not to fight (for the Negroes cannot make any resistance against horsemen with fire-arms) but to pillage these defence less people, to carry them off as slaves, burn their towns, kill the aged and infants, destroy their crops, and inflict on them every possible misery'.[24] A column of a hundred or more bare-foot captives joined by iron rings around their necks would be driven by men with whips through jungle, savannah or desert for hundreds of miles – more than a thousand from the Congo to Kilwa on the Indian Ocean – until their destination was reached weeks or many months later. And often that proved to be only the start of a turbulent sea voyage across the Red Sea or the Indian Ocean, lying in chains at the bottom of a decrepit boat. In 1888 a Catholic missionary described the slave market in Ujiji, on the eastern shore of Lake Tanganyika. It was 'crowded with slaves, joined by cords or chains in long lines, and with others revealing signs of starvation … Nearby was a cemetery where the dying as well as the dead were left for the hyenas'.[25] Ujiji, incidentally, is the place where Henry Morton Stanley, of 'Dr Livingstone, I presume?' fame (though he probably never said this at the time, but invented it later [26]) had found the great anti-slavery campaigner in 1871.

Far more perished *en route* than the approximately 10% (sometimes as high as 20%) who died during the 'Middle Passage' across the Atlantic. Dr Gustav Nachtigal, who in 1870 accompanied a slave caravan to Kuka on the shore of Lake Chad 'observed such hardships that for every slave who survived, he estimated that three or four had died or, desperate to escape, had disappeared.'[27] 'For every ten slaves who reached Cairo' from central Africa east of Lake Chad, it was reported in 1866, 'fifty had died along the way.'[28] It is estimated that for every slave brought to the island of Zanzibar, which by 1840 had become the largest slave market in the east and the world's main supplier of cloves, six times that number were killed by the slavers en route, and hundreds of villages burnt to the ground as a warning against resistance.[29] An even greater rate of attrition on the trek to Zanzibar was considered by Livingstone to be the true figure: 'the price paid for every living slave was at least ten dead.'[30] A late nineteenth century writer came to the same conclusion: 'the sale of a single captive for slavery might represent a loss of ten in the population – from defenders in attacks on villages, the deaths of women and children from related famine, and the loss of children, the old, and the sick unable to keep up with their captors or killed along the way in hostile encounters or dying of sheer misery.'[31]

The Scale of the Iniquitous Trade

The success of a nation depends on a critical size of its population, as indicated in chapter 2. What effect did the slave trade have on African demography? Many never left Africa at all, but finished up along the shore of the Mediterranean from Morocco to Cairo or along the edge of the Sahara, where during the last decade of the nineteenth century an estimated 100,000 were employed by Tuareg masters.[32] Down the east African coast from Malinde to Mombasa and on the nearby islands of Pemba and Zanzibar some 769,000 imported slaves were working on plantations of grain and cloves respectively during the nineteenth century.[33] Whether the destination was within Africa or beyond its shores, of course, made no difference to the decay of the communities whence the captured were abducted. In Bahr El-Ghazal, in southwest Sudan, for example, 'Continued raiding for slaves … had so depleted the Bari people that the effects would still be evident in the 1920s.'[34]

The Atlantic slave trade escalated rapidly in response to the growth of plantations in Brazil, the West Indies and the southern states of North America. Canadian historian Paul Lovejoy has calculated that 409,000 souls were transported out of sub-Saharan Africa between 1450 and 1600, 1,348,000 between 1601 and 1700, 6,090,000 between 1701 and 1800, and 3,366,000 between 1801 and 1900 – a total of 11,313,000.[35] These figures are compatible with Roger Anstey's estimate, mentioned above, of 3.6 million slaves transported between 1761 and 1810 when the trade was at its height. During the closing years of the eighteenth century nearly 80,000 slaves were being exported annually according to Roland Oliver.[36]

The regions most affected during the eighteenth century were the west-central coast (present-day Angola, Republic of Congo and the Democratic Republic of Congo) which lost 2,331,800 of its inhabitants; the Bight of Benin (mainly today's Togo and Benin) 1,223,200 lost; the Bight of Biafra (mainly the Niger delta) 901,100 lost; and the Gold Coast – mainly today's Côte d'Ivoire and Ghana – 881,200 lost.[37] The years 1801 to 1867 saw a further 1,613,200 transported from the west-central coast; 546,200 from the Bight of Benin; 453,700 from the Bight of Biafra; and 68,600 from the Gold Coast. In addition, 407,537 were taken from the south-east of Africa, whence the slaves were being exported to Brazil around the Cape of Good Hope in order to avoid Britain's Royal Navy that was patrolling the waters off West Africa. Together with 176,200 removed from Upper Guinea and 113,900 from Senegambia, the total number taken for the trans-Atlantic trade between 1801 and 1867 was 3,313,600.[38]

Removal of these numbers of men, women and children represents a significant reduction in the resident population.

Roland Oliver mentions the fact that in a region Upper Volta (present-day Burkino Faso) the population declined by 17 percent during the second half of the nineteenth century alone.[39] On the other hand, Roger Anstey calculates that the entire area of Gold Coast, Bight of Benin and Bight of Biafra, that was losing around 14,000 of its population every year between 1761 and 1810, was just about rejuvenated by the natural growth rate. In contrast the 30,000 taken annually from the west-central coast constituted a net decrease in population. Overall, the Atlantic slave trade 'particularly before 1810, is likely to have been an important cause of population decline.'[40]

Figures for the Arab trade across the Sahara to the Mediterranean (in which Africans themselves participated) from the coast of the Red Sea to Arabia, and from East Africa across the Indian Ocean to Persia, India and beyond are more difficult to obtain, especially prior to the nineteenth century. Moreover they don't take account of the huge losses en route. American historian Ralph Austen estimates that a total of 4,820,000 slaves were led across the Sahara between 650 and 1600, 1,600,000 transported across the Red Sea during this time, and 800,000 from East Africa between 800 and 1600, making a total of 7,220,000 up to 1600. For the seventeenth century, Paul Lovejoy who considers the precision of Ralph Austen's figures debatable, has come up with 700,000 along the Sahara, 100,000 across the Red Sea and the same number from East Africa, making a total of 900,000. For the eighteenth century his numbers are 700,000 across the Sahara, 200,000 across the Red Sea and 400,000 from East Africa. Whereas the Atlantic trade peaked in the eighteenth century, the Arab trade continued to expand throughout the nineteenth. Lovejoy's figures for this are 1,200,000 along the Sahara, 450,000 across the Red Sea and 442,000 from East Africa (for which a greater accuracy is now justified).[41] David Livingstone estimated that by the 1870s some 12,000 to 20,000 slaves were being exported annually out of east Africa.[42]

So the total for the Arab slave trade between 650 and 1900 can be put at 11,512,000. This, you will note, is virtually the same as the 11,313,000 quoted above for the number of slaves transported across the Atlantic in just four and a half centuries. Both these figures, it has to be said, have been considerably inflated by writers with a lesser regard for accuracy. However the Arab trade did not stop there. The French scholar Raymond Mauvy estimates that a further 300,000 slaves were exported along the three routes during the first half of the twentieth century. His estimates for the earlier years are higher than those of Ralph Austen and Paul Lovejoy, so that he comes up with a total of 14,000,000 from the seventh century onwards.[43] The true extent to which sub-Saharan Africa was depleted of its population over the centuries will never be known. What is clear is that the population of Africa as a percentage of world total declined by almost a half (13.4% to 8.8%) between 1750 and 1850, whereas that of Asia, Europe, Latin America and North America grew steadily during this time.[44] Not until the twenty-first century would Africa experience the kind of population increase typical of Europe during the nineteenth and twentieth centuries.

The Economics of the Slave Trade

I mentioned above that the price a slave in West Africa might fetch in the early days was the equivalent of $4. Were these captives being sold for too little? The price increased considerably after 1750 and by 1770, King Tegbessou of Dahomey (despite his predecessor's well-intentioned ideas mentioned above) was earning some £250,000 per year through this trade.[45] Such income was not invested in agriculture, mining or other activity that might have boosted West Africa's development. Instead the revenue was used to buy guns and ammunition with which to enslave yet more men and so increase profits further. As has been pointed out, 'increases in the international demand for enslaved Africans induced a reallocation of resources in Africa towards slave production and away from other economic pursuits'.[46]

So far as the Arab trade to North Africa, Arabia and across the Indian Ocean is concerned, local African chiefs appear not to have benefitted at all. The human booty was taken by force, not exchanged for any goods, and the profits were firmly in the hands of Arab traders from Zanzibar and elsewhere along the coast of East Africa.

Persistence of Slavery in Africa

The abolition of the Atlantic slave trade meant that chiefs and kings, who had made a handsome profit from the sale of slaves to Europeans, simply reemployed these unfortunates for other purposes. 'The production of slaves for the Americas also produced slaves for Africa. It is difficult to prove that the Atlantic slave trade *caused* the transformation of slavery in Africa, but it is likely', according to Paul Lovejoy, who points out that during the period 1905-1913 a quarter of the population of French Western Sudan (today's Senegal and Mali) were in slavery.[47] The situation in the Congo was even worse. One of the aims of the West Africa Conference in Berlin in 1884 had been to rid the region of the Arabian slave trade. The results were the exact opposite. Having given legitimacy to European seizure of the Congo, the inhabitants were forced to work as porters, construction workers (of the railway between Matadi and Leopoldville that by-passed the cataracts on the Congo River) and collectors of ivory and rubber. Half the population – some 10 million men, women and children – are reckoned to have died between 1880 and 1920 as a result of the regime's enforcement measures.[48]

Some of the grisly details will be described in the following chapter. Elsewhere outright slavery continued unabated. A Danish traveller to Libya reported that in 1930 a slave market was still being held every Thursday in Kufra.[49] In northern Nigeria slavery did not become illegal until 1936.[50] A friend of mine reported that when he visited Senegal in 1959, 'Mauritian Arabs … were attacking and capturing black tribesmen where the Sahara ended and tropical Africa began; they then shipped them across the Sahara with camel trains to Arabia as slaves (using) sandstorms as cover.'[51] In Liberia during the 1960s, within a country founded specifically for the benefit of freed or escaped slaves, 'it was estimated that one quarter of the labour force were coerced, living and working in conditions close to slavery.'[52] In East Africa, matters were even worse. In 1990 there were said to be 'between 100,000 total slaves and 300,000 part slaves and former black slaves in the service of Arab masters.'[53]

Conclusion

To what extent did the consequences of interlopers on sub-Saharan soil hold back the development of its people? Internal slavery, after all, had been endemic since early times. But the export of slaves by Europeans in West Africa, and by Arabs in Central and East Africa, certainly limited the natural growth and vigour of the population. The unimaginable suffering endured by slaves during the Middle Passage and the cruelty inflicted on them at their respective destinations is, of course, a separate matter: man's inhumanity to man is evident the world over. However 'The most important result of slavery, perhaps … is the devaluation of the black man in terms of his human worth which it entailed, and which began to be elaborated in the west into a powerful racism as a means of justifying and rationalizing the terrible commerce….'[54] This in turn led to the colonisation of Africa, as described in the next chapter.

End Notes

[1] J J Rousseau: *Le Contrat Social* (book I, chap iv), quoted in Anstey (1975) p 120

[2] Anstey (1975) p 38. According to Lamb (1983) p 146, 'One out of every seven Africans who took that journey [out of Senegal] died at sea, a victim of disease or maritime disaster'.

[3] Burns (1972) p 65

[4] Niven (1964) pp 130-148

[5] Ewen Callaway: Freedom in exile. *Nature* **540**:184-7 (2016)

[6] *The Independent*, Friday 8 August 2014.

[7] Allen (1849) p 13

[8] Anstey (1975) p 51

[9] Hobsbawm (1977) p 381

[10] Allen (1849) p 20 *et seq.*

[11] Elisée Soumonni: *The compatibility of the slave and palm oil trades in Dahomey, 1818-1858*; in Law (2002) p 86

[12]Abaka (2005)

[13] Gareth Austin: *Between abolition and* Jihad*: the Asante response to the ending of the Atlantic slave trade, 1807-1896*; in Law (2002) p 100 *et seq*

[14] Richard Gray and David Birmingham: *Economic and Political Consequences of Trade in Africa*; in: Richard Gray and David Birmingham, eds: *Pre-colonial African Trade: Essays on Trade in Central and Eastern Africa before 1900* (Oxford University Press, London, 1970) pp 18-19. Quoted in Anstey (1975) p 69

[15] Diop (1987) p 3 *et seq*

[16] *ibid* p 153

[17] Segal (2001) p 35

[18] *ibid* p 123

[19] *ibid* p 4

[20] Lamb (1983) p 300

[21] see http://www.modernghana.com/news/102692/1/ghana-apologizes-to-slaves-descendants.html

[22] Iliffe (1995) p 146

[23] Collins and Burns (2014) p 280

[24] Segal (2001) p 135

[25] *ibid* p 157

[26] Jeal (2007) p 117 *et seq*

[27] Segal (2001) p 63

[28] *ibid* p 151

[29] Ransford (1983) p 49

[30] Segal (2001) p 159

[31] *ibid* p 62

[32] *ibid* p 176

[33] *ibid* p 60

[34] *ibid* p 153

[35] Collins and Burns (2014) p 213

[36] Oliver (1991) p 123

[37] figures from Paul Lovejoy, quoted in Collins and Burns (2014) p 216

[38] figures from Paul Lovejoy, quoted in *ibid* p 225

[39] Oliver (1991) p 121

[40] Anstey (1975) p79 *et seq*

[41] Segal (2001) p 56

[42] Boucher (1985) p 217

[43] Segal (2001) p 57

[44] see GeoHive:
http://www.geohive.com/earth/his_history1.aspx

[45] see https://visionaryfoundation.wordpress.com/2014/11/11/the-economics-of-trans-atlantic-slave-trade/

[46] Warren Whatley and Rob Gillezeau: *The Impact of the Slave Trade on African Economies* see http://www-personal.umich.edu/~baileymj/Whatley_Gillezeau.pdf

[47] Segal (1995) p 5

[48] Hochschild (1999) p 233

[49] Segal (2001) p 143

[50] Iliffe (1995) p 206

[51] von Maltzahn (2016) p 138

[52] Acemoglou and Robinson (2012) p 258

[53] *Africa Report*, Sep-Oct 1990, p 7

[54] Irele (1981) p 92

Chapter Seven
INTERLOPERS:
COLONISERS AND MISSIONARIES

At the end of the nineteenth century a European writer remarked that 'The eighteenth century stole the black man from his country; the nineteenth century steals his country from the black man.'[1] The traffic in slaves (though not slavery itself) was abolished by Denmark-Norway in 1803, by Britain in 1807, by the Netherlands in 1814 and by Portugal and Spain (in a manner of speaking) in 1815. Although the French Republic had abolished the slave trade throughout its territories already in 1794, Napoleon reinstated it eight years later; it was abolished for a second time only in 1848. It was the elimination of the trade that turned European merchants on the one hand, and African chiefs on the other, towards non-human traffic.

Colonialism

Causes

The dramatic decline in the export of slaves from West Africa during the nineteenth century was matched by a burgeoning of agricultural and mineral (largely gold) products. Palm oil, rubber, gum arabic, cloves and ivory (that had been an African export for more than a thousand years) were among the goods being sent abroad. They were exchanged, as during the slave trade, for glass beads, glazed calico, bits of cloth and other trivial items that could be cheaply produced in Europe (as well as for guns). Towards the end of the nineteenth century brass rods of 2 feet in length were being used to pay the workers in the Congo.[2] 'Legitimate commerce' now encouraged Africans to diversify their exports. In a previous chapter I mentioned William Falconer's views in regard to the intellectual advantages of commerce,[3] which he expressed specifically in regard to Africa.

Exporting goods instead of people made sense in any case, and led to an expansion of agriculture throughout West Africa. In Senegal, for example, the chiefs turned to the cultivation of peanuts and other groundnuts. This would prove highly profitable when it was found that the oil obtained from groundnuts could be used by Europeans in the manufacture of soap and other commodities. However there were downsides to such switches in trade as far as the foreigners' dealings with the locals were concerned: 'whereas the slave trade strengthened the elite, the peanut trade put money, and thus guns, in the hands of peasants.'[4] This, according to some historians, led directly to European intervention.[5] The re-employment of slaves for agricultural purposes meant that 'slavery, rather than contracting, appears to have expanded in Africa throughout the nineteenth century. … Though much of European penetration into Africa was justified on the grounds that slavery had to be combated and abolished, the reality was different.'[6] Indeed, the death rate among plantation workers pressed into service in German East Africa (today's Tanzania) during the early years of the twentieth century was the same (7-10%) as that of the slaves who had died on board ship during transportation to the Americas.

The distinction between being a slave and an indentured worker is subtle. In order to maintain discipline and a high rate of productivity, the European companies sent soldiers as well as commercial administrators. The writer Joseph Conrad's description of a voyage down the coast of West Africa at the end of the nineteenth century, in the voice of the fictional character Charles Marlow, is evocative: 'I left in a French steamer, and she called in every blamed port they have out there, for, as far as I could see, the sole purpose of landing soldiers and custom-house officers. I watched the coast. … Here and there greyish-whitish specks showed up, clustered inside the white surf, with a flag flying over them perhaps. Settlements – settlements, some centuries old, and still no bigger than pin-heads on the untouched expanse of their background. We pounded along, stopped, landed soldiers; went on, landed custom-house clerks to levy toll in what looked like a God-forsaken wilderness, with a tin shed and a flag pole lost in it; landed more soldiers – to take care of the custom-house clerks, presumably.'[7] In the Congo the soldiers were part of the *Force Publique*, the so-called police force that helped the administration to achieve its goals. For this the officers – Africans as well as Belgians – used the *chacotte*, a whip of rawhide hippopotamus skin. If this did not work, a bullet would do the trick in so far as it discouraged others from resisting (a hundred lashes of the *chacotte* achieved the same result). As mentioned in the previous chapter, some ten million Africans died from one insult or another over a forty-year period.

European explorers (and occasional slavers) had been penetrating parts of West Africa for years. By the end of the eighteenth century some had made contact with tribes several hundred miles inland from the coast in present-day Senegal, Ghana and Nigeria.[8] But now it was trading companies favoured by their respective governments that began to encourage their nationals to sign agreements with local kings and chiefs. Soon the concessions included certain rights over the land itself. Europeans started to take more interest, not just along the coast **(Fig 7.1)** but in the interior of Africa, 80 % of which was still under native kings and chiefs up to the 1870s. Venturing inland up rivers like the Congo, Niger or Zambezi, however, was not without hazard: over 60 percent of such adventurers died in the attempt.[9]

Within a mere twenty years, between 1878 and 1898, the entire continent would be partitioned and claimed by Europeans. So it was inevitable that the former slaving nations – Britain, France and Portugal, but also Belgium, the Netherlands, Italy and Spain – found themselves competing for a slice of the action. Suddenly Germany, that after its unification and subsequent victory over the French in 1871 saw itself as a prominent European power, felt left out. The wily German Chancellor, Prince Otto von Bismarck, had a plan to rectify this. Only three years earlier he had opined

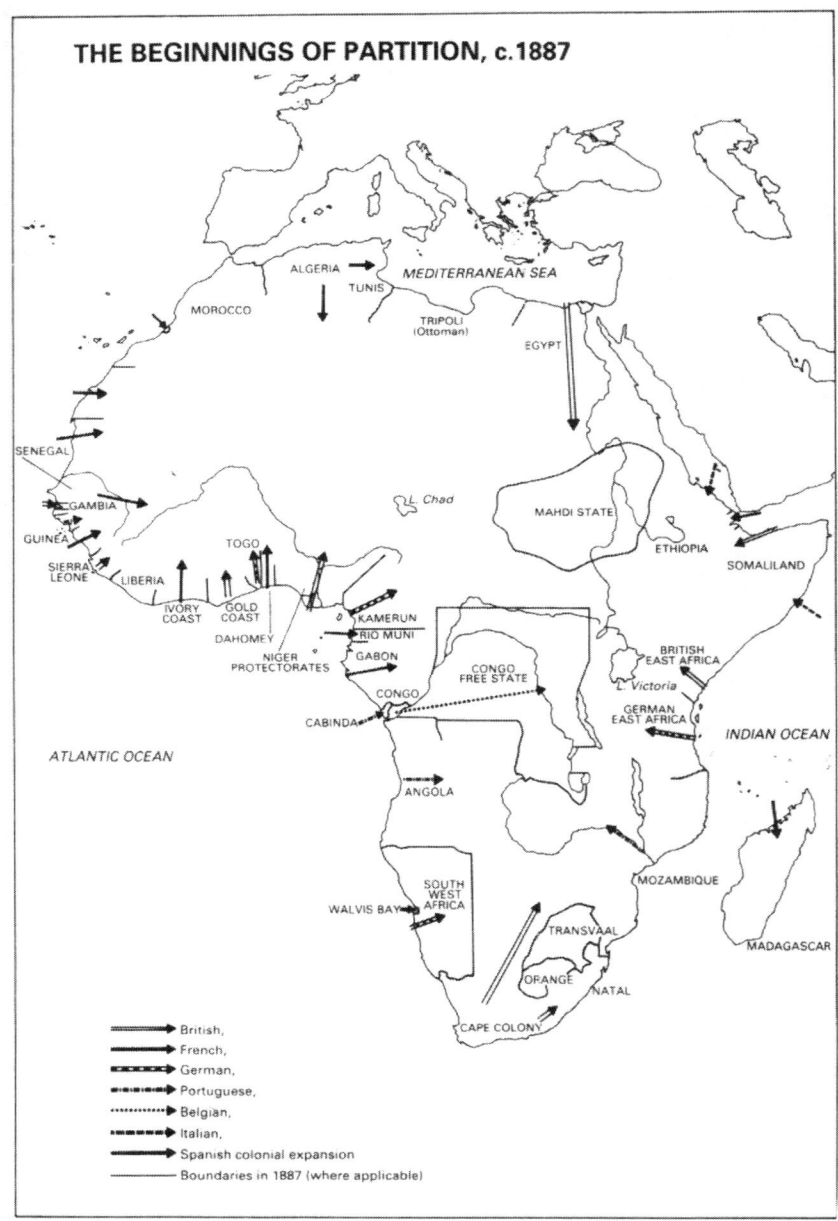

Figure 7.1.

that 'The advantages which people expect from colonies for the commerce and industry of the mother country are mainly founded on illusions, for the expenditure occasioned by the establishment, support, and especially the maintenance of colonies very often exceeds the gain which the mother country derives from them, as is proved by the experience of England and France in their colonial policy.'[10] Bismarck's conclusion was clear: 'So long as I'm Chancellor, we shan't pursue a colonial policy.'[11]

What made him change his mind? The fact that German firms from towns like Bremen and Hamburg were beginning to trade actively in West Africa, even outnumbering the British in the port city of Lagos, was perhaps less important than the fact that German explorers, like Gerhard Rohlfs who was the first European to cross the Sahara from north to south (reaching Lagos in 1867), were opening up the interior. Then there were German protestant missionary societies in South West Africa (today's Namibia) and the Gulf of Guinea (today's Togo) who might need protection. The most decisive factor was probably the worsening economy, with talk of revolution, which hit Germany during the early 1880s. Creating opportunities for emigration to Africa would act as a 'safety valve for the state: Only through colonies could Germany be made safe against social revolution.'[12]

Bismarck's plan was simple. He had already invited the leading nations of Europe, namely Austro-Hungary, Britain, France and Russia, to a Congress in Berlin in 1878 at which they discussed the situation in the Balkans. Bismarck had played the disinterested host. Africa was barely mentioned, but the chancellor had managed to establish himself as an experienced player in diplomacy. It was therefore easy for him, six years later, to summon representatives from fourteen nations that included Austro-Hungary, Belgium, Britain, Denmark, France, Italy, the Netherlands, Portugal, Spain and Sweden-Norway (then in union), plus the Ottoman Empire and the United States, to a West Africa Conference. The focus would be on regularising the position of the Congo, in which a Belgian trading company, privately sponsored by its king Leopold II, was causing some alarm, and on suppressing the East African slave trade through Zanzibar. The venue would again be Berlin. The date was fixed for the 15th of November 1884. Most of the participants would be onlookers as they had no colonial ambitions in Africa. But Bismarck was no longer the disinterested host.

In May of that year Dr Gustav Nachtigal, a German explorer currently in Lisbon had received a secret cable from Bismarck. He was to proceed to West Africa on the pretence of exploring some of the lands bordering the Gulf of Guinea. Bismarck informed Nachtigal that he had been appointed Imperial Consul-General for the west coast of Africa. His mission was to sign treaties with the local chiefs in three coastal regions. The chiefs in each area had been active in the Atlantic slave trade but were now exporting agricultural produce instead. The first location was the narrow strip of unclaimed land known as Little Popo, situated between the Gold Coast (British) and Dahomey (French). The second was the coastal region of Cameroon, five hundred miles to the east that bordered on the Niger Delta (within the British sphere of influence) to its west. The third was Angra Pequena, the coastal lands between the Portuguese colony of Angola to its north and the British Cape Colony to its south. Nachtigal was successful in all three aspects of his mission, largely because no one was expecting a German incursion here. The treaties were ratified in Berlin and the territories annexed. They were named Togoland (today Togo), Kamerun (Cameroon) and South West Africa (today Namibia) respectively.

The participants at the West Africa Conference in Berlin may have been surprised at Germany's incursion into Africa, but there was not much they could do about it. Most of them were in the process of grabbing territories on behalf of their own governments. The French were unwilling to leave the entire Congo in Belgian hands: their man Pierre Savorgnan de Brazza had explored much of the land north of the right bank of the Congo River. Henry Morton Stanley, who was the first to explore the entire Congo River, was employed by the duplicitous King Leopold II.

Stanley had started at Nyangwe on the Lualaba River, which Livingstone thought was the headwater of the Nile. Stanley felt that the Lualaba could become the Congo, even though it flowed northwards whereas the Congo enters the Atlantic flowing south. He proved his point in 1877 by navigating down the Luabala in boats that had been carried, together with arms and other equipment, by more than two hundred porters (half of whom died from accident or disease during a journey that took nearly three years to complete) all the way from the east coast off Zanzibar. After some 300 miles down the Lualaba Stanley encountered a series of rapids (Stanley Falls) that had to be by-passed on foot through jungle country peopled by unfriendly (and cannibalistic) warring tribes. At the lower end of the rapids (Stanleyville) the river flows westward in a wide 1,200 mile arc until it reaches a wide lake (Stanley Pool) above yet more cataracts. These the expedition by-passed on the left bank, finally reaching water that was navigable all the way to the sea. It was this approximately 200-mile stretch of land along the left bank up to Stanley Pool that Leopold commissioned Stanley to explore in readiness for a railway to be built up to the point (Leopoldville, later Kinshasa) at Stanley Pool where the river becomes navigable once more. The Portuguese, who had been the first to delve into the lower waters of the Congo back in the fifteenth century, also wanted a slice of the action. All had been participating in the 'Scramble for Africa', and now wanted their incursions ratified.

After considerable wrangling, the conference drew to a conclusion with the signing of the Berlin Act on 26 February 1885. France would have a good chunk of territory on the right bank of the lower Congo that became French Equatorial Africa, later the Republic of Congo. Portugal was fobbed off with little. The bulk of the territory (later Zaire; now the Democratic Republic of Congo) was left in Belgian hands. It had ostensibly been developed as a philanthropic enterprise, the Comité d'Etudes du Haut Congo (later the International Association of the Congo), though in reality it was under Leopold's control. Bismarck was one of the few to have seen through the king's machinations, jotting down 'swindle' and 'fantasies' on the map he had received from Leopold,[13] but he kept his reservations to himself. All countries would have the right of navigation and trade up rivers like the Congo and the Niger. The question of the eastern slave trade was brushed over in fine words by Bismarck: the conference had "shown 'much careful solicitude' for the moral and physical welfare of the native races, and the Chancellor cherished the hope that this principle would 'bear fruit' and help introduce the populations to the advantages of civilization."[14] The fact that not a single member of the 'native races' had been invited to the conference, and that its resolutions had been passed without consulting – or even informing – any of the 'populations', bothered none of the participants.

A second missing component emerged only some months later. Bismarck had omitted to inform the delegates that even while they were in session, he had approved a treaty that a young German adventurer named Carl Peters had signed with a representative of the Sultan of the island of Zanzibar. The effect of that flimsy document was to place the entire territory on the mainland over which the Sultan exercised control, from Mount Kilimanjaro to the coast, in German hands. Since East Africa had not been on the agenda of the conference, the European Powers subsequently had no option but to accept this *fait accompli*. The territory became known as German East Africa (later Tanganyika, then Tanzania as **Tan**ganyika merged with **Zan**zibar in 1964). By the beginning of the twentieth century, most of the African continent of Africa was under European control **(Fig 7.2)**. The only white areas (apart from Libya which was then part of the Ottoman Empire and Morocco which would become a French colony in 1904) were Liberia in the west, the newly-created nation for freed American slaves, and Ethiopia in the east, the birthplace of humanity. I describe the fortunes of both in the following chapter.

THE MAP COMPLETED, c.1902

CEUTA (Sp.)
MELILLA (Sp.)
MALTA
MEDITERRANEAN SEA
MADEIRA
MOROCCO
TUNIS
IFNI
CANARY IS
TRIPOLI (Ottoman)
RIO DE ORO
ALGERIA
EGYPT
GAMBIA
FRENCH WEST AFRICA
ERITREA
PORT GUINEA
ANGLO-EGYPTIAN SUDAN (Condominium)
(Fr.)
SIERRA LEONE
TOGO
NIGERIA
ETHIOPIA
Br. SOMALILAND
GOLD COAST
LIBERIA
FRENCH EQUATORIAL AFRICA
FERNANDO PO
SP. GUINEA
KAMERUN
UGANDA
SAO TOME
BRITISH EAST AFRICA
ATLANTIC OCEAN
CABINDA
CONGO STATE
GERMAN EAST AFRICA
ZANZIBAR
INDIAN OCEAN
ANGOLA
NORTHERN RHODESIA
COMOROS
SOUTHERN RHODESIA
MOZAMBIQUE
SOUTH WEST AFRICA
WALVIS BAY
BECHUANALAND
MADAGASCAR
SWAZILAND
SOUTH AFRICA
BASUTOLAND

British control
French control
German control
Potuguese control
Belgian control
Italian control
Spanish control

N = NYASALAND

Figure 7.2.

Half a century earlier, the explorer David Livingstone (see below) had espoused three 'Cs' to be the aims of his mission in Africa: Christianity, civilisation and commerce. Bismarck and other European leaders used these sentiments (inverting the order and putting commerce first) to justify their presence in Africa. The French, during the nineteenth century, officially viewed colonialism through even more rose-tinted spectacles: 'Colonialism was seen as a mark of civilization, of national grandeur, of science and progress. The nation, which emerged out of the French Revolution, brought *liberty* and not *oppression*, *development* and not *exploitation*, to the peoples it was "liberating".'[15] Not so their prime minister Jules Ferry, who made no bones about the colonists' objectives: 'The higher races have a right over the lower races; they have a duty to civilize the inferior races', he told the Deputies in the National Assembly in 1885.[16] Paul Déroulède, a soldier with right-wing views, who nevertheless opposed colonialism, subsequently told Jules Ferry: 'I've lost two children, and you offer me twenty servants.'[17]

The idea that African nations like Songhay in the west or Great Zimbabwe in the south had been as 'civilised' as European nations in their day, and should be left to develop on their own, seems not to have occurred to men like Bismarck or Jules Ferry. I should explain the inverted commas over 'civilised'. Strictly speaking, only the Graeco-Roman culture was civilised, in the sense that it upheld the rights of the individual citizen (*civis*), slaves being excluded from citizenship. It is this concept, especially in terms of democratically elected governments, that resurfaced in Western Europe during the eighteenth, nineteenth and twentieth centuries and spread to North America and Australasia thereafter. But the colonists did not consider the rights of individuals, any more than did the pharaohs of Egypt, the kings of Nubia, Aksum, Ghana, Mali, Songhay, Great Zimbabwe or, for that matter, those who governed over the people in the early cultures of Mesopotamia, India, China, central and south America or indeed of many European monarchies before the nineteenth century. I have used the word 'civilisation' in earlier chapters more for convenience than for accuracy in order to describe the cultures that emerged in sub-Saharan Africa and elsewhere.

Another reason for the expansion of colonialism was British opposition to slavery. Frederick Lugard, son of an army chaplain stationed in India, epitomises the combination of soldier, explorer and administrator. In 1888 he was asked by missionaries in Nyasaland (today's Malawi) to help rid the countryside of marauding Arab slave traders around Lake Nyasa. He obliged and was severely wounded for his efforts. 'He returned to England a convert to the case for the British government to intervene in Africa. Imperialism was the only antidote to the East African slave trade.'[18] Entrepreneurs like Cecil Rhodes put it more simply: 'Africa is still lying ready for us', he said, 'it is our duty to take it'.[19]

A few Africans actually *sought* European governance. Samuel Ajayi Crowther, future bishop of south-western Nigeria told Queen Victoria in 1850 that 'The slave trade on … the African coast would be at an end if Lagos, the stronghold of its greatest support', despite the British navy's embargo, 'was destroyed'.[20] King Acqua, who ruled in Cameroon prior to its unexpected annexation by Germany, approached the same monarch in 1880 to ask for protectorate status: 'Dearest Madam, We we servants have *join* together and thoughts its better to write you a nice loving letter … We *wish* to have your laws in our towns. We want to have every *fashion* altered, also we will be according to your Consul's word.… We have spoken to the English consul plenty times about having an English *government* here… When we heard about Calabar River,' (in today's Nigeria) 'how they have all English *laws* in their towns, and how they have put away all their *superstitions*, oh, we shall be very glad to be like Calabar now.'[21] It didn't do him any good. Four years later the country was forcefully appropriated by Germany.

For most African chiefs, European domination of their territories was abhorrent. It was also illegal. Some were induced to sign agreements they did not understand. In other cases the

Europeans simply reneged on their promises. Cecil Rhodes in Matabeleland (later Southern Rhodesia, now Zimbabwe) was particularly adept at this. Then again, troops were occasionally sent in to take over areas on one pretext or another. The feelings of Muhammad Muntaga, brother of Sultan Ahmadu, are typical. In 1883 he wrote 'to the uncircumcised … Colonel Desbordes, may God confound and bring ruin on your friends … No one is more of a malefactor, no one more of a traitor, no one more wicked than you.'[22]

Some Africans tried to oppose the newcomers. In the delta of the Niger the locals, fearing for their own trade in palm oil, in 1895 attacked the Niger Company set up by George Goldie, soldier turned commercial entrepreneur. Then they relented. Their king wrote to the Prince of Wales, begging to be forgiven for his subjects' attack on the Company. They were 'now *very sorry indeed, particularly* in the *killing* and *eating* of parts of its employees … We now throw ourselves entirely on the mercy of the *good old Queen*, knowing her to be a most kind *tender-hearted* and sympathetic *old mother.*'[23]

The only successful opposition to the interlopers occurred in Ethiopia, where the 100,000 strong force of Memelik (Menilek) II notably defeated an Italian incursion in 1896. Italy had already negotiated a right to occupy Eritrea to the north (assisted by the British, whose main aim was to keep the French out of Egypt and the Egyptians out of Ethiopia), but wanted more. They tried again to achieve this under Mussolini in 1936 but were defeated by British forces together with Ethiopian patriots five years later. To the west, the Italians managed to wrest Cyrenaica from the Ottoman Turks in 1912 and to acquire Tripolitania and Fezzan (the three constituting today's Libya) by treaty and other means. They held on to their possessions until defeated, again by British forces, in 1943. The inherent love of culture among Italians does not sit easily alongside militarism. When news of the 1896 defeat reached Italy, 'Shouts of "Viva Menilek" were heard in the streets of Rome and in other Italian cities. Nearly 10,000 people signed a petition calling for Italy's total withdrawal from Africa.'[24] Heirs to the martial leadership of Scipio Africanus or Julius Caesar have not reappeared.

During the 1820s, the Kru people living along the south westerly tip of West Africa were surprised to see a new kind of interloper arriving on their shore. The Kru were good sailors, and had long been taken on by the captains of slaving ships as crew; (in order to ensure that they were not confused with the unfortunate cargo being transported, the Kru had a vertical line tattooed on their forehead). So they were well aware of the fate that awaited their brothers below deck. What astonished the Kru was that the newcomers were black like themselves, but they were *arriving*, seemingly on their own accord, not departing in chains. Who were these people, and from where did they come? They proved to be freed or escaped slaves, and they came from the United States of America, where the American Colonization Society was helping them to resettle in Africa. The Society was motivated not so much by the altruism of its members, as by the slave-owning Southerners who did not want emancipated slaves living within their communities. By 1847, when the territory became an independent nation, thousands of former slaves and freed men, calling themselves 'black pioneers' had arrived. They had named their new home Liberia (for obvious reasons) and their capital Monrovia (after US President James Monroe, for less obvious reasons). None of the European powers dared interfere in Liberia, though it wasn't for want of trying. British, French, German and Spanish governments all had a go and the first two managed to wrest territory off Liberia through treaties forced on the young and impoverished country. She lost 50 miles of coastline and productive hinterland to the British colony of Sierra Leone in 1885 and 2,000 square miles of hinterland to French West Africa in 1907. Her fate is told in the next chapter.

Consequences

The policies of the colonists were all extractive (see chapter 2), as they had been under the chiefs who preceded them as ultimate rulers. Only in Bechuanaland (today's Botswana; see chapter 9) was the more inclusive regime of King Khama II continued, under the title of protectorate rather than colony. The Belgians were the most extractive. King Leopold II made himself a fortune out of exporting ivory and rubber. He was lucky in that the equatorial rain forests of the Etat Independant du Congo (as Leopold named it once the Berlin Conference had allocated it to him) or Congo Free State – a euphemism if ever there was one – are rich in wild rubber (*Landolphia*). This grows as a vine on other trees. The rubber tree itself (*Landolphia kirkii*) grows more slowly and requires maintenance. Leopold was aware that the price of rubber, which soared during the 1890s as the demand for automobile tyres became insatiable, would fall once the yield from rubber trees introduced from South America into Burma and Malaya began to compete. The land controlled by Leopold, one of the largest (1.5 million square miles) in the whole of Africa, lies south of the Congo River and stretches eastwards into the interior as far as Uganda, Rwanda, Burundi and Tanzania. As mentioned above, the coastal region to the north of the Congo was claimed by the French and is now the Republic of Congo, while Belgian Congo (Leopold sold his 'holding' of the entire Free State to the Belgian Government for 95 million francs in 1908) became the Democratic Republic of Congo at independence in 1960. For a time the former Belgian and French colonies were known after their capitals as Congo-Léopoldville and Congo-Brazzaville (named after the French explorer of that name). In 1971 the Democratic Republic of Congo changed its name to Zaire, but is now back again as DR Congo.

Roger Casement, who in 1898 was appointed British Consul for the Congo Free State, was employed as supervisor for the Compagnie du chemin de fer du Congo that would eventually build the rail link to Léopoldville. He was appalled to learn of the exploitation of the natives working on the rubber plantations further up river and in 1903 wrote a report to the Belgian authorities. In the words of one who had managed to escape, 'We get no pay. We get nothing … we starved. Wild beasts – the leopards – killed some of us while we were working away in the forest and others got lost or died from exposure or starvation and we begged the white men to leave us alone, saying we could get no more rubber, but the white men and their [black] soldiers said: Go. You are only beasts yourselves. … We tried, always going further into the forest, and when we failed and our rubber was short, the soldiers came to our towns and killed us. Many were shot, some had their ears cut off, others were tied up with ropes around their necks and bodies and taken away. The white men at the posts sometimes did not know of the bad things the soldiers did to us, but it was the white men who sent the soldiers to punish us for not bringing in enough rubber.'[25]

Another account was recorded by a Swahili-speaking American who was employed by the administration. The speaker is a woman named Ilanga. 'We were all busy in the fields … when a runner came to the village saying that a large band of men was coming, that they all wore red caps and blue cloth (the outfit of the *Force Publique*), and carried guns and long knives, and many white men were with them, the chief of whom was Kibalanga (the African name for a *Force Publique* officer called Oscar Michaux, who once received a Sword of Honour from Leopold's own hands). … … We were not long seated (in our houses) when the soldiers came rushing in shouting, and threatening Niendo [their chief] with their guns. They rushed into the houses and dragged people out. Three or four came to our house and caught hold of me, also my husband Oleka and my sister Katinga. We were dragged into the road, and tied together with cords around our necks, so that we could not escape. We were all crying, for now we knew that we were to be taken away to be slaves. The soldiers beat us with the iron sticks from their guns, and compelled us to march to the camp of Kibalanga, who ordered the women to be tied up separately, ten to each cord, and then the men in the same way. … We then set off marching very quickly. My sister Katinga had her baby in her arms, and was not compelled to carry a basket; but my husband Oleka was made to carry a goat. … We had nothing to eat, for the soldiers would give us nothing. … The next day we continued the march, and when we camped at noon were given some maize and plantains, which were gathered near a village from which the people had run away. So it continued each day until the fifth day, when the soldiers took my sister's baby and threw it in the grass, leaving it to die, and made her carry some cooking pots which they had found in the deserted village. On the sixth day we became very weak from lack of food and from constant marching and sleeping in the damp grass, and my husband, who marched behind us with the goat, could not stand up longer, and so he sat down beside the path and refused to walk more. The soldiers beat him, but still he refused to move. Then one of them struck him on the head with the end of his gun, and he fell upon the ground. One of the soldiers caught the goat, while two or three others stuck the long knives they put on the ends of their guns into my husband. I saw the blood spurt out, and then saw him no more, for we passed over the brow of a hill and he was out of sight. Many of the young men were killed the same way, and many babies thrown into the grass to die. … After marching ten days we came to the great water … and were taken in canoes across to the white men's town at Nyangwe.'[26]

Joseph Conrad considered this mistreatment as 'the vilest scramble for loot that ever disfigured the history of human conscience and geographical exploration' [27] and in 1903 wrote to Casement, saying that 'It is an extraordinary thing that the conscience of Europe which seventy years ago has put down the slave trade on humanitarian grounds tolerates the Congo State today. It is as if the moral clock had been put back.'[28]. The legacy of brutality and corruption in that part of the world is very much alive a century on: some 5 million people – men, women and children – are believed to have died so far as a result of ongoing civil war in DR Congo, and a thousand women a day are reputedly raped by rampaging soldiers. Eighty per cent of the population was living on 50 cents a day in 2003, while politicians were driving by in new Mercedes cars.[29]

The outright slavery that flourished along the Niger Bend in the 1890s did not worry the French either. 'In general the slave trade flourished under the walls of the new French forts just as it had flourished under the town walls of Ahmadu [Sultan of the Islamic Tukolor empire south of the Senegal river, based on Segu on the Niger], and Samori [in the mountains of Guinea]. It paid better than any other business; [Captain Louis] Archinard gave it his blessing by taking the traditional 10 per cent tax.'[30] Indigenous soldiers were themselves allowed 'to take as many captives as they could … It was only in 1901 that French government directives were issued for the suppression of the trade.'[31] The British were equally ambivalent. When Lugard, the opponent of the Arab slave trade, found himself back in Africa as British High Commissioner for the former Sokoto Caliphate, that would become the northern part of Nigeria by 1906, he somewhat surprisingly decreed that 'To prematurely abolish the almost universal form of labour contract, before a better system has been developed to take its place, would not only be an act of administrative folly, but would also be an injustice to the masters, since Domestic Slavery is an institution sanctioned by the laws of Islam, and property in slaves was as real as any other form of property among the Mohammedan population at the time that the British assumed the Government.'[32]

The French were less extractive than the Belgians, except in their part of the Congo along the river's right bank, where enforcement of labour was as ruthless as that in the Belgian part along the river's left bank and the huge area to the south. Algeria, occupied on a pretext in 1830, was administered as a Department of France itself, with representation for Africans, from 1848 until independence in 1962. Nevertheless they were second-class citizens, considered incapable of self-government. This was the general opinion throughout all of Africa. Not until the second half of the twentieth century would that view be modified.

Another consequence of colonialism was the spread of disease. The availability of quinine during the nineteenth century had enabled Europeans to enter tropical Africa without fear of dying of malaria. But their arrival in considerable numbers brought problems for the Africans, as germs to which they were unaccustomed took hold. Just as smallpox, tuberculosis, measles and whooping cough brought from Europe to the Americas may have caused more deaths there than the Black Death did in Europe,[33] so the same diseases brought havoc to Africa.

'The immediate consequences of the final breaching of the old African seclusion was epidemiological disaster. ... The inhabitants of the Belgian Congo before 1880 were estimated to number about 40 million; by 1910 the figure had dropped to 15.5 million, and was 9.25 million in 1933. The record from French West Africa is still more shattering: ... the population of one area was 20 million in 1911; by 1921 it was reduced to 7.5 million and was down to 2.5 million in 1931. ... [34] The author of these statistics does not mention the wanton killings that surely contributed to the earlier decline.

Carving up Africa according to European interests meant ignoring tribal entities that had existed for centuries. Around 10,000 kingdoms and smaller units of self-government were amalgamated into less than 40 colonies. Some of these combined tribes of long-standing enmity, in others tribal boundaries between friendly tribes were severed. In Mali, for example, the predominantly Mande population was merged with Tuaregs (who had invaded the country centuries earlier) from the north. In the Gold Coast the Akan who populated the Ashante Empire based on Kumasi were forced into union with the Ewe to the east, the Ga along the coast to the south, the Dagomba in the Volta River region to the north, as well as with other minor groups. At the same time some Akan now found themselves in Côte d'Ivoire, while a quarter of the Ewe, together with some Ga, finished up in Togo. In the Congo basin, the unification of more than 200 separate tribes, created tensions that continue to this day. In Nigeria the Yoruba in the south west were amalgamated with Hausa from the north, Igbo from the south east, as well as some Fulani (who are spread throughout the Sahel from Senegal and Guinea in the west to the Sudan in the east, from Mali and Niger to the north to Cameroon in the south). Together with several other distinct tribes, this made Nigeria the most populated country in the whole of Africa. But the merger of the Muslim

Hausa with the other, predominantly Christian, clans led to religious conflict that successive administrations have been unable to quell. Even today 250 different ethnicities, speaking 500 languages, make up the Nigerian population.

So on it went throughout the continent. Needless to say divisions on the one hand, and mergers on the other, caused considerable friction when the newly created states achieved independence half a century later. Resentment by one group and hostility towards another continue. In Kenya antagonism between Luo to the west and Kikuyu to the east is holding back the economy. Following the 2007 presidential election between Mwai Kibaki (Kikuyu) and Raila Odinga (Luo), that was 'won' by the incumbent Kibaki, rioting broke out to such an extent that a thousand people were massacred and hundreds of thousands displaced. A particular example concerns The Gambia and Senegal. Both border the Atlantic, but tiny Gambia on the Gambia River is completely surrounded by its larger, horse-shoe like neighbour with access to the Atlantic along the Senegal River in the north and the Casamance River in the south. It was pure horse trading that resulted in the fairly homogenous population being split between France (Senegal) and Britain (Gambia). 'The arrangement was regarded as both temporary and unsatisfactory, but with the colonial powers seemingly uninterested in further rationalization of the map, or even in cooperation during the colonial period, the existing frontiers have survived by default.'[35]

Another point is that the populace in general continued to show allegiance to their chiefs, rather than to the respective government, because chiefs look after their own clans more sympathetically than any government official. Something along these lines was pointed out by men like Joseph Casely Heyford, a perceptive author, lawyer, educator, and politician born in the British Gold Coast in 1866. By disregarding 'Africa's ancient and honourable traditions and institutions of statecraft' that had evolved over many centuries, and by failing to rebuild and modernise them, 'the British had abetted their disintegration by assuming they were dealing with a savage people.'[36] It was an error that local politicians, after independence, would repeat: the views of the majority were ignored time and again, as one-party government, military rule or whites-only government were introduced (see chapters 9-14).

The Europeans also played off one part of a country's population against the other. On the one side were the chiefs and 'men of quality' like academics and lawyers; on the other side were the mass of the people, led by radical politicians such as Julius Nyerere in Tanganyika (later Tanzania), Kwame Nkrumah in the Gold Coast (later Ghana), Kenneth Kaunda in Northern Rhodesia (later Zambia), Jomo Kenyatta in Kenya and Ahmed Sékou Touré in Guinea. The former group were happy to side with their colonial masters and to approach potential independence slowly and with caution. The latter were not prepared to wait and agitated for independence at the earliest possible moment. In the end, they won out.

The colonists built medical centres, hospitals and schools, but these were mainly for the benefit of the Europeans who were administering the different nations. In Kenya during the 1950s, for example, the colonial government spent $180 a year on the education of each white child, $65 on each Asian child and $5 on each African child.[37] Of the schools that were built for the population as a whole, most catered for primary education only. Secondary schools were few in number, though some exceptionally good ones emerged as pointed out below. The French and British contribution to education eclipsed all others, with the French system the better of the two. However the anticlericalism that erupted in France in 1903 had a devastating effect on its mission schools: most were closed. As a result, Islamic teaching was strengthened, a consequence that the French now have reason to regret. Nevertheless, by the 1920s 'the French educational system has adapted courses of instruction to the needs of the African much more successfully than has been done in any other territory in Africa. … Texts and courses have been designed to fit native needs.'[38]

The Germans had little regard for the education of their African subjects. In German East Africa a thousand missionary schools (half Protestant, half Catholic), accommodating some 62,000 pupils were built. The population in 1913 was 7.5 million, so that less than 1 percent of the population was catered for. Of these schools, less than 3 percent were 'upper', providing anything beyond the maximum of four years of primary (elementary) education. In German West Africa (today's Namibia), the situation was even worse. For a population of between 25,000 and 40,000 in 1904 (which was all that remained after the Herero uprising of the previous year had been brutally put down with the loss of between 24,000 and 100,000 African lives), there was just one 'upper school'. The number of pupils attending it was twelve.[39]

Since Africans were considered unfit for higher education, few universities were built. The French founded the University of Algiers in 1909, where its most famous alumnus was the writer Albert Camus. The British established a technical school in Kampala, Uganda in 1922 that later became Makerere University. They also opened a college at Achimoto outside Accra in the then Gold Coast in 1924. In Nigeria, Yaba College was set up in Lagos in 1932; it moved to Ibadan in 1948 to become Ibadan University. The teaching and administrative staffs at all these centres were, of course, mainly European. In South Africa several good universities, such as Cape Town, Pretoria, Stellenbosch and Witwatersrand, were founded. None was open to Africans, who were able to attend only the less prestigious University of Fort Hare. In fact the best way for an African to gain access to higher education was to go to Europe or America, and several of the future leaders did just that. Not until the second half of the twentieth century would the European view that Africans were unable to benefit from education, and hence incapable of self-government, be modified.

The change occurred particularly after the Second World War, in which many Africans had fought and died on behalf of the Allies. So the British founded new university colleges in their colonies in order to 'promote a "responsible class" to whom, sooner or later, they could safely hand political independence'. They based the new universities on the Oxbridge model 'in the belief that the function of a university in Africa was to create and sustain an intellectual élite'. The result was that students and teachers became 'isolated from the life of the common people in a way which has had no parallel in England since the Middle Ages.'[40] This, as much as anything, led to the emergence of an educated upper class that was often in conflict with radical politicians in the early years of independence.

Infrastructure was also improved. Electricity grids were constructed to link major cities, even though over 90% of the population lived in the countryside. By 1900 Durban in South Africa was linked by underwater telephone to Europe. Roads, railways and ports were built in order to export the produce and minerals plundered by the interlopers (though in several instances the railways also allowed native farmers to export their crops). It did not always go smoothly for the colonists however. In the French Congo, for example, twenty-one of the original forty companies lost money and nine had gone bankrupt by 1906. The railway to the coast was not completed until 1934, by which time it had cost the French taxpayer 231 million francs. So far as the Africans were concerned, 17,000 of the conscripted workmen died of malnutrition and disease.[41] The fate of workers in the neighbouring (Belgian) Congo Free State has already been mentioned. During the depression of the 1930s, the price of African goods dropped sharply, bringing economic downturn and unemployment. Indeed the allegation that the European powers profited enormously from colonisation is as unwarranted – except in a few cases like that of the Congo Free State – as their purported huge revenue from the Atlantic slave trade.

Of course *some* income from African trade filtered through to the colonial powers. Take the Gold Coast as an example. Cocoa has been its major export for over a century (Africans themselves drink little chocolate). Around 1900, 2,000 tons of cocoa a year were being exported. By 1910 this had risen to 40,000 tons a year and in 1960 (three years after independence) 350,000 tons were exported. This made Ghana the largest cocoa producer in the world (more recently slipped into second place, behind Côte d'Ivoire). Who benefited from this? The amount remitted to the farmers themselves was controlled by the Cocoa Marketing Board. They saw little of the profit. In 1953, for example, the cocoa producers received £28 million out of sales worth £74 million. Most of the money went directly to London where a cocoa reserve fund was set up. Following Britain's dire financial situation at the end of the war in 1945, its government felt justified in keeping it. The government of the Gold Coast (power shared between the Governor and the newly-formed Convention's People's Party led by Kwame Nkrumah) was allowed to use only a small part of this reserve in order to buy 'hard currency' to fund its infrastructure projects. So in 1953 the Gold Coast was allowed to keep just 21 percent of the £25 million earned in sales to the USA and other dollar area countries. The following year this had dropped to 16 percent of £20 million earned. Another aspect of Europeans benefiting from African production is that they often make up the higher echelons of the workers. Again in the Gold Coast, where gold was its second major export, half of the earnings in the mining industry in 1949 went overseas. This means that virtually all the profits were paid to European technicians and executives.[42]

A comparable situation existed in French-controlled West Africa. In Senegal, for example, 'The ... economic beneficiaries of the colonial system were the French firms. In the precolonial period commerce had been dominated by the mulatto population, but they gradually lost ground to the Lebanese and small French businesses on the one hand, and to the large French companies, particularly CFAO (Compagnie Française de l'Afrique Occidentale) and SCOA (Societé Commerciale de l'Ouest Africain) which dominated the import-export trade, on the other.'[43] What I have described illustrates the sort of profit made by European governments and their nationals throughout Africa.

In exchange, of course, the colonial powers contributed toward the management of their respective colonies, as indicated above.

In general the French and British spent the most, the Belgians and Portuguese the least. In the Belgian Congo (successor to the Congo Free State) the Brussels government avoided all expenditure on health, education and welfare by passing responsibility to the various missionary groups that the Catholic and Protestant churches had set up. The same was true of Ruanda-Urundi (today's Rwanda and Burundi), that had been part of German East Africa prior to the First World War: less than a hundred Africans there had progressed beyond secondary school by 1961. In Guinea-Bissau on the west coast between Senegal to the north and Guinea to the south, three hundred years of colonial rule by Portugal produced very little advancement. In 1974 there were just fourteen university graduates, an illiteracy rate of 97 percent and only 265 miles of paved road in a country spanning 14,000 square miles – roughly the size of Belgium.[44]

Does foreign domination necessarily stifle the creative potential of an invaded country? Not at all. Take Sicily as an example. The Greeks started settling there during the eighth century BC, followed by Romans, Vandals, Ostrogoths, Arabs and Normans. In the twelfth century it found its own identity as the Kingdom of Sicily, but the rulers were successively Spanish, German and French. Only after 1861 would Sicilians be ruled by an Italian monarchy. The foreigners brought culture of one sort or another and allowed local arts to flourish. The Greeks built theatres – that in Syracuse could accommodate over 2,000 spectators, every stone seat carved into the rock of the sloping hillside still there today – and fostered the studies of Archimedes; the Romans, as elsewhere, adapted Greek architecture to their own style; the Normans incorporated the Islamic iconography of the Arabs into the Palazzo dei Normanni and the church of Monreale in Palermo; baroque architecture flourished under Spanish rule; in the nineteenth century Vincenzo Bellini wrote opera and Wagner, on a visit to Palermo, composed the second act of Lohengrin; and in the twentieth century Luigi Pirandello and Salvatore Quasimodo won Nobel Prizes for their literature. All the foreigners, apart from the Arabs, were European. In Africa the same Europeans introduced no culture whatsoever. Apart from a few rudimentary churches built by missionaries, all the colonists did was to inhibit indigenous progress through the imposition of inferiority on the natives.

Missionaries and Murderers
Christian

Christianity spread early into Africa. It became the state religion in Aksum in 330 AD, fifty years before it was ratified as the state church within the Roman Empire (though Constantine had decriminalised the practice in 313 AD). Christianity proliferated little outside Aksum, and the religion, in contrast to that of Islam, lay dormant in most of the continent. The first mission consisted of a handful of Roman Catholic priests (together with 500 soldiers), sent out in 1481 to Elmina on the Gold Coast by the King of Portugal. Over the following two centuries the mission expanded westwards as far as Sierra Leone, but it then began to fizzle out. By 1723 the priests, by now largely Capuchin friars, had gone. Their impact on the population had been negligible. The Dutch settlers who had appeared at the Cape in South Africa during the previous century kept themselves pretty much to themselves. Their Boer descendants were not interested in proselytising anybody. So long as their British and African neighbours did not interfere with their God-given right to settle *where* they wanted and to govern their territories (that housed a majority of Africans) *how* they wanted, they were satisfied.

Not until the nineteenth century, when Europeans started to explore the interior of Africa, would Christianity begin to take hold. Protestant missionaries of various stripes began to accompany the inquisitive travellers. But it was slow going: by 1872, for example, less than a hundred out of sixty thousand inhabitants in the British colony of Lagos had been converted.[45] Explorers and missionaries were often the same person. David Livingstone is a case in point. The Scotsman was sent out by the London Missionary Society, though is said to have converted just one man in the entire region of Bechuanaland (now Botswana);

but since that man was a tribal king, his influence was considerable (the convert subsequently lapsed). Livingstone's motto, as mentioned above, had been 'Christianity, civilisation and commerce', but he was no more successful with the other two. His legacy lies elsewhere. In east and central Africa, where he spent most of his time, commerce was dominated by the slave trade. The slavers were ruthless Muslim Arabs (often of African blood), aided by Indian traders on the coast, who operated between the interior and Zanzibar, whence much of their cargo was exported to Arabia and beyond. Livingstone opposed the practice as vehemently as possible, bearing in mind that some of the Arab traders often brought him medicines and food.

But others plundered Livingstone's own resources. In the last letter ever written by him (on 21 November 1872), that subsequently reached England together with his dead body, he complains of 'being cut off from the world by a slave-trading coterie of banian British subjects [actually Indian traders] and mainland Arabs who plundered my stores and strove by the destruction of my letters to prevent evidence of their deeds going to the coast. They managed to make me lose two years of time – to entail at least two thousand miles of useless tramping, risk of violent death four several times and the loss of how much money I cannot tell'.[46] In an earlier letter eventually taken back to England by Stanley, Livingstone wrote to the Editor of the *New York Herald* (the paper that had commissioned Stanley to search for Livingstone) condemning the East African slave trade outright: 'The whole traffic, whether on land or ocean, is a gross outrage of the common law of mankind … Many have but a faint idea of the evil that trading in slaves inflicts on the victims and on the authors of the atrocities'[47] … 'I come back to the slaving question and if I am permitted in any way to promote its suppression I shall not grudge the toil and time I have spent. It would be better to lessen human woe than discover the source of the Nile.'[48] Given that he was a Christian missionary, that is hardly a surprising sentiment. It is for Livingstone's abhorrence of the slave trade that he is revered by Africans to this day.

His second contribution, of course, was as an explorer. Exploration was the way to introduce the '3 Cs' into Africa. As Stanley told the members of the Scottish Geographical Society in 1884, '… David Livingstone has declared that the end of the geographical feat is the beginning of the commercial enterprise.'[49] Livingstone made the first crossing of the African continent (like most explorers on foot most of the way) from Luanda (Angola) on the Atlantic to Quelimane (Mozambique) on the Indian Ocean between 1853 and 1856. A subsequent crossing in the opposite direction (following one completed by Verney Lovett Cameron in 1875 [50]) would be made by Stanley between 1874 and 1877 from Zanzibar via the Great Lakes region, where he had found Livingstone in 1872, and down the Congo to the Atlantic. In fact none of these voyages should claim priority. According to American writer Adam Hochschild, '… the first recorded crossing of central Africa, unacknowledged by Stanley and almost all the other white explorers, had been made half a century earlier by two mulatto slave traders, Pedro Baptista and Anastasio José,' [51] though others believe that in their trek from west (Angola) to east (Mozambique) they only got as far as Tete, not quite on the Indian Ocean.[52]

Livingstone had mapped the Zambezi river a decade earlier (losing his wife to malaria in the process) and named its great waterfall after Queen Victoria. On reaching the shores of Lake Nyasa (now Lake Malawi) Livingstone is said to have enquired its name: the locals, thinking he was asking what this was, replied 'Nyasa', which means 'lake'. A similar story is told about the first European immigrants in Australia. Seeing the strange animals hopping around, one man pointed at them and raised his eyes, in expectation that a nearby group of aboriginal settlers would tell him what these animals were called. 'Kangaroo', one of the settlers said. The word actually means 'what is he saying?'

Livingstone's obsession with the source of the Nile is not to be dismissed lightly. After the much publicised (by Stanley) meeting with the Welsh-born American at Ujiji near the western shore of lake Tanganyika in November 1871, Livingstone refused to return to England, and instead persuaded Stanley to help him ascertain, once and for all, the source of the Nile. They searched the area to the north of the lake, but found no out-flowing waters. Stanley had had enough (he had a scoop to file, after all) and the two men parted the following March. Stanley promised to return with dentures for his friend (Livingstone had lost most of his teeth, but that was the least of his troubles). The intrepid Scot would not give up, and continued to explore the area to the south west of the lake. Another year in the tropics proved too much for his disease-ravaged body. Dysentery and intestinal haemorrhage led to his death on the first of May 1873. Livingstone's memory is revered in Africa as much as it is in Britain. Today more than two dozen towns, schools, clinics, and other sites in Botswana, Burundi, Ghana (he never actually came near the Gold Coast), Malawi, South Africa, Tanzania, Uganda, Zaire, Zambia and Zimbabwe bear his name. There is even a Livingstone College in Salisbury, North Carolina, USA. This is where Livingstone's son Robert, who had fought on the Union side in the American Civil War, was captured and died of his wounds.[53] Livingstone realised that 'the day for Africa has yet to come.'[54] Many are still waiting, but I believe it is finally on its way.

The intentions of the missionaries may have been entirely benign (they introduced, among other things, the ox-plough and provided medicines considerably more efficacious than the treatments handed out by traditional healers), but they were not always welcomed. During the second half of the 1880s a powerful ruler, King Kabaka Mwanga of Buganda, held sway in that part of today's Uganda. Of Mwanga's father, King Mutesa I, it was said that 'There was much that was good and lovable in him but his education had been a training in cruelty, brutality and lust.'[55] The son would out-perform the father in each of these three traits. In 1885, James Huntington, recently appointed Bishop of East Equatorial Africa by the Church Missionary Society in England, was approaching his intended diocese on the northern shores of Lake Victoria, when he was imprisoned by the king's men. But then he received good news. 'He was to leave his prison at last.

They took him through the forest to rejoin the porters of his caravan. The shock of that meeting must have been terrible. The porters were indeed there, but naked and bound in the clearing, like sheep in a pen. The soldiers stood ready with their spears. As they tore the clothes from his back, the bishop managed to shout, "Tell the King that I am about to die for his people, that I have brought the road to Buganda with my life". He knelt in prayer. Then a signal gun was fired. With a wild shout the soldiers leapt on the bishop, leapt on the trembling porters, hacking and spearing till the gap in the forest was choked with dead.'[56]

King Mwanga did not mellow with time. The following year a young page, who had converted to Christianity, refused to accede to the king's advances and was beaten. 'But the incident and the refusal of the other pages to be defiled by the King, seemed to have finally unhinged Mwanga. On 25 May [1886], in a paroxysm of rage, he had ordered all Christian "readers" at court to be seized. Some were castrated, others hacked to death, their bodies left to the vultures. On 3 June, one large group – eleven Protestants and thirteen Catholics – was taken and burnt on a funeral pyre at Namgongo. What was most astonishing about these terrible events, astonishing even to the executioners, was that the young boys died singing and praising the white man's God. Many had been offered freedom if the abjured Christianity. They chose martyrdom.'[57] There is now a shrine at Namgongo, and the event is commemorated annually to this day.

Muslim

Muslim scholars, clerics and traders (again, in this case, often the same person), as well as men-at-arms, started arriving in Africa 1400 years ago. 'It was intermittently by conquest but more lastingly by the diffusion of ideas that Islam had spread through large areas of black Africa.'[58] They mainly came south to sub-Saharan Africa from the Mediterranean coast along two routes: from the Berber states in the west to the empires of Ghana, Mali and Songhay; and from Egypt through Nubia to the empire of Kanem-Bornu (centred on present-day Chad) and the Hausa kingdoms (in northern Nigeria and surrounding areas). They were as well intentioned as the European missionaries of the nineteenth century. They did not even actively seek to convert anyone: many Africans did so of their own accord. As Edward Blyden has pointed out, '… the Negro who accepts Mohammedanism acquires at once a sense of the dignity of human nature not commonly found among those who have been brought up to accept Christianity.'[59] Moreover in contrast to Christianity, '… what really took place, when the Arab met the Negro in his own home, was a healthy amalgamation, and not an absorption or an undue repression.'[60]

In ancient Ghana, the Arabs initially lived separately from the natives. Gradually their African hosts began to appreciate their literacy, code of conduct, love of learning and culture. Soon much of the Sahel (the area from the Sahara in the north to the tropical rain forest in the south, from the Atlantic in the west to the Red Sea in the east) had become islamised. We owe the description of life in this region largely to Muslim writers, as the natives had no script. Some chroniclers, like Al-Bakri, never set foot in Africa: his account of the region was written entirely from the comfort of his native Cordoba. Others did. Ibn Battuta's portrayal of life in Mali, including the cities of Gao, Jenne and Timbuktu, during the early fourteenth century remains one of the best-documented accounts available to historians.[61] Two hundred years later Leo Africanus, a Moor who was born in Granada but spent most of his life in North Africa, also wrote about the Sahel, though again in his case much depends on the accounts of others. In his account of life in the 'Kingdom of Melli', which probably refers to the area visited by Ibn Battuta, he mentions the influence of Islam in relation to what are probably early forms of a university: 'Here are great store of temples, priests and professors, which professors read their lectures in the temples.'[62]

Edward Blyden, delivering a lecture in Sierra Leone in 1884, can barely contain his fervour on behalf of Islam: 'Between Sierra Leone and Egypt the Mohammedans are the only great intellectual, moral, and commercial power. The tribes intervening have for more than 300 years been under the influence of Islam. It has taken possession of, and has shaped the social, political, and religious life of the most intelligent tribes. Its adherents control the politics and commerce of nearly all Africa north of the Equator. The Mohammedans … have given the initiative of intellectual progress to the tribes of the interior. It is through them that the natives have acquired all they have of knowledge of the outside world, or of past history, sacred or profane. They have given unity to the great tribes of the continent, and have placed millions of Africans – by means of their language, letters and books – under the same inspiration. Suppose Africa had been obliged to wait till now for knowledge of letters and books from Europeans, what would have been the condition of things, at this moment, in the interior?'[63] This from a man who was himself as devout a Christian as anyone of his day.

So Islam created a beneficial stimulus on the early nations of sub-Saharan Africa. Kings and chiefs had ruled on the basis of particular lineages, as in Europe. 'By contrast, Islam provided a more cohesive force and a stronger basis for empire-building.'[64] Some writers consider that Islamic influence affected the countries north of the Sahara more than those below it. But 'Mauretania, Senegal, Gambia, Guinea, Mali, Niger, Nigeria, Chad, Sudan and Somalia are all countries where Islam has been established for six to eight centuries, and where the main direction of trade, travel, forced migration and cultural influence has been northwards across the desert. It is the Islamic factor in all its historical depth that makes the North African countries inescapably a part of Africa, whatever other affiliations may be claimed for them.'[65]

How times have changed. When I visited Ibadan University in the 1980s (see chapter 14) there were merely robbers on the road from Lagos to contend with at night. Now religious fanatics like the members of Boko Haram roam the countryside intent on mayhem. In the Sudan the government of Omar al-Bashir has oppressed the non-Muslims living in the Darfur region in the south (now a separate country) for over a decade. Half a million died at the hands of Arab militia and three million fled into the interior, to be housed in make-shift camps. Fanatical *jihadists*, inspired by the Wahabi doctrine emanating from Saudi Arabia, Qatar and United Arab Emirates that galvanised the likes of Osama bin Laden, tarnish the reputation of Islam. They terrorise peaceful citizens across the Sahel, from Mali and Nigeria in the west, to Kenya and Somalia in the east. They have forgotten that 'Islam has had a long commitment to religious pluralism. Muhammad (recognised) Jews and Christians as protected peoples … and there are few scriptures in the great religions of the world that can match the reverence with which the Qur'an speaks of other religious traditions.'[66] The culture that enlightened Muslims brought to sub-Saharan Africa over the centuries, their terrorist successors, in 2013 and beyond, destroyed.

What If?

What if the colonisation of Africa at the end of the nineteenth century had not happened? If the relaxed conditions prevalent during the early years of that century, at least in British West Africa, had prevailed? Having finally been freed of slavery, the inhabitants might have gone on to sooner and more effective independence without having to suffer a second assault on their liberty. In the east, the natives were subject to seizure by Arab traders well into the twentieth century. For suggesting the former scenario I will describe events that began in Sierra Leone and involved one of its most inspired citizens.

Sierra Leone was the place from which slaves were first transported westwards across the Atlantic Ocean on English ships. In 1562 Sir John Hawkins took three hundred innocent souls by force and sailed with them to St Domingo where he exchanged them for sugar and ginger, hides and pearls, with which he returned to England the following year. Two centuries later, Sierra Leone was the first place where escaped or freed slaves from North America found haven. They had been arriving along the coast, at what would become Freetown, since 1787, having traded their freedom for service in the British army during the American War of Independence. They finished up in London whence they were sent to establish a new colony in Sierra Leone. The resident Temne were not welcoming and drove the first lot of migrants away by burning their homes. Next came former slaves who had sought liberty in Nova Scotia, Canada. In 1800 a group (known as Maroons), who had rebelled in Jamaica, arrived. Eight years later, when the slave trade was abolished by Britain and its navy was seizing vessels bound for the Americas, the occupants of those ships were brought to Freetown. The French were resettling slaves freed by them in the similarly-named port of Libreville in Gabon.

Over the next decade or so, the number of such 'recaptives', or 'Creoles' as their descendants were called, came to outnumber all previous immigrants. Few understood each other since their tribal origins spanned the entire coastline of West Africa: sixty different languages could be heard in Freetown. So English became the common language. The British supervised the colony in a pretty benign way. Schools were established by the Church Missionary Society (CMS) at which the teachers included former 'recaptives' alongside English and German missionaries. The aim was to give the children an education that would enable the brightest to continue at higher establishments. Some went abroad, others to Fourah Bay College, established in Freetown in 1827 by the CMS. This produced among its alumni a President of Sierra Leone and several leading academics. The students at the CMS school 'had the chance of a better education than many white children in contemporary rural England – who were merely being trained to take a docile, subordinate place in a stratified society.'[67]

A few Creoles rose to positions of high office. John Carr, an Afro-Trinidadian, became Chief Justice of the Colony, another Afro-West Indian became Colonial Secretary and another, William Fergusson, finished up as Governor – the only African ever to have held such office. None of this would happen half a century later, as British and other European colonists tightened the screws on their 'inferiors'. Views like those of Colonel D'Arcy, Administrator of the Government of the Gambia in 1865, would fall on deaf ears: 'After many years of intercourse with the race … I am convinced that the liberated Africans contain in themselves all the elements of a commercial people. … As it takes three generations at home to make an English gentleman, so likewise does it take three generations to make an intelligent, well-educated African gentleman.'[68]

Africanus Horton

One well-educated African gentleman (after barely one generation) was James Africanus B Horton (1835-1883). He was born in the hill village of Gloucester, five miles up from Freetown, to a recaptive carpenter and his wife, both of Igbo origin (in south-east Nigeria). After school in Gloucester, James attended Fourah Bay College, paid for by the afore-mentioned John Carr. Among his teachers was the Rev Edward Jones, an Afro-American from South Carolina, reputed to be the first African to have graduated from an American university (Amherst, in 1826).[69] The young African was well served by his teachers who equipped him with knowledge of Latin, Hebrew and Greek (in order to read the Old and New Testaments in their original languages) as well as mathematics and geography. Such a background would qualify him for entry into a British university, but where would the money come from? The British government, as it turned out. The administration was aware that few of the doctors it sent out to Sierra Leone survived more than a year before succumbing to malaria or yellow fever. The natives, on the other hand, appeared to display some immunity to tropical diseases. In 1855 it decided to send three of the most able Africans to study medicine in Britain. Horton was one.

He qualified for Membership of the Royal College of Surgeons at King's College in London, where he was awarded the prize in surgery. This was followed by an MD at Edinburgh University. Here Horton was the only student of his year to be awarded honours in the practice of medicine. His thesis, for which he was commended, was subsequently published as *The Medical Topography of the West Coast of Africa; with Sketches of its Botany* (John Churchill, London 1859). On the strength of it, the Botanical Society of Edinburgh elected him a foreign member. As was the custom for medical graduates of the time, he was commissioned into the British army as staff-assistant surgeon (eventually rising to a rank equivalent to Lt Colonel). He was one of only two Africans to serve as an officer in the medical department of the British Army during the entire nineteenth century. At the behest of his superiors he spent the next twenty years shuttling along the coast line of West Africa between Bathurst (The Gambia), Freetown (Sierra Leone), the Gold Coast and Lagos (present-day Nigeria).

His duties were concerned mainly with the health of the residents – he was one of the first to emphasize the importance of sanitation in preventing infectious diseases – but in 1873, as commandant of the fort at Sekondi (Gold Coast), he also successfully defused a revolt by some belligerent natives. Instead of praise he received blame for negligence from his senior officer, Colonel Harley, who was abetted by Horton's own (English) sergeant. Being an African in charge of Europeans was not easy. Fortunately the governor, John Pope Hennessy, supported Horton against his enemies. To Harley, Hennessy wrote that Horton had 'hitherto shown himself to be one of the best officers in Her Majesty's Service on the Gold Coast' and that he was not prepared to accept an unsupported opinion to the contrary [70] and to Lord Kimberley, Secretary of State for the Colonies in London, he commented on 'the high opinion I entertain of Dr Horton's ability and zeal. Indeed I regard him as one of the most useful officers on the Coast of Africa.'[71]

Horton showed an almost Leonardo-like curiosity and the desire to document whatever came his way. He used a leave of absence in London to expand an earlier work (*Political Economy*) into *West African Countries and Peoples* and to write two further books, *Physical and Medical Climate and Meteorology of the West Coast of Africa* and *Guinea Worm, or Dracunculus*. His interests included mineralogy, to the point that he bought several iron mining rights in the Gold Coast, from which he hoped to profit (he didn't). He preceded Mohammad Yunus, the Bangladeshi Nobel Laureate in economics, by more than a century in setting up a bank in Freetown (the first in the region) in order to advance credit to farmers and others and thereby promote economic development. He realised that expanding education, that had benefitted him so successfully, throughout West Africa was key to its future, and lobbied government ministers in London accordingly. At the same time he petitioned them in regard to Resolution 3 of the House of Commons Committee – 'that the object of the policy of the Government should be to encourage in the natives the exercise of those qualities which may render it possible for it more and more to transfer to them the administration of all the governments, with a view to our ultimate withdrawal from all, except, perhaps Sierra Leone.'[72] Self-government for the peoples of the Gold Coast and Lagos, as well as Sierra Leone, should indeed be the primary aim. His pleas received polite acknowledgement, but no more.

Horton championed the capabilities of Africans in a way that forestalled the concept of *negritude* by Léopold Sédar Senghor and Aimé Césaire (see chapter 13) by a hundred years. As an obituary pointed out, 'his lifework was to endeavour, not only by his writings, but by his everyday action, to vindicate his country and race from misconstruction and insult, and to improve and maintain the capacity and destiny of the Negro to play an independent and important part in the future history and well-being of the world.'[73] So today 'Africans, pessimistic about the future of their continent and sceptical about the mental and moral endowments of their race, may find an inspiration in his unstinted optimism about Africa and Africans.'[74] To me, Horton's most perceptive attribute was that 'he did not regard racial characteristics as fixed and unalterable. He believed that the variations between human groups depended on nurture and environment, and that any "race" could be improved by education, and degraded by the lack of it.'[75] He might well have written chapter 3.

During the early nineteenth century, then, encouraged by a few enlightened members of the British establishment, '...the Creole bourgeoisie in Africa – at least the reflecting part of it – had begun to move from a position of unconditional acceptance of European civilization to one that was more qualified, ambivalent and even sometimes critical.'[76] Horton was not only the first African to benefit from such intellectual and occupational freedom, he was also among the last. By 1902 African doctors were no longer able to enter the West African Medical Service. For on the 26th of February 1885 in Berlin, Joseph Conrad's 'moral clock' [27] had indeed been put back – not just in the Congo, but throughout most of Africa, by seventy years.

To return to my question. What if the imposition of European opinion in the 1880s in regard to the African's ability to manage his own affairs had not shackled him to second-class status? Would Africans have been economically better off by the middle of the twentieth century, when they finally achieved independence? Would Swaziland have become the new Switzerland? It is unlikely. At best they might have been no worse off.[77] Europe grew economically because of the industrial revolution that started in England and soon spread across the whole of Western Europe. Between 1000 and 1820, the average west European GDP per capita grew less than 3-fold; but over the next 130 years alone it increased nearly 4-fold. In China, isolated from foreign contact, the GDP per capita grew 1.3-fold between 1000 and 1820, but over the next 130 years actually declined back to where it had been in 1000 (because of population growth without compensating economic growth). The average African GDP per capita stayed constant between 1000 and 1820, but over the next 130 years it doubled.[78] So colonialism produced an increase that was equal to half of that achieved in Western Europe between 1820 and 1950.

I am not for a moment arguing that colonialism was a good thing. It produced untold misery and loss of life. But to suggest that in the absence of European interlopers Africa would have prospered economically is unrealistic. Look at Ethiopia (formerly Abyssinia), the only African country to resist colonisation, and Liberia. Both remained among the poorest countries throughout the nineteenth century and beyond.

However it has also to be pointed that indigenous, small scale African enterprise helped to drive the economy forwards during the colonial period (essentially 1880 to 1950). 'Except for a few places in Africa ... plantation agriculture was unknown. Cash crops were grown by peasant farmers on their own individual plots, using traditional farming methods and practices. In other words, the natives prospered using their own existing indigenous system with only minor modifications and improvements. ... The fundamental point is that African nations had the *economic freedom* to decide for themselves what crops they could cultivate – cash crops or food crops – and what to do with the proceeds. ... Though this freedom was circumscribed under colonialism in central and southern Africa, the peasants prospered during the colonial era. Why, then, were they unable to continue prospering after independence? The answer is obvious: Their economic freedom was somehow snatched from them.'[79]

It is improbable that Africa on its own would have produced an industrial revolution – it only happened once in the entire history of the world. But application of industrial technology is something that could have been initiated in sub-Saharan Africa. It didn't happen under colonialism, and it hasn't happened since independence (except in South Africa). It is certainly a reason for the region's lack of growth.[80] Some consider there to have been three industrial revolutions. The first, that occurred between about 1750 and 1830, is the one to which I have just referred. It produced the exploitation of steam power which was then used in railways, steamships, and factories. The second revolution occurred in the United States as well as in Western Europe between about 1870 and 1930. It encompassed the application of electric power for light, heat, transport and a myriad of other things. The third revolution has been taking place in the United States, Western Europe and Japan since the 1950s. It concerns the application of electronics for computers, the internet and emails, mobile telephones, and so forth (they're even talking about a fourth revolution – in digital technology). Unlike the first two, the third revolution is having an immediate impact globally: on Africa as well as on the other continents. Agriculture is an area where its application is of particular importance.[81] Another reason to be optimistic about the future of sub-Saharan nations.

Conclusion

Colonialism restricted expansion within tropical Africa for a number of reasons. First, the incidental introduction and spread of novel microbes had a devastating effect on the health of the native population. Second, the arbitrary division of the continent into colonies that was based solely on horse-trading between European nations destroyed boundaries between tribes that had evolved over centuries, and made governance after independence more difficult. Third, the second class status imposed on Africans in their own country had a devastating effect on their hopes and aspirations for a better life. Only a few, the future leaders of their respective countries, would begin to formulate their dream: the overthrow of the colonial masters. Economics aside, the overall effect of European meddling in African affairs has undoubtedly been negative.

End Notes

[1[Quoted by Blyden (1967) p 337

[2] Conrad (2007) p 123

[3] Curtin (1965) p 69

[4] quoted by Law (2002) p 3

[5] see, for example, Martin Lynn: *The West African palm oil trade in the nineteenth century and the 'crisis of adaptation'* in Law (2002), p 57 and A G Hopkins: *The 'New International Economic Order' in the nineteenth century: Britain's first Development Plan for Africa* in Law (2002), pp 240-264

[6] Acemoglu and Robinson (2012) p 257

[7] Conrad (2007) p 15

[8] see map in Curtin (1965) p 21

[9] Jeal (2007) p 91

[10] Helmuth Stoecker: *The Historical Background* in Stoecker (1986) p 17

[11] Pakenham (1991) p 203

[12] according to influential newspaper articles at the time; Helmuth Stoecker: *The Annexations of 1884-1885* in Stoecker (1986) p 22

[13] Jeal (2007) p 287

[14] Pakenham (1991) p 254

[15] Pascal Blanchard, Sandrine Lemaire, Nicolas Bancel and Dominic Thomas: *The Creation of a* Colonial Culture *in France, from the Colonial Era to the 'Memory Wars'* in Blanchard (2014) p 2

[16] *ibid* p 9

[17] *ibid* p 12

[18] Pakenham (1991) p 413

[19]. James (216) p 89

[20] Cunliffe-Jones (2010) p 49

[21] Pakenham (1991) p 182 *et seq*

[22] *ibid* p 171

[23] *ibid* p 464

[24] Zewde (1991) p 83

[25] Pakenham (1991) p 598 *et seq*

[26] Hochschild (1999) p 132 *et seq*

[27] quoted by Owen Knowles in his introduction to Conrad (2007) p xiv

[28] Pakenham (1991) p 656

[29] Ayittey (2005) p 13

[30] Pakenham (1991) p 370

[31] Segal (2001) p 175

[32] *ibid* p 178

[33] De Fries (2014) p 95

[34] Ransford (1983) p 76

[35] Dilley and Eades (1994) p xxxvi

[36] Davidson (1998) p 235

[37] Lamb (1983) p 156. Such discrimination would be continued in South Africa throughout its apartheid years; during the 1980s the government spent $677 a year to educate a white child, $277 for a coloured child (mixed ancestry) and $66 for a black child: Lamb (1983) p 326

[38] Vaillant (1990), p 56

[39] Wolfgang Mehnert: *Education Policy* in Stoecker (1986) p 221

[40] Eric Ashby, quoted in Davidson (1973) p 1640

[41] Pakenham (1991) p 640

[42] Davidson (1973) pp 105-112

[43] Dilly and Eades (1994) p xxix

[44] Lamb (1983) p 5

[45] Blyden (1967) p 50

[46] Boucher (1985) p 219

[47] *ibid* p 213

[48] *ibid* p 204

[49] Jeal (2007) p 295

[50] Vernon Lovett Cameron: *Across Africa* (Harper and Brothers, New York, 1877)

[51] Hochschild (1999) footnote to p 28

[52] Oliver and Atmore (1981) p 43

[53] Niven (1964) p 154

[54] Ransford (1983) p 222

[55] Niven (1964) p 39

[56] Pakenham (1991) p 306

[57] *ibid* p 314

[58] Segal (2001) p 177

[59] Blyden (1967) p 9, quoting from R Bosworth Smith's lectures on *Mohammed and Mohammedanism* delivered at the Royal Institution in 1874.

[60] *ibid* p 12

[61] Dunn (1986) and Mackintosh-Smith (2002)

[62] from *The history and description of Africa and of the notable things therein contained / written by al-Hassan ibn Mohammed al-Wezaz al-Fasi, a Moor, baptized as Giovanni Leone, but better known as Leo Africanus; done into English in the year 1600 by John Pory; and now* *edited, with an introduction and notes, by Robert Brown* (Hakluyt Society, London, 1896); quoted by Blyden (1967) p 195

[63] Blyden (1967) p 226 *et seq*

[64] Ayittey (1992) p 72 *et seq*

[65] Oliver (1991) p 255

[66] Aslan (2005) p 262

[67] Fyfe (1972) p 21

[68] Horton (1868) p 22

[69] Fyfe (1972) p 26

[70] *ibid* p 108

[71] *ibid* p 108

[72] Horton (1868) p vii

[73] Fyfe (1972) p x

[74] Horton (1970) p 17

[75] Fyfe (1972) p 70

[76] Irele (1981) p 95

[77] Lamb (1983) p 139

[78] see http://en.wikipedia.org/wiki/List_of_regions_by_past_GDP_%28PPP%29_per_capita

[79] Ayittey (2005) p 353

[80] See, for example John Page (2014): *Africa's Failure to Industrialise: Bad Luck or Bad Policy?* https://www.brookings.edu/blog/africa-in-focus/2014/11/20/africas-failure-to-industrialize-bad-luck-or-bad-policy/

[81] Juma (2011)

Chapter Eight
INDEPENDENCE:
POLITICS AND PHILANTHROPY

T he end of the Second World War in 1945 spurred Africans throughout the continent to escalate their efforts to rid themselves of their colonial masters. Many had fought for them (with veiled promises of self-government after the war), as they had done in the First World War. Aspirations for independence at that time had been disregarded at the Versailles conference in 1919, and this was being repeated at the United Nations in 1946. For over a century the educated upper classes and the local chiefs within the British colonies had been mollified with knighthoods and investitures at Buckingham Palace. In French possessions, Africans had been able to vote for, and send delegates to, the National Assembly in Paris. Some of these deputies even became ministers and served in French cabinets, but the representation was nominal. At the beginning of the Fourth Republic in 1946, 18 million Africans in French West Africa were represented by just six deputies; in metropolitan France the same number of voters could count on more than a hundred deputies to speak on their behalf. The mass of the African people were not satisfied by such crumbs from the respective governments in Europe. The granting of independence to India in 1947 caused them to redouble their demands for independence. In the French colonies, the defeat of their colonial masters in Vietnam at the battle of Dien Bien Phu in 1954 showed what could be achieved by militant action. No longer would Africans endure second class citizenship. The map of Africa would change dramatically over the ensuing years **(Fig 8.1)**.

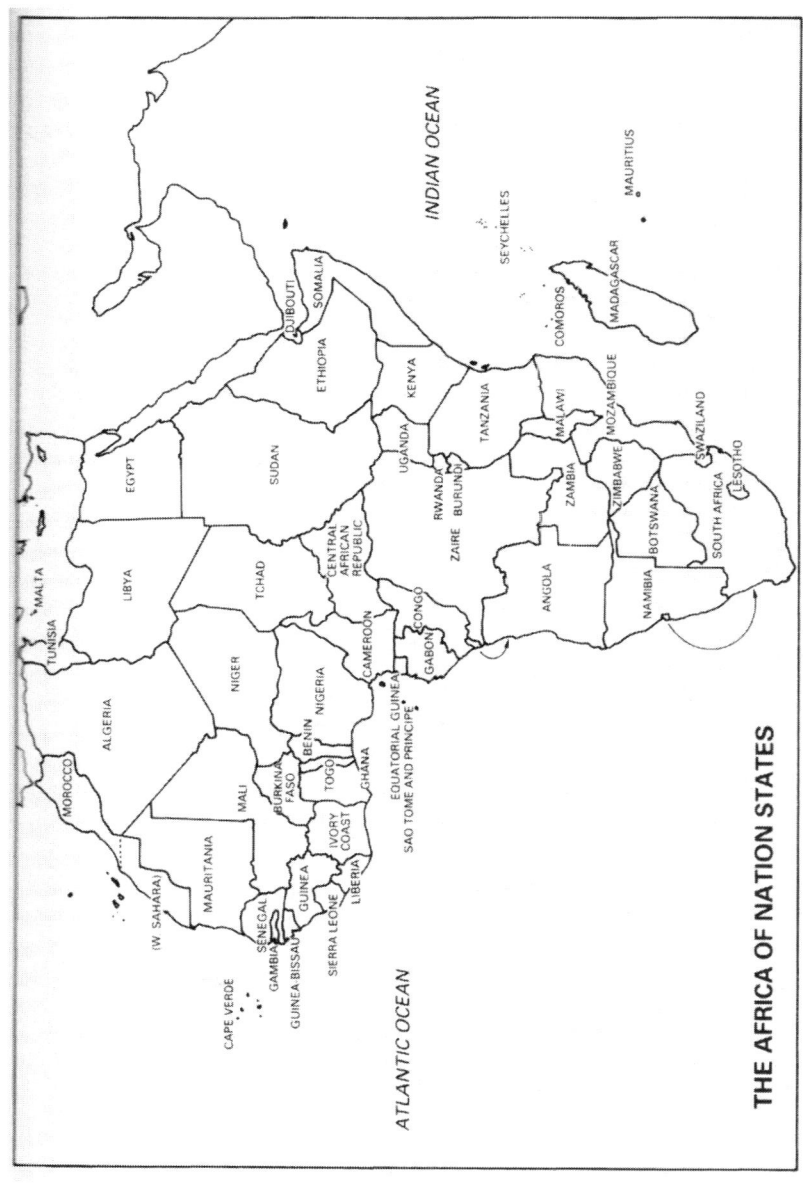

THE AFRICA OF NATION STATES

Figure 8.1.

The Politics of the New Leaders

Because the colonists were considered capitalists (which they largely were), socialism seemed the right policy after independence. Four leaders, in particular, espoused this view, which was formally expressed by the Arusha Declaration of 1967. This is an admirable document, potentially a model for good governance.[1] The document was drafted by Julius Nyerere, a Tanzanian chief's son who started life as a teacher, then studied at Makerere University (in Kampala, Uganda) and Edinburgh University, before being elected Tanzania's first president. Two of the others were Kwame Nkrumah, an academic from Ghana (see chapter 10) and Léopold Sédar Senghor, as much poet as politician, from Senegal (see chapter 13). The fourth was Ahmed Sékou Touré, an impoverished descendant of a Guinean chief, who became politically active early on, was elected Guinea's deputy to the French national assembly, and was four times elected president of his country (unopposed each time).

The intellectual rigour in the minds of these four men provides as good a rebuttal as any that black Africans are less intelligent than Europeans. Yet they, like Marx and Engels before them, were wrong in their assumptions. Socialism does not lead to economic success, especially in a newly-created country. Tanzania, Ghana, Senegal and Guinea, as well as Congo and DR Congo, Libya, Tunisia and Zambia, did not prosper. Rhodesia, South Africa and Botswana, on the other hand, thrived because men like Cecil Rhodes, Jan Smuts and Seretse Khama had other views. The fact that these three countries lie on the border between tropical and sub-tropical Africa also helped.

Initial success followed by a decline reflects the situation in sub-Saharan Africa as a whole. Between 1965 and 1980, for example, the average GDP per capita of sub-Saharan Africa grew by 1.5% per year. During the 1980s it fell by 1%.[2] A major reason for this reversal was a dramatic increase in the population, which by itself surely attests to a country's success, not its failure. Even countries like Kenya and Côte d'Ivoire, which are within tropical Africa, continued to prosper. Thereafter things began to fall apart, and their economies also declined. In Kenya it was because its president Daniel arap Moi (who followed Jomo Kenyatta) initiated one-party state, diverted the finances to himself and his cronies, tortured opponents and was prepared to see living standards (for those not in power) decline. By 2011 it was one of the poorest countries in Africa. Côte d'Ivoire, under its first president Felix Houphouet-Boigny, was also a one-party state (that enabled him to win election after election over more than 30 years), but was economically successful during most of this time. As China under Deng Xiaoping showed, one-party state and economic progress are not incompatible. After the mid-1990s, however, success turned gradually to failure and the Human Development Index for Côte d'Ivoire is now one of the lowest in Africa (Table 3).

Excuses

When socialist policies proved to be flawed and governments became discredited, you might have thought that the populace would have been given a chance to elect leaders of a different stripe. Not so. As George Ayittey, a son of Ghana and an economist of stature, has pointed out, this is the first of three myths and distortions propounded by African leaders to explain the poor performance of their respective countries:

Myth 1: Democracy Is Alien to Africa

'Ghana's first head of state, Dr Kwame Nkrumah, was probably also the first to expound this view. ... Many other modern African leaders used this same "African tradition" to justify their autocratic rule. No such justification is defensible.'[3]

Promoting socialism in the first place was said to be part of the African tradition. But Ayittey disagrees.

Myth 2: Socialism and One-Party Rule Are Indigenous African Ideology

'Kwame Nkrumah first espoused this idea: "The choice of (socialism) is based on the belief that only a socialist state can assure Ghana a rapid rate of economic progress without destroying that social justice, that freedom and equality, which are a central feature of our traditional way of life". ... Such a rationale for socialism stemmed from a complete misunderstanding of indigenous economic institutions and the native system of government ... There was no organized opposition in the indigenous African political system simply because there was no need for opposition. The traditions of free expression and consensus ensured that in the process of governance each person's viewpoint was heard, regardless of his wealth, status, or membership in an organisation. There were no winners or losers.[4] To be fair, Nkrumah also considered capitalism to be 'too complicated a system for a newly independent nation. Hence the need for a socialist society.'[5] When socialism proved not to bring economic success, the military stepped in. They argued that military rule reflects African values. This leads to Ayittey's third myth:

Myth 3: Military Rule is Uniquely African

'But an exhaustive study of indigenous African political systems does not reveal soldiers or men in uniform serving as chiefs or heads of village governments. The heads of these governments were always civilian. ... Such rule was as alien to Africa as was colonial rule.[6]

Consequences

A more charitable viewpoint is expressed by John Iliffe, a British historian who has made Africa his speciality. As mentioned above, he argues that population growth, resulting from better medical facilities, is one of the major reasons for the disappointing performance of the newly independent nations during the second half of the twentieth century. (*Under* population, due to droughts and consequential famines, has been proposed for the region's failure in earlier times). The provision of doctors in tropical Africa increased from one per 50,000 people in 1960 to one per 20,000 by 1980. Throughout this period free education soared: primary schooling expanded four-fold, secondary schooling six-fold, and university education twenty-fold. Better-educated mothers, in concert with better immunisation procedures administered by twice as many nurses, led to a thirty percent decrease in infant mortality. So the population grew three-fold between 1950 and 1990. But this out-ran the ability of the state to provide free education, and for this reason, as well as because of the increase in oil prices during the late 1970s, the economy suffered: sub-Saharan GDP per capita declined by one percent a year during the 1980s. This had an adverse effect on the provision of medical care.

In Ghana, for example, expenditure on health declined by sixty percent between 1974 and 1984. 'Eight years later the country had some 50,000 cases of yaws, a disease of poverty supposedly eradicated before independence, and its child mortality rate had risen. Tuberculosis, cholera and yellow fever became more prevalent in sub-Saharan Africa, while each year an estimated 20,000 to 25,000 victims contracted sleeping sickness. Roughly one African in six suffered a clinical case of malaria each year.'[7]

Education throughout sub-Saharan Africa was constrained in the early years of independence – as it had been during pre-colonial and colonial times – by a lack of schools and teachers. Is formal teaching always a necessity? For some bright, inquisitive youngsters, it seems not. Professor Sugata Mitra has found that simply giving Indian children from the poorest villages and backgrounds a computer and access to the internet, their curiosity will stimulate them to acquire knowledge.[8] If it works in rural India, why not in Africa? I see this rather as an adjunct to secondary schooling, not as an alternative. Didactic education is surely necessary for other reasons, such as instilling a sense of discipline and acquiring real knowledge. But there is no doubt that teaching through IT has a future in schools throughout sub-Saharan Africa, and many nations are bringing IT into the curriculum.

There was also a dramatic decline in food production – the core of sub-Sahara's economy – during the early years of independence. By stifling peasant farming through state control, the outcome was the same as it had been in the USSR: a loss of productivity. At independence, sub-Saharan Africa could feed itself. Thereafter the per capita food output declined annually by around 1% until the mid-1980s. The reason is clear. 'For the first two decades of independence, African governments neglected or exploited peasant farming, concentrating on large-scale agricultural enterprises, whether socialist villages, state farms, irrigation schemes, or private estates. Socialist villages and state farms were uniformly disastrous. Large irrigation projects could be profitable ... but the huge sums invested to exploit West Africa's unpredictable rivers would probably never repay.'[9] It must also be acknowledged that a series of droughts and resultant famines occurred across sub-Saharan Africa during the 1980s: in Mali and Mauretania in the west, and in Ethiopia and Mozambique in the east. Although the onset of such disasters cannot be blamed on politicians, the inability to deal with the consequences does reflect poorly on their competence. Thirty years after independence, agriculture was still failing to feed the continent's growing population. 'In 1990, over 150 million Africans were hungry; as of 2010, the number had increased to nearly 239 million. Starting in 2004, the proportion of undernourished began increasing ... prompting 100 million people to fall into poverty. One third of people in sub-Saharan Africa are chronically hungry.'[10] As pointed out in chapter 5, politicians like President wasee Mutharika in Malawi, are beginning to change this dismal outlook.

Much of the infrastructure put in place by the colonists also declined after independence. By the time the Belgian Congo gained its independence in 1960, 31,000 miles of roads had been constructed. Twenty years later, barely ten percent of these were fit for vehicular traffic. Even projects begun under the newly independent governments failed. During the early 1970s, the visionary (but unsuccessful, even by his own subsequent account) Julius Nyerere of Tanzania helped neighbouring Zambia to export its valuable copper deposits without having to go through white-dominated Southern Rhodesia or South Africa. He persuaded the Chinese to build a 1,160 mile railroad from Kapiri Mposhi in the Zambian copper fields to the port of Dar es Salaam at a cost of $400 million. A noble enterprise that would create jobs for hundreds of his people. Within a few years the railroad was breaking down due to lack of maintenance (and theft) and the Chinese had to be called back to run it as best as possible. So jobs that might have gone to Tanzanians desperately seeking work went instead to foreigners. Only in one instance did a newly-elected president actually strive to retain European expertise. It was Jomo Kenyatta, first president of Kenya, who realised that those foreigners in his country who had decided to stay, in spite the Mau Mau terrorist attacks against them prior to independence in 1964, might be used to train Africans in technical and managerial skills. He also spurned the socialist policies of his contemporaries and focussed instead on traditional, small scale farming. For several years Kenya's economy bucked the trend. Alas it was Kenyatta's successors who during the 1980s returned the economy to typically dismal proportions. Yet 'Almost any country in Africa could have done at least as well as Kenya if it had had a Jomo Kenyatta.'[11]

The authoritarian rule imposed in many countries after independence contrasted with the relative freedom that had existed in traditional African societies and had not entirely been eroded by colonialism. In former times a king or chief could be removed if his policies proved ruinous. In general he would be advised by an inner or privy council, and the views of all its members would need to be satisfied. 'Under most traditional African constitutions, bad or ineffective rulers were more readily removed from office than most modern constitutions allow. Divine kingship does not absolve a ruler from removal if he fails to live up to his responsibilities or constitutional duties. Important decisions were made only after necessary discussions and conclusions had been made.'[12] As the African historian P D Curtin has pointed out, 'Africa's great achievement in law and politics was probably the stateless society, based on cooperation rather than coercion, not to mention the fact that the African states had been so organised as to preserve local autonomy.'[13]

The same was true at lower levels. In a council of elders, representing the different familial lineages in a village, or in a meeting of the villagers themselves in a homogenous community, all the participants could influence the outcome. In fact the reason why decisions were often delayed is that the head of each assembly had to convince its members of his proposals. It wasn't a question of simply counting votes. Opponents as well as supporters had to be persuaded that a proposed plan was the right one, and this could take days or weeks. And in an African setting, it worked. Moreover 'Most analysts now agree that although colonialism was evil, it offered comparatively more freedom than did many independent African countries in the 1980s. ... By 1990 the political regimes instituted in most African countries were indistinguishable from the abominable system of apartheid or institutionalized racism in South Africa.'[14]

Such sentiments have been expressed even by former presidents, who when in power promoted the opposite. Julius Nyerere, president of Tanzania from independence in 1962 to 1984, harassed the peasants and forced them on to collective farms, bulldozing their villages on the way, in order to realise his goal of African socialism. As in the Soviet Union during the 1930s, collectivisation led to poverty and economic decline. The country had to import maize and other grains (paid for by Western aid) in order to prevent mass starvation. The average person was 5% worse off in 1984 than he had been in 1962. Although Nyerere recognised already in 1961 that 'Self-government is an expensive business, and there is no one to pay the cost but ourselves',[15] not until 1998 did he admit that 'Colonialism ... was replaced by a combination of neo-colonialism and government by local elites' of whom he, of course, was one 'who too often had learned to despise their own African traditions and the mass of the people who worked on the land'. He also said 'Africa will have to rely on Africa. African governments will have to formulate and carry out policies of maximum national and collective self-reliance. If they do, Africa will develop; if they don't, Africa will be doomed.'[16] Most Africans are still waiting for this 'delayed success'.

The old system had worked pretty well in pre-colonial times, but in the newly independent nations the relationship between politicians and their extended family, clan or tribe was one of the reasons why fraud became endemic. Those with access to government ministers used their positions to lobby for financial favours, which the officials found difficult to refuse. There simply wasn't enough to be distributed fairly among all. Because the leaders 'did not command the authority of their colonial predecessor, whose confidence had been assured by the military and economic power of their imperial governments' they were unable to 'govern without the more devious means of corruption, bribery, intimidation, and, frequently, violence. These methods became increasingly accepted, both within Africa and in the eyes of foreign donors.'[17] It is a topic to which I shall return in a subsequent section.

Another feature of earlier times that some of the new leaders and their colonial predecessors tried to suppress was the freedom to trade and make a profit in the traditional markets of villages and towns. Profit was private property – unable to be claimed by the chiefs – and could be used for whatever purposes the trader desired. Generally it was reinvested, used for household expenses, or shared out among the members of a particular family or clan. Women were the main traders, and for those not working in the fields, sitting at their stalls took up most of their day. Even in Muslim-dominated centres such as Timbuktu, Kano or Mombasa, the rural markets were run by women. Markets were a focal point in the life of the community. Politics were freely discussed, and decisions taken, without influence from above. In the run up to independence, 'support for the nationalist movements … came in considerable measure from the donations of the market women.'[18] Free enterprise and free trade still exist, but they have been curtailed by the socialist principles of the politicians in several of the newly independent states, as well as by ensuing martial rule and civil wars.

Martial Rule

So far as authoritarian rule is concerned, the West must bear some of the blame for its uncritical support of dictatorships. In Uganda, for example, more than 800,000 people perished at the hands of three of its presidents: Idi Amin (1971-79), Milton Obote (during his second presidency of 1980-85) and Tito Okello (1985-86). When Idi Amin, as chairman of the AOU (Organisation of African Unity and fore-runner to the African Union), addressed the UN General Assembly in 1975, he denounced the 'Zionist-US conspiracy' and advanced the view that Israel should be annihilated. The UN General Assembly, with the delighted support of its Arab members, 'gave him a standing ovation when he arrived, applauded him throughout his speech, and rose to its feet when he left. The next day, the UN Secretary-General and the President of the General Assembly gave a public dinner in Amin's honor.'[19]

But Idi Amin was not the worst in the number of people he caused to die at his hands. Between him and erstwhile leaders in Equatorial Guinea, Ethiopia, Nigeria and Somalia, 2.2 million people perished. If you add man-made famines (over 2 million deaths between 1980 and 2000), together with civil and other wars (Angola, Burundi, Congo, Côte d'Ivoire, Liberia. Mozambique, Rwanda, Sierra Leone and Sudan: 15.6 million), you reach a total of 19.8 million deaths.[20] Now recall the estimate of those who perished as a result of the Atlantic and Arabian slave trade: between 11 and 12 million westwards and some 11.5 eastwards. This was over a period of 300 years and 1,200 years respectively. In other words the number of those who perished as a result of the slave trade over many centuries is approximately the same as the number whose deaths can be ascribed to the incompetence or blood-lust of leaders in post-independence sub-Saharan Africa over just *five decades*. And it's still on-going: a million South Sudanese face starvation in 2017 [21] as a result of the ethnic civil war led on the one side by President Salva Kiir, a Dinka, and on the other by former Vice-President Riek Machar, a Nuer.

According to George Ayittey, out of 52 African countries in 1990, 44 can be classified as Repressive, Very Repressive, or Brutally Repressive, with 2 as Whites Only (South Africa and Namibia in 1990), and just 4 as Indigenously African (Consensual Democracy): Botswana, Mauritius, Senegal and The Gambia. In fact during the 1990s 'not a single black African dictatorship was democratized, despite massive foreign aid, Western tutelage, and quiet diplomatic pressure, not to mention the numerous constitutions ostensibly drafted for this purpose. Rather there were movements in the opposite direction as military dictatorships replaced civilian governments in Burkina Faso (1983), Burundi (1987), the Central African Republic (1981), Ghana (1981), Nigeria (1983), Guinea (1984), Guinea Bissau (1980), Lesotho (1986) and Sudan (1989). Since 1957 there have been more then 150 African heads of state. Only six in the history of postcolonial Africa relinquished political power voluntarily.'[22] As Bishop Desmond Tutu put it in 1987, 'It is sad that South Africa is noted for its vicious violation of human rights. But it is also very sad to note that in many black African countries today, there is less freedom than there was during that much-maligned colonial period.'[23]

Coups d'état by the military were a regular feature of the newly-independent nations. In 1958, General Ibrahim Abboud overthrew the civilian government in the Republic of the Sudan. In 1963 Colonel Christophe Soglo did the same in Benin. That year Sergeant (later General) Etienne Eyadema overthrew the government in Togo. In 1965, after a second coup, Colonel Joseph Mobutu took over in the Democratic Republic of the Congo, that he renamed Zaire (32 years later it was back to its earlier name). In 1966 Lt. Colonel Joseph A. Ankrah unseated Kwame Nkrumah in Ghana (see chapter 10). The same year Lt Colonel Yakubu Gowon overthrew another general in Nigeria. In 1967 Brigadier David Lansana took over in the middle of an election in Sierra Leone. The following year Major Marien Ngouabi, fresh out of prison, ousted the acting head of state in the People's Republic of Congo (the French, not the Belgian, Congo). Also in 1968 Colonel Moussa Traoré overthrew the president of Mali. The next year Major General Mohammed Siad Barre wrested power from the government in Somalia (renamed the Somali Democratic Republic by him). The 1970s saw but two coups: one in Rwanda in 1973 (see chapter 11) and one in Chad in 1975.

Civil Wars

Another form of strife that affected the ability of post-independence nations to prosper was a series of civil wars: in the Sudan, in the Congo and in Nigeria. The dispute in the Sudan was essentially between the Muslim, Arab-dominated government in Khartoum and the Christian or animist people, comprising a number of different 'African' (as opposed to 'Arab') groups living in the south western region of Darfur. It is pretty clear that the former were harassing and abusing the latter. The so-called First Sudanese Civil War lasted from 1955 (before independence was granted) until 1972 and culminated in the establishment of the Southern Sudan Autonomous Region. It wasn't very autonomous, and harassment by the government forces continued during an eleven-year period of 'peace'. Apart from ethnic tensions between the Arab northerners and their southern neighbours, much of the conflict was about oil. Most of the wells are in the Darfur region, but the fuel needs to be transported east across Sudan to reach the sea ports. In 1983, war (Second Sudanese Civil War) broke out again, with enmity between the two sides spurred on by the Sudanese leader Colonel Omar al-Bashir. The conflict ended only in 2005, when Southern Sudan was granted independence from the rest of Sudan. Over the preceding half century more than two million southern Sudanese had been killed and four million had become refugees. Regrettably, conflict within South Sudan itself continues to this day: now on largely tribal lines between Dinka and Nuer.

I referred in the previous chapter to the way that the colonial powers arbitrarily joined together areas populated by different ethnic groups into a single nation. The Belgian Congo, comprising hundreds of different ethnic groups, is a good example. In 1960 it gained independence of the mother country. The newly-elected prime minister, Patrice Lumumba, was soon deposed on the orders of the president, Joseph Kasavubu. During the ensuing political and tribal upheaval, Lumumba was arrested by soldiers loyal to Joseph Mobutu, the man he had appointed as his Army Chief of Staff. The following year Lumumba was handed over to the authorities in Élisabethville, capital of the province of Katanga in the south east of the country. On 17 January he was murdered by Katangan troops. In the meantime tensions with the central government had flared up to such an extent that Katanga, which had already moved towards secession under its leader Moiré Tshombe, confirmed its independence of the rest of the Congo. From the Katangan point of view, with its mines rich in copper and cobalt, and thus accounting for half of the Congo's wealth, this was a fairly smart move. Needless to say, it led to violent fighting between Katangan forces, swelled by mercenaries from Britain, France, Rhodesia and South Africa, and a United Nations force sent in to retake the errant province. The following year the UN force succeeded, and Katanga was back as part of the Congo.

Another civil war occurred in the tribally diverse country of Nigeria. In 1967 the Igbo, who dominate the south east of the land where the waters of the Niger River empty into the sea, were encouraged to secede from the rest of the country (see chapter 14). The man responsible for this was Odumegwu Ojukwu, a military officer and politician, who became leader of the break-away Republic of Biafra. It lasted just three years. By 1970 the region was back as part of Nigeria. But a million had lost their lives in the process. The early years of independence in these areas of sub-Saharan Africa were clearly not happy ones. Yet conflict in all three – South Sudan, Congo and Nigeria – continues to rumble on.

Military governments like to have martial hardware at their beck and call (for oppressing civilians, not for fighting wars with neighbouring countries: there have been very few wars between the different African nations over more than a century). In 1973, African countries spent $3.8 billion on arms. Ten years later the figure was $16.9 billion. It then fluctuated somewhat, but was still $12 billion in 1987. The latter amount is roughly five times what Africa was requesting in financial aid per year, and is a larger sum than that spent on education and health combined. $1 million, which was the cost of a tank at that time, would have provided 1,000 classrooms for 30,000 children. One helicopter would have paid the salaries of 12,000 schoolteachers.[24] So African countries wasted the opportunity provided by aid intended for improving infrastructure, by investing instead in unnecessary military hardware. No wonder the most able people despaired at their government's stupidity and went abroad, mainly to Europe and North America, to lead more fulfilling lives. 'The post-colonial experiment in nationhood was failing miserably. Many African countries were being dominated by their military. Professionals, artisans, educators, and skilled workers were all packing up and leaving. It was the beginning of the phenomenon widely referred to as the brain drain. In a short space of time, the continent lost its most vital human resource, all the people who were desperately needed to drive forward Africa's growth and development.'[25]

Aid: *Timeo ... dona ferentes* (I fear those bringing gifts)

'I am strongly inclined to do away with distribution of grain, because through dependence on them, agriculture was neglected' said the emperor Augustus.[26] The newly independent nations of Africa and their western backers would have done well to recall this, as well as the title of this section. Instead of using the aid – contributed largely by foreign governments – to boost the economy by improving education, health and infrastructure, it has been frittered away. As the president of Senegal, Abdouaye Wade, pointed out in 2002, 'I've never seen a country develop itself through aid or credit. Countries that have developed – in Europe, America, Japan, Asian countries like Taiwan, Korea and Singapore – have all believed in free markets. There is no mystery there. Africa took the wrong road after independence.'[27] In *Dead Aid*, its author analyses the problem with clarity: 'What is perhaps most amazing is that there is no other sector, whether it be business or politics, where such proven failures are allowed to persist in the face of such stark and unassailable evidence. So there we have it: sixty years, over US$1 trillion dollars of African aid, and not much good to show for it. Were aid simply innocuous – just not doing what it claimed it would do – this book would not have been written. The problem is that aid is not benign – it's malignant. No longer part of the potential solution, it's part of the problem – in fact aid *is* the problem.'[28] There are four main reasons for this.

First, aid is used by military dictatorships, and even by democratically elected governments, to buy military hardware. Some of the figures were mentioned a couple of paragraphs up. In chapter 11, I will refer to a specific case – that of Rwanda – in which foreign aid was used to buy weapons in order to commit the worst genocide since the Second World War.

The second reason is corruption. The US Senate Committee on Foreign Relations estimated in 2004 that $100 billion of World Bank money has been siphoned off by corrupt officials. Other analyses reach a similar conclusion. 'Of the US$525 billion that the World Bank has lent to developing countries since 1946, at least 25% (US$130 billion) has been misused.'[29] Part of this figure includes expenditure on arms, and part includes misspending by donor nations. But while countries like China, Indonesia and Thailand are guilty of corruption, the overall effect has been to improve their economies. In Africa, 'at least US$10 billion – nearly half of Africa's 2003 foreign aid receipts – depart Africa every year. … It is truly tragic that while stolen aid monies sit and earn interest in private accounts abroad, the countries for which the money was destined have stagnated, and even regressed.'[30]

The third reason is legal diversion of aid money away from its intended recipients. 'Many studies estimate that only about 10 or at most 20% of aid ever reaches its target. There are dozens of ongoing fraud investigations into charges of UN and local officials siphoning off aid money. But most of the waste resulting from foreign aid is not fraud, just incompetence or even worse: simply business as usual for aid organisations'. In the case of a particular tranche of aid money to Afghanistan, which is probably typical of aid to other countries, 20% was taken off as UN head office costs in Geneva, 20% of the remainder taken by sub-contracted NGOs in Brussels, and several smaller amounts by a further three layers of official bureaucracy.[31] Foreign aid for a particular project is frequently used to pay foreigners working in the receiving country. I recall a conversation several years ago with an American contractor who told me of a particular project in Egypt that was being funded largely by the USA. A generous gesture, you may say, until it became clear that most of those being paid to work on the scheme were actually US citizens seconded to Egypt for the duration of the project.

The fourth reason is that donor organisations and countries give aid – without much care as to how it is administered – in order to claim the moral high ground. Bob Geldof's *Band Aid*, to raise awareness of the Ethiopian famine in 1984, raised an estimated $24 million, and encouraged others like *Live Aid* to raise further amounts. Together they are said to have raised $150 million. Some of this money undoubtedly helped the starving victims of the famine, but did little to encourage Ethiopia and other countries to reform and to improve their ability to avert future crises. On the other hand it did encourage governments to donate (from taxation of their own people, of course). So African dependency on western generosity endured. Bob Geldof continues to shame individuals and governments to give more to Africa: *Don't they know it's Christmas* is back on screens and in record shops. But little of such aid has been invested in improving infrastructure.

Hospitals were so poorly supported that in Zambia, for example 'It is hard for the villagers of Chamkombe ... to see how foreign aid from well-meaning Western sources has made much difference. At the main provincial hospital in Kasama, there has been no water for three years. Patients usually sleep two to a bed, with others on the floor. They must arrange with relatives or friends to have water brought to them.'[32] In several instances, lawless warlords simply steal the aid: 'International relief for the poor, starving population is an inexhaustible source of profit to the warlords. From each transport they take as many sacks of wheat and as many liters of oil as they need. For the law in force here is this: whoever has weapons eats first. ... The dilemma faced by international organizations? If the robbers aren't given their cut, they will not let the shipments of aid get through, and the starving will die. Therefore you give the chieftains what they want, in the hope that at least the leftovers will reach those suffering from hunger.'[33]

Some of these four reasons have been summed up by George Ayittey in a perceptive analogy: 'A bucketful of holes can only hold a certain amount of water for a certain amount of time. Pouring in more water makes little sense as it will all drain away. To the extent that there are internal leaks in Africa – corruption, senseless civil wars, wasteful military expenditures, capital flight, and government wastes – pouring in more foreign aid is futile.'[34] The Index of Economic Freedom, compiled by the Heritage Foundation and the Wall Street Journal led to a similar conclusion in 2001: '.... sub-Saharan Africa's poverty is not the result of insufficient levels of foreign aid; on a per capita basis, many sub-Saharan African countries are among those receiving the world's highest levels of economic assistance. Rather, the main cause of poverty in sub-Saharan Africa is the lack of economic freedom embroiled in policies that these countries have imposed on themselves' – shades of Acemoglu and Robinson – 'as well as the rampant corruption systemic in many of these countries.'[35]

The Chinese take a different view towards aid, in so far as they share in the rewards. In other words they give in exchange for commercial deals. Their purchase of commodities such as oil and heavy metals is accompanied by investment in infrastructure. In the 1970s they built the railway mentioned above that links Tanzania with land-locked Zambia, site of some of the world's largest copper mines. China is now the world's largest investor in Africa: copper and cobalt in the Democratic Republic of Congo as well as in Zambia, textiles in Lesotho, timber in the Central African Republic and railways in Uganda. But its biggest investment is in oil-rich countries like Angola, Nigeria and Sudan. Angola alone provides some 20% of China's oil imports. In 2006 President Hu Jintao summarised his country's 'aid' programme at a Sino-African summit as follows: 'China has firmly supported Africa in winning liberation and pursuing development ... China has trained technical and other professionals ... It has built the Tanzam railway and other infrastructure projects and sent medical teams and peace-keepers to Africa. ... We, the leaders of China and. African countries, in a common pursuit of friendship, peace, cooperation and development, are gathered ... to renew friendship, discuss ways of growing China-Africa relations and promote unity and cooperation among developing countries.'[36] Edward Blyden, writing in 1884, was more prophetic than he realised: 'It has been predicted that the Negro race will die out of Africa. ... The suggestion has been made to supersede them by Chinese'.[37]

Aid is not the only way in which western countries retard African development. Exporting goods from Africa represents an uphill playing field, in so far as the developed nations impose stiff tariffs on imports that are likely to damage their own economies. It is true that the European Union has been trying for over a decade to reach a trade agreement with ECOWAS (Economic Community of West African States) by offering tariff-free imports of agricultural produce, but its altruism is circumscribed. Its Common Agricultural Policy 'treats Africa as an economic colony. Brussels applies tariffs to tomato sauce, but not to tomatoes; to chocolate, but not to cocoa beans; to roasted coffee, but not to green coffee. Africa, in other words, is expressly discouraged from developing secondary industries that would add value to its commodities. According to Calestous Juma of Harvard University, the entire continent of Africa earned £1.8 billion from coffee exports in 2014. In the same year, Germany alone, earned £2.9 billion from coffee re-exports.'[38]

Countries that Escaped European Colonization

Before concluding this chapter, the fate of the two countries that never fell under European domination during the nineteenth century needs to be considered. They are Liberia and Ethiopia.

Liberia

Little struggle was required to move from control by the American Colonization Society in 1821 to independence in 1847. The constitution was modelled on that of the United States (which, because of its acceptance of slavery, was the only major country not to recognise the new nation; it changed its mind only in 1862). There was a Senate, a House of Representatives, an elected President and Vice-President, and so forth. Even the capital Monrovia – no more than a village – was designed along the lines of Washington, DC (but more than a hundred years later it still had no public transport, few houses with electricity and fewer still with running water). What of the indigenous tribes, most of whom lived in the hinterland? Were they now masters of their own destiny? Not at all. The American immigrants, who accounted for no more than 1 % of the population, forced them to live in one of sixteen 'tribal areas' and then largely ignored them. Those who were born free in the USA also disparaged recently-liberated slaves whom they considered (rightly) to be 'a set of worn-out, miserable wrecks of humanity.'[39] One American immigrant who might have been entitled to feelings of superiority – not because of back ground but on account of his intellectual ability – was Edward Wilmot Blyden (1832-1912).

Edward Blyden

He was born in St Thomas in the Danish West Indies (today's American Virgin Islands). His parents were free-born and literate: his father a tailor and his mother a school teacher. Like Africanus Horton, he claimed descent from the Igbo (Ibo) tribe that has dominated the land around the lower reaches of the Niger for thousands of years. He considered himself a pure Negro, and would become 'the greatest Negro champion of his race in the nineteenth century,'[40] as well as 'the first African writer and intellectual to enjoy a truly international reputation.'[41] He denigrated those of mixed ancestry (despite marrying one himself) and developed a pathological hatred of mulattos that lasted his entire life. Elsewhere, of course, the opposite view prevailed. Under apartheid in South Africa, for example, 'coloreds' would be allowed privileges denied to 'blacks'.

After a brief spell in Porto Bello, Venezuela, the family returned to St Thomas where Edward attended school in the morning and worked as an apprentice tailor in the afternoon. His talents and a gift for oratory were recognised by the local vicar, Rev John Knox, who supported Edward's desire to become a clergyman. Accompanied by Knox's wife, the eighteen year-old set off for the United States to enrol at Rutgers' Theological College where Knox had studied. Like Léopold Sédar Senghor (chapter 13) in the following century, his aspiration was denied (in this instance, because of his colour). Two other theological colleges in the 'tolerant' American North took the same view. Staying any longer in the USA was, in any case, risky. As the recent film *Twelve years a slave* showed so vividly, blacks living in northern states were in danger of being captured by ruthless criminals and sent south into slavery. Blyden decided to accept the American Colonization Society's offer to repatriate him in Liberia. He began a new life in Monrovia in January of 1851.

Without resources, yet wanting to complete his education, Blyden found work as a part-time clerk in a merchant company. The rest of his time was spent at a small Presbyterian school together with twelve other pupils. He studied theology, including the Hebrew language, the classics, geography and mathematics. He was already fluent in Spanish and would subsequently learn Arabic. His progress so impressed the Principal (Rev D A Wilson) that he was offered a full-time scholarship – paid for by the Rev John Knox and his congregation back in St Thomas, together with funds from the Presbyterian mission. Within three years Blyden was himself teaching at the school and even standing in for the frequently indisposed Rev Wilson.

Blyden considered it his mission to dismiss the prevailing view that Negroes were unable to manage their own affairs. Instead he promoted the idea that Africans were as capable as anyone. 'The African has no superior among the races and is in advance of some', he wrote.[42] Liberia was the one place where this might be realised and he urged 'the young men and women of Liberia to apply themselves to study … so as to secure the success of Liberia and the perpetuity of her institutions.'[43] High ideals for a twenty-four year old to preach to his seniors.

In 1858 Blyden's other dream was realised, and he was ordained a Presbyterian minister. That year he succeeded Rev Wilson as Principal of the school. Two years earlier he had married Sarah Yates, a girl of mixed parentage, who was the niece of the Vice-President of Liberia. The union was not a happy one. Blyden's hatred of mulattoes was one reason, and one is entitled to ask why he married her in the first place. Sarah did not share in her husband's intellectual pursuits and he was often away on lecture tours and government assignments. The result was that twenty years later he took up with a black schoolteacher from Louisiana, but without divorcing his wife. This led to charges of infidelity, and he resigned from the church in 1886.

From the time he set foot in Liberia, then, Blyden devoted himself to establishing a new nation of American Negroes in West Africa. It was not an arduous task. In contrast to the millions of Syrians who are today escaping from brutal repression by their president and heading for Europe, the migrants arriving in Liberia from America were but a trickle. A mere 15,000 were reportedly helped by the American Colonization Society to settle in Liberia between 1821 and 1860.[44] Blyden had tried hard to increase the numbers, but the finances of the Society and Blyden's desire to have only pure Negroes limited his efforts. More importantly, the wish of American Negroes to migrate to Africa fluctuated according to their status at home. After the defeat of the slave-owning South and the Civil Rights Act of 1875, numbers waned. When that act was declared unconstitutional by the Supreme Court in 1883, they rose again. But the movement never came to resemble anything like the migration of Anglo Saxons from Europe to North America two centuries earlier.

During the 1860s Blyden's influence grew steadily. He had served as Editor of the *Liberia Herald* during the previous decade and had seen the publication of *A Voice from Bleeding Africa on behalf of her exiled children*, the first of the many lectures, articles, pamphlets and books he would produce during his lifetime. He was appointed Liberian Commissioner to the United States, a role by which he was able to lobby for the resettlement of American

Negroes in Liberia. He began to fulfil his ambition of becoming an academic as well as a politician. He was appointed Professor of Classics at the recently-established Liberia College (the second oldest institution of higher learning in sub-Saharan Africa after Fourah Bay College in Sierra Leone), a post he held concurrently with being Liberian Secretary of State. He revelled in working from morn to night, dispelling the myth about Negro lethargy that typified the thinking of whites during the nineteenth century.

In 1870 Edward James Roye was elected the fifth president of Liberia. Claiming pure Igbo descent, he naturally earned Blyden's admiration. But there was a problem. A wealthy man in his own right, Roye realised that what Liberia needed was a large influx of money in order to improve infrastructure and education. He managed to secure a £100,000 loan from Britain, but at an unsustainably high (7%).rate of interest. He further alienated his countrymen by unilaterally declaring that his Presidency would be increased from two to four years. An election was fought in 1871. Liberia's first president, Joseph Jenkins Roberts, returned to challenge Roye, and won. Roye had tried to prevent the election but found himself outvoted by the Senate and the House of Representatives who declared his presidency to be over and sent him to jail. Roye managed to escape but was killed in the attempt. Blyden's support of Roye was well known, and his assertion that 'decadent mulattoes in important positions accounted in part for Liberia's want of enterprise and progress' [45] did not help. He was pursued by the populace who proposed his lynching. Blyden managed to extricate himself and sought shelter in neighbouring Sierra Leone.

Here he was offered work by the Church Missionary Society. The CMS was aware of Blyden's publication of 'Mohammedanism in West Africa' by the *Methodist Quarterly Review* earlier that year. This led the British government to appoint him as Agent to the Interior. His role was to teach Arabic at Fourah Bay College, so that Africans might be better able to interact with Muslims living in the interior. On the other hand Blyden's proposal to establish a new university run entirely by black scholars from across the world fell on deaf ears. While in Sierra Leone, Blyden launched and edited a newspaper in Freetown under the title *Negro*. But the promoter of Negro ability and competence soon fell out with his benefactors on account of their patronising attitude towards black Africans. He returned to Monrovia towards the end of 1873.

Blyden spent the next decade based in Liberia. He travelled extensively during this time. On behalf of the American Colonization Society he made several trips to the USA as part of his drive to enthuse American Negroes to emigrate to Liberia. He went to London in 1877 as Liberian Ambassador to the Court of St James, the first African ever to be appointed to such a role (his surprising view that 'there was no Negro in America yet fitted for a high diplomatic position' [46] obviously applied only to others). In London Blyden was welcomed not only by members of the establishment, from Queen Victoria downwards, but by leading intellectuals also. The philosopher Herbert Spenser considered it 'Quite a new thing to find members of your race writing as you have done on questions of race, and I consider it very useful.'[47] He was back in Liberia within two years (though he would return briefly to Europe as Liberian Minister Plenipotentiary and Envoy Extraordinary to London and Paris in 1905). Throughout this time he was busy teaching at Liberia College, of which he became President in 1880. His presidency was somewhat short-lived, as squabbles with newly-appointed mulatto professors caused him to quit four years later. In the meantime his literary output continued to expand. Neither activity prevented him from dabbling once more in politics and he served in the cabinet for two years as Minister of the Interior. In 1885 he contested the election for President. His defeat was not unexpected in view of his continuing antipathy to mulattoes who made up the bulk of the people. It was just as well, for his obstinacy and failure to see the merits of an argument other than his own would have made him a poor holder of that office. Smarting from his defeat, he went back to Sierra Leone.

Freetown had become the second home to which he would return whenever matters in Monrovia became unpleasant for him. Wherever he was, his pen and his voice remained active. In 1887 he published *Christianity, Islam and the Negro Race* in which (as quoted in the previous chapter) he showed that 'when the Arab met the Negro in his own home,' the result was, in contrast to Christianity, 'a healthy amalgamation, and not an absorption or an undue repression.'[48] He taught English to Muslim students in Sierra Leone, and founded a school in Lagos, where he was appointed Agent of Native Affairs. He lectured to audiences across the United States (urging black students to come to Liberia and to enrol at Liberia College) and Europe (praising both the British and the French for their policies in West Africa). He particularly encouraged Britain's Colonial Office to provide higher education for Negro Mohammedans in northern Nigeria: 'They are not most effectually conquered or ruled by arms. Money and books, trade and literature, will do more to win them to allegiance and devotion than any other agency.'[49]

By the time he was in his late seventies, Blyden's health began to suffer. He was also short of money. A small pension that he had been awarded by the Liberian government was removed when his involvement in a border dispute between Liberia and Sierra Leone appeared to favour the latter country. He managed to get himself to Britain in order to remove an aneurism on his knee at the Royal Southern Hospital, Liverpool. Fifteen weeks later he returned to Freetown. The fine words, statues and stained glass windows that were erected after his death did little for him at the time. He died in relative penury six months before his eightieth birthday.

Blyden's incisive literary style, coupled with a deep knowledge of ancient writings and a lively interest in current affairs, makes him the equal of contemporaries like Waldo Emerson in America or Thomas Carlyle in Britain. But literary giants don't change a country. Tolstoy's influence on the coming revolution in Russia was minimal, and Nadine Gordimer's books during the apartheid years left the Afrikaner unperturbed. J E Casely Hayford (Ghanaian polymath when the country was still the British Gold Coast), himself a supporter of pan-Africanism, may have considered Blyden to have been 'the voice of one crying in the wilderness of all these years, calling upon all thinking Africans to the roots whence they were hewn by the common Father of the nations ... to unlearn all that foreign sophistry has encrusted upon the intelligence of the African,'[50] but the aspirations of the movement's author fell on stony ground. As recently as 1963, though, a commentator referring to the former colonies of French Equatorial Africa (now Republic of Congo, Gabon, Central African Republic and Chad) was starry-eyed enough to write that 'There remains, however, every reason to suppose that they will in time together join a much larger African federation, which may well contribute to the unification of the whole continent.'[51]

The Twentieth Century

Liberia's performance as a new nation during the twentieth century was as unremarkable as it had been during the nineteenth. Independence of European colonialism was not enough to propel the young nation to success. Squabbling between the indigenous population and their American masters ('Americo-Liberians'), between one ethnic group and another among the natives, between the True Whig Party and its opponents, was one reason. Lack of economic development was another. When Barbara Greene visited the jungle hinterland of Liberia with her cousin, the novelist Graham Greene, in 1935, conditions in the villages were primitive, and not much better in the coastal towns of Grand Bassa and Monrovia. The title of her published journey – *Land benighted* [52] – is apt.

The country was held together by an able and well-meaning president, William Tubman, elected seven times between 1944 and 1971. His successor William Tolbert (the father-in-law of Tubman's son Shad), who served until his overthrow (and murder) in 1980, was of a different disposition: anyone caught begging for bread or water was shot. 'Unremarkable' was no longer an applicable word. The coup d'état against Tolbert's government was led by Master-Sergeant (later Field Marshal

Brigadier-General) Samuel Doe, who was named President by his compatriots of the People's Redemption Council the following day. He was the first Liberian of pure native (Krahn) descent to hold the post. Mass executions of former Tolbert supporters, vindictiveness against members of tribes other than Krahn, and corrupt and repressive government led to a counter coup against Doe. This was organised by a former Doe supporter turned antagonist, Charles McArthur Ghankay Taylor. Taylor led a Libyan-supported group named National Patriotic Front of Liberia, and, as President of Liberia, would go on to terrorise not only his own citizens, but those of neighbouring Sierra Leone as well. It was one of his acolytes, Prince Yormie Johnson, who captured, tortured and murdered Doe (Taylor was operating from the countryside outside Monrovia at this time). Between Doe, Johnson and Taylor, the rule of law was substituted by indiscriminate fighting and murder. Monrovia's public buildings were reduced to rubble.

According to Anthony Daniels, a doctor who visited Monrovia in 1991, '… houses were ruins … mere shells … their tin roofs were torn off, their windows blown out. Their doors, lintels, beams and window frames had been extracted for use as firewood … there was not a stick of furniture left … the University of Liberia … was abandoned, deserted … All the buildings were pock-marked by bullets. … the Harvey S Firestone Science Building … had been completely destroyed, reduced to rubble, probably by direct hits from rockets. … the library … was peppered by bullet holes … … the Maternity Hospital … had neither roof nor windows … the destruction … was the product of labour, intense and systematic. The hospital had been dismantled, piece of equipment by piece of equipment, and then mutilated … Human excrement covered the ground, together with growth charts, health education pamphlets, pills, broken pieces of equipment, syringes, bandages and other dressings. One or two obstetric chairs, their covers slashed, their mechanisms destroyed, were to be seen, tipped over into the mess around them.' … 'the John F Kennedy Hospital … a gift from the United

States to Liberia in the early sixties ... deteriorated rapidly: a visiting team of foreign doctors was horrified to discover that not a single lavatory or water tap was working throughout the hospital's four floors. ... the hospital was now completely deserted ... part of the ground floor, dark as night and dank as a jungle, was flooded. ... in the small garden in front of (St Peter's Lutheran Church) there are two slight mounds, long and narrow. These are the mass graves for about half of the six hundred people who took refuge in St Peter's and were massacred there at the end of July 1990.'[53]

The country began to return to normality in 2003, when Taylor resigned to seek refuge in Nigeria. After a short interregnum, Liberia elected its first female president, Ellen Johnson (no relation) Sirleaf. Taylor was subsequently arrested, convicted of war crimes and crimes against humanity by the UN-backed Special Court for Sierra Leone in The Hague. He is now in prison in the UK, serving a 50 year sentence, President Sirleaf was re-elected in 2011, the year in which she was joint winner of the Nobel Peace Prize. Democracy has returned to Liberia, but economically the country is the seventh poorest (out of 230) in the world.

Ethiopia

Today's Ethiopia encompasses the area that was Aksum (chapter 4), plus a sliver of land to the west and a large region to the south, making the country more than twice the size of Aksum, [54] and one of the most populous in Africa. This expansion, that took place over the centuries from around 1200 AD onwards, was not due so much to invading settlers from Arabia or Egypt, as to an enlargement of the original state. The impetus came largely from the Cushitic-speaking Oromo in the south, one of the most prominent of the more than sixty ethnic groups in Ethiopia (the other major grouping being that of the Semitic-speaking Amhara in the north. As mentioned in chapter 4, 'Evidence is strong that the Afro-Asiatic (Hamitic-Semitic) group of languages developed and fissured in the Sudan-Ethiopian borderlands. There Proto-

Cushitic and Proto-Semitic began their evolution'[55]). Most of the Oromo, but no means all, were early converts to Islam. They established their own kingdoms over the years, and would harry the nominal rulers of the country – heirs to the Christianized Solomonic emperors of Aksum [56] – until the country was ostensibly unified under the Emperor Tewodros II following his coronation in 1855. It had been a long struggle.

There had been countless battles between local kings and the emperor, among provincial rulers themselves, between Muslim emirs and the Christian emperor, as well as incursions by Egyptians and Arabs, by Turks and Europeans. In 1528, for example, Ahmad ibn Ibrihim al-Ghazi defeated the army of Emperor Lebna Dengel. The latter turned to the Portuguese for help. This persuaded Ahmad ibn Ibrihim to seek Turkish support, and he won again in 1542. A year later the tables were turned and Emperor Galawedos, Lebna Dengel's successor, routed Ahmad ibn Ibrihim's troops. By the middle of the sixteenth century 'the country had lost hundreds of thousands of lives, a measure of confidence in itself and its religion, and much of its capital. Ethiopia would not be able to follow Europe into commercial and then industrial capitalism.'[57] This remark applies pretty well to all the other kingdoms that declined after an earlier period of greatness and success. It epitomizes one of the main reasons for sub-Saharan Africa's failure.

Yet leaders like Tewodros II well recognized Ethiopia's shortcomings. He tried hard to acquire European expertise from the British, admitting in his letters to Queen Victoria that he was 'blind' and 'ignorant'. He compared the 'darkness' of Ethiopia to the 'light' of Europe.[58] It did him no good: technical aid was not forthcoming. In fury he imprisoned the British Consul, Captain C E Cameron. Retribution was quick. A force of 32,000 men under command of Sir Robert Napier entered Ethiopia from the coast in January of 1868 to rescue the Consul and other Britons held by Tewodros II. The prisoners were readily given up but a fiery battle ensued, which Tewodros' troops lost. An honorable man, he blew out his brains with one of a pair of ornamental pistols that had been presented to him by Queen Victoria.[59] The entire rescue campaign was covered by the *New York Herald's* irrepressible correspondent, Henry Morton Stanley. Tewodros' actions suggest that if the British and other European governments had done more to help African nations to modernize, much of the failure of the newly independent countries might have been avoided. But it also required the will to change society. As the American scholar and expert on African history, Harold Marcus, commented, 'Unlike the Japanese state, the Solomonic empire would not undergo the social revolution required to attain security though industrial modernization.'[60]

In the meantime discord continued, not just between Muslim and Christian, but among Christians themselves. During the seventeenth century an argument erupted between the ecclesiastics of Shewa province in the centre of the country and those of Tigray province in the north. The Shewans asserted that Christ was born three times: first in eternity, then in Mary's womb through the Holy Spirit, then by physical delivery. The traditionalist Tigrayans dismissed this heresy. To add to this controversy, Roman Catholics, partly through recently-arrived Jesuits, proclaimed the entire Ethiopian Church, that worshipped the Judaic Sabbath (as well as the Christian Sunday), to be erroneous. Civil war broke out, and further bloodshed was prevented only by the action of Emperor Fasilidas: he expelled the Jesuits. Although the country would become a Soviet Union-backed dictatorship under Mengistu Haile Mariam in 1974, the tenets of Ethiopian Christianity live on, and not only in Ethiopia. Observance of the Sabbath and Judaic dietary restrictions are practised by millions of Christians throughout the world.[61]

The defeat by Emperor Menilek II's forces of Italian troops under General Oreste Baratieri at Adwa in 1896 had prevented Ethiopia from becoming an Italian colony, and Menelik [62] had tried hard to modernize the country. The first hospital was built (with help from the Russian Red Cross) and compulsory vaccination introduced – half a century before the rest of the world resorted to this measure (in order to eradicate smallpox). A modern bank (precursor to the Bank of Abyssinia) was established. Menelik sought to introduce compulsory education, but the lack of teachers stumped him. At least he tried. Menelik was succeeded by his grandson Lij Yasu. Lij had leanings towards Islam, which alarmed his Christian family to the same extent that Protestant Britain during the seventeenth century was terrified by James II's attraction to Catholicism. Lij was ousted by the nobles – like James II – and replaced by Menilek's eldest daughter Zewditu. She became Ethiopia's first female ruler since the legendary Queen of Sheba. On her death in 1930 a distant relative, who had been Regent during her reign, was crowned Emperor as Haile Selassie (Hayla-Sellase) I.

Although himself an autocrat, Haile Selassie I was (at least in some ways) a reforming ruler. He was lucky to inherit exceptionally high revenues from the sale of coffee that had, together with slaves, long been Ethiopia's main export. The latter trade was still extant in 1912 when 40,000 peasants in south western Ethiopia were enslaved and sent into servitude in Addis Ababa – which translates as 'New Flower' – the capital city since 1892. Menilek II had formally ended the trade throughout Ethiopia in 1903, but it did not officially cease until Haile Selassie abolished the slave trade entirely during his time as Regent. At this stage he also managed to secure Ethiopia a seat on the League of Nations. More importantly it was under Selassie's rule that the country was finally unified, with the freedom of provincial governors to act unilaterally curtailed.

But trouble was looming, once more from outside. The Italians had regained a foothold in Eritrea as well as in Somaliland, and abetted by Mussolini's shenanigans at home, an Italian force entered Ethiopian territory in 1935. Haile Selassie tried his best, but his meagre force was no match for Italian fire-power, numerical superiority, bombs and mustard gas. He abdicated in 1936 and King Victor Emanuel III became the country's nominal ruler with Marshal Rodolfo Graziani as his viceroy. Bands of patriotic Ethiopians continued to harass the intruders wherever possible. The foreigners responded by burning the rebels alive in their huts and by indiscriminate slaughter of women and children. But the economy and infrastructure improved. In 1941 Haile Selassie, accompanied by British troops under the command of Major Orde Wingate (who would be instrumental in driving the Japanese out of Burma three years later and have a school in Addis Ababa named after him), entered western Ethiopia from the Sudan. Within months, the Italians were gone and Eritrea was once more a part of Ethiopia: the country had regained access to the Red Sea.[63]

Haile Selassie continued his autocratic reign until Lt Col Mengistu's coup in 1974 brought eight hundred years of dynastic rule to an end. Under the so-called People's Democratic Republic of Ethiopia, supported by the Soviet Union which had replaced the United States as financial donor, life worsened. A famine between 1983 and 1985 that was caused only in part by drought, affected the lives of some eight million people, of whom a million died. Another famine, resulting entirely from an even worse drought than that of 1983-1985, is beginning to hit the country in 2016. In 1991 a faction calling itself the Ethiopian People's Revolutionary Democratic Front toppled Mengistu, who fled the country. He was subsequently indicted on charges of genocide. Today Ethiopia is known as a Federal Democratic Republic, with (dubious) free elections. Its regime has still been classified as 'authoritarian' by the Economist Intelligence Unit's Index of Democracy 2010, which ranked it at 118 out of 167 (actually above many other African countries as well as China).[64] In most league tables, though, Ethiopia, like Liberia, languishes near the bottom. The argument that in the absence of European colonialism African nations would have prospered is difficult to sustain. On the contrary, during the twentieth century, many 'bemoaned the backwardness of independent Ethiopia, compared with colonial Africa.'[65]

Conclusion

Men of vision, like Kwame Nkrumah of Ghana and Léopold Sédar Senghor of Senegal, led their countries to independence with aspiration and fine words. The 1960s, during which most

African countries achieved independence, represented a decade of hope. Reality then set in and the 1970s and 1980s were beset by economic decline. 'Development strategies mostly failed to deliver higher living standards, with the exception of Botswana and Mauritius. By 1980 many countries south of the Sahara had a per capita income that was below the level at independence.'[66] The same point has been made by Africanist Roland Oliver: 'According to a long-term survey published by the World Bank in 1989, the per capita income in the whole of sub-Saharan Africa, excluding only South Africa, grew by 2.7% per year during the 1960s, levelled off to zero during the 1970s and fell by 1.2% per year during the first half of the 1980s. This meant that ... by the middle of the 1980s most [African countries] had fallen well behind all but the poorest countries of southern Asia.'[67]

Some North African countries fared better, but not by much. The comparison between sub-Saharan and some Asian economies, though, is stark. At independence Ghana had the same GDP per capita as South Korea ($200). Forty years on, the figures were $420 for Ghana and $4,400 for South Korea.[68] As mentioned in chapter 2, social cohesion or 'inclusivity' is one of the main reasons for a nation's success. This was displayed only in countries like Botswana and Mauritius. Elsewhere single party government, coups d'états and ethnically motivated civil wars failed to redeem the initial optimism. They made matters worse. Observers could justly say that few African countries benefitted from independence: living conditions uniformly declined. Africa South of the Sahara was indeed a failed region. Not until the 1990s did matters start to improve. In Ghana, for example, parliamentary democracy was reinstated in 1993; the following year Senegal and other francophone countries devalued the currency (the CFA franc) by 50% and the ailing economies began to pick up; 1994 also saw free elections and the end of apartheid in South Africa. Such pivotal changes for the better (with notable exceptions in Rwanda and Somalia during the early 1990s) underlie my optimism for sub-Saharan Africa's future. Some countries, like DR Congo, still languish near the bottom of any league table, and overall sub-

Saharan Africa is way below the world average (see Table 3). But several countries are managing to pull out of failure. Of Botswana, Ghana and Rwanda it can be said that they have 'great expectations' (chapters 9 to 11). This would have been true of South Africa (chapter 12) during the second half of the 1990s. Since then, however, it has reflected the beginnings of failure rather than the continuation of success. For that reason I have titled chapter 12 'Diminishing success', though if it pulls out of its present problems it can regain 'great expectations'. For Ethiopia (see above), Senegal (chapter 13) and Nigeria (chapter 14) the expectations are less. Liberia (see above) doesn't come close.

End Notes

[1] see http://en.wikipedia.org/wiki/Arusha_Declaration

[2] Iliffe (1995) p 252

[3] Ayittey (1992) p 65

[4] *ibid* p 66 *et seq*

[5] Segal (1963) p 260

[6] Ayittey (1992) p 69 *et seq*

[7] Iliffe (1995) pp 243-264

[8] Leslie (2014) pp 157-162

[9] Iliffe (1995) p 267

[10] Juma (2011) p 7

[11] Lamb (1983) p 65

[12] Daniel Boamah-Wiafe: *Africa: The Land, People, and Cultural Institutions* (Wisdom Publications, Omaha, 1993) p 169; quoted by Ayittey (2005) p 21

[13] P D Curtin in J Ki-Zerbo (ed) *Methodology in African Prehistory: UNESCO General History of Africa, Vol I* (London, 1981), 58; quoted in Garlake (2002) p 9

[14] Ayittey (1992) p 12

[15] Segal (1963) p 126

[16] *PanAfrican News*, September 1998, quoted by Ayittey (2005) pp 9 and 401

[17] Collins and Burns (2014) p 363

[18] M I Herskovits and M Harvitz, eds: *Economic Transition in*

Africa (Northwestern University Press, Evanston, Ill, 1964) p 377; quoted by Ayittey (2005) p 348

[19] Ayittey (1992) p 120

[20] figures presented by George Ayittey at the San Francisco Freedom Forum on 28 Sep 2012; see http://bit.ly/TcG1NN

[21] see 'Famine alert' in *Nature* **542**: 397 (2017):

[22] Ayittey (1992) p 116 *et seq*

[23] quoted by Ayittey (1992) p 131

[24] figures taken from Ayittey (1992) p 153

[25] Mahama (2012) p 243

[26] according to Suetonius in *The Lives of the Caesars*, quoted by Conway (2012) p 63

[27] Moyo (2010) p 149

[28] *ibid* p 47

[29] *ibid* p 52

[30] *ibid* p 57

[31] Acemoglu and Robinson (2012) p 452

[32] *New York Times* of June 5, 1990, p A13

[33] Kapuscinski (1998) p 255

[34] Ayittey (1992) p 337

[35] Ayittey (2005) p 16

[36] Moyo (2010) p 104

[37] Blyden (1967) p 238

[38] Daniel Hannan, writing in the *Sunday Telegraph* (UK) of 16 July 2017

[39] Lynch (1967) p 10

[40] *ibid* p 3

[41] Irele (1981) p 96

[42] Lynch (1967) p 18

[43] *ibid* p 19

[44] Dunn and Holsoe (1985) p 8

[45] Lynch (1967) p 53

[46] *ibid* p 123

[47] *ibid* p 181

[48] Blyden (1967) p 12

[49] Lynch (1967) p 203

[50] *ibid* p 245

[51] Segal (1963) p 219

[52] Greene (1938)

[53] Daniels (1992) pp 35, 36, 38, 39, 44, 47. 48, 49, 50; and pp 137, 139, 140 and 147

[54] The area approximating to that of Aksum has been called Abyssinia since early times. The name derives from the Arabic *Al-Habasha*, *Habshat* being the name of the tribe from Yemen that is said to have settled there in pre-Christian times. The name has subsequently been indiscriminately used to refer to the entire area of Ethiopia.

[55] Marcus (1994) p 3

[56] When in 1270 Yekuno Amlak proclaimed himself emperor (having murdered his predecessor), 'the new monarch encountered considerable resistance and, in order to win over Tigray with its many Axumite traditions, he and his supporters began to circulate a fable about his descent from King Solomon and Makeda, Queen of Saba [Sheba], a genealogy that ... gave him traditional legitimacy and provided the continuity so honoured in Ethiopia's subsequent national history' [Marcus (1994) p 16]

[57] Marcus (1994) p 34

[58] Zewde (1991) p 37

[59] Jeal (2007) p 72

[60] Marcus (1994) p 106

[61] under the aegis of communities such as the Seventh Day Adventists, The Living Church of God, The United Church of God, Philadelphia Church of God and others.

[62] Niven (1964) p 56

[63] Eritrea became an independent country again in 1993, and Ethiopia is once more land-locked

[64] http://graphics.eiu.com/PDF/Democracy_Index_2010_web.pdf

[65] Zewde (1991) p 84

[66] Yanacopulos and Joseph (2006), p 147

[67] Oliver (1991) p 244

[68] Ayittey (2005), p 2

Chapter Nine
GREAT EXPECTATIONS: BOTSWANA

B otswana is a country that bucks every trend seen elsewhere in Africa. While its economy was rated a 'basket case' at independence in 1966, its GDP per capita since then has risen to be one of the highest on the continent.[1] The level of corruption is the lowest in all of Africa: in 2014 it was the same as that of Portugal and better than most Eastern European countries.[2] Its Development Index, that incorporates life expectancy, education and income indices (Table 3), in 2010 was the second highest in sub-Saharan Africa (behind Gabon).[3] It is 'the only country in southern Africa, and one of the very few in Africa itself, that has escaped war, misrule, or internal strife.'[4] Why is this?

Khama III

To explain these apparent contradictions, we must turn to the nineteenth century, and the rule of Khama III, also known as Khama the Great He was *kgosi* (translated loosely as ruler, chief, or king, though none of these terms quite encapsulates the role of *kgosi*) of the Bamangwato from 1875 to 1923, when he died in his late eighties. The Bamangwato are one of many Bantu-speaking tribes that inhabit the southern third of continental Africa. They are concentrated in the northern half of what, during colonial times, was called Bechuanaland (an English corruption of *BaTswana's* land – that of the *Tswana* people, one of whose tribes are the Bamangwato). Most of Bechuanaland is covered by the Kalahari Desert – a not entirely inhospitable area since it provides good grazing for cattle when it rains. This varies in different regions between 100 and 500 mm per year, and may be compared with the Sahara which receives only between 20 mm 100 mm of rain per year. Nevertheless it is the Kalahari Desert that accounts for the relatively low population density then as now. Readers may be familiar with the indigenous inhabitants of the Kalahari who have been there for the last 40,000 years, known variously as Bushmen, San or Kung, and idealised in the writings of Laurens van der Post.

Khama III inherited none of his father's characteristics. Sekgoma the First was a chief of the old order: feudal and warring in outlook, with a fondness for the liquor that the Europeans had brought to the region. The son espoused a different European habit: Christianity, introduced by the London Missionary Society and its chief exponent, David Livingstone. Through Khama's influence, Christianity spread among his people: today more than 70 percent of Botswana's population worship some form of this religion. To the consternation of many, Khama introduced strict prohibition of all alcoholic beverages save locally brewed beer (this embargo has not survived). In return he gave the Bamangwato something much more valuable: protection from the racist policies of Bechuanaland's neighbours, namely Boers in the Transvaal to the south east and Cecil Rhodes' British South Africa Company in Matabeleland (later Southern Rhodesia) to the north east.

By 1885 both were proposing to take over Bechuanaland, and the British Government, that controlled Bechuanaland, was listening. Although apartheid policies in Matabeleland and the Transvaal were not then apparent, Khama's instinct warned him of subsequent danger. Khama was a shrewd man (he also foresaw the – unsuccessful as it turned out – Jameson Raid that took place ten years later). In order to prevent any potential annexation of territory in 1885 he decided to go to the very top: to the Colonial Secretary, Joseph Chamberlain, in London. Together with the chiefs of two neighbouring tribes, Khama travelled to Cape Town and then by steamer to London. Joseph Chamberlain was not a man known to change his mind, especially at the behest of a trio of African chiefs. But Khama persevered and was able to persuade Chamberlain not to agree to the proposals of the British

South Africa Company and the government of Transvaal. The chiefs were then received by Queen Victoria at Windsor Castle, where gifts were exchanged. They returned triumphantly to Bechuanaland.

The territory occupied by the Bamangwato and neighbouring tribes in the north of Bechuanaland now became Bechuanaland Protectorate. It was governed by Great Britain as a protectorate, rather than as a colony (a somewhat subtle distinction). Two other protectorates in southern Africa were Basutoland (established in 1884; after independence called Lesotho) and Swaziland (established in 1902; it retained its name on independence). Both are within what would become South Africa, and both suffered as a result during the apartheid years. Bechuanaland Protectorate was able to resist South African pressure much more successfully. The southern part of Bechuanaland became British Bechuanaland, which was incorporated into the (British) Cape Colony (South Africa after its independence) in 1895.

Khama's inspired rule is best summed up in a letter that Sir Henry B Loch, the High Commissioner for the three protectorates, who was stationed in Cape Town, wrote to Khama's neighbour, Lobengula, chief of the Matabele in Bulawayo. Lobengula had long been a thorn in Khama's side, but he was eventually defeated by the clever chief of the Bamangwato. Even worse was to come for Lobengula, though, as Cecil Rhodes began to outwit him time after time. Sir Henry Loch wrote to him: 'In Khama's country the white men and the black men live side by side as friends ... because Khama rules his people with justice, and protects all who come into his country. That is why the English people are friends of Khama. They respect and honour him for his fair dealings as between man and man, and because he protects the lives and the property of his people.'[5]

Seretse Khama

Bechuanaland has been fortunate in its leaders right up to the present time. Although Khama III's son and heir, Sekgoma Khama II, did not distinguish himself (he had been an irritant to his father for much of his life), another Bamangwato, who was in the cast of Khama III, emerged. This was Sekgoma's son, a boy called Seretse, born in 1921. When Sekgoma died in 1925 after only two years on the throne, Seretse became *kgosi*. At four years of age he was too young to reign, and Sekgoma's younger brother, Tshekedi Khama (Seretse's uncle) was appointed regent.

Seretse's education, like that of others of his class, took place in South Africa: first at a number of boarding schools and then at the South African Native College at Fort Hare (also known as Fort Hare University College) – all of course segregated and catering only for blacks. Yet the education they received was so good that black Africans from all over southern Africa studied there. The list of Fort Hare alumni reads like a Who's Who of leading figures: Kenneth Kaunda, Seretse Khama, Nelson Mandela, Robert Mugabe, Joshua Nkomo, Julius Nyerere, Oliver Tambo, Desmond Tutu, among others.

On graduation in 1944, Seretse moved to Oxford (Balliol College) to continue his education. He left after a year and transferred to the Inner Temple in London to read for the bar. England was a cold and dreary place compared with sunny Bechuanaland Protectorate. Food was scarce (the Second World War may have just ended, but rationing was still in place and items like meat would continue to be restricted for another decade). Most of all, Seretse was lonely: his royal background did not impinge on the average Englishman; the colour of his skin did. An event then occurred that changed not only Seretse's life (for better), but that of Bechuanaland Protectorate itself (for worse). He met, fell in love with, and promptly proposed to an English girl. She was Ruth Williams, 24 years old to Seretse's 27, worked in the foreign claims department of a firm of Lloyd's underwriters, had met Seretse at an event organised by the London Missionary Society and reciprocated his overtures. Good for them, you might say.

Not so in 1948. The Church of England – yes, the Anglican Church which nowadays has more adherents in Africa than in England and the rest of the world put together – objected. In fairness, it was being lent on. When Seretse's uncle Tshekedi, the Regent, had been approached by his nephew for permission to marry Ruth, he was horrified. He cabled his lawyer in Cape Town, who told the High Commissioner for Bechuanaland Protectorate, Sir Evelyn Baring (whom we shall meet again shortly) to stop the marriage. Baring contacted the Deputy Under-Secretary of State for Commonwealth Relations in London, who passed the matter to the Africa section of the London Missionary Society. Following a meeting at Mission House, three men (one of whom Seretse had actually invited to the wedding) asked the vicar of St George's Campden Hill, who had agreed to marry the couple, to stop the marriage. The vicar said he would consult the Bishop of London, who was about to conduct an ordination service at nearby St Mary Abbotts Church. The Bishop's response was in the negative. Unable to reverse the decision of the Regent in Bechuanaland, the High Commissioner in South Africa, the leading members of the London Missionary Society and the Bishop of London, the couple married quietly in a civil ceremony at Kensington Registry Office.

Three weeks later Seretse returned alone to Bechuanaland. In accordance with Bamangwato custom, a *kgotla* or tribal meeting was called in order to confirm him as *kgosi*. It took place in front of the traditional *kgosi*'s residence (currently occupied by Regent Tshekedi) on a hill top in the diminutive and dusty capital Serowe. Tshekedi advised against such a course of action: a white woman as a *kgosi*'s wife would be inappropriate. He had told Seretse to either divorce Ruth or renounce his title. Seretse would have none of this. He now asked the crowd of nine thousand or so people who had travelled from far to attend the *kgotla*, to sit down on the grass. He then invited 'those who want me and my wife' to stand: the entire assembly, with few exceptions, rose to its feet. After they had reseated themselves he asked those who objected to his wife to stand up: only forty did so. The Acting Deputy Resident Commissioner, Vivien Ellenberger, commented that 'It was a stirring spectacle, a magnificent expression of public sentiment' and consequently reported to his superiors in London that, in his opinion, Seretse was a 'fit and proper person to be Chief.'[6]

The High Commissioner for Bechuanaland and the other two Protectorates, Sir Evelyn Baring, disagreed. Stationed still in South Africa as his nineteenth century predecessors had been, Baring had formed a close friendship with Dr Daniel Malan, the prime minister of South Africa, who was steering his country along increasingly stringent *apartheid* lines. Spurred to action by Malan and his counterpart in Southern Rhodesia, Sir Godfrey Huggins, Baring wrote to the Secretary-of-State for Commonwealth Relations in London, Philip Noel-Baker. Seretse Khama he never even bothered to meet. Baring's letter to Noel-Baker was unequivocal: 'I need not, I am sure, emphasise how repugnant mixed marriage of this nature is to the great majority of people in Southern Africa. It is apparently the immediate official recognition of Seretse and his wife which arouses most criticism'. Criticism, of course, by whites outside Bechuanaland, whose own citizens averred that 'The administration is ours as the Bamangwato, it has no connection with other countries outside the Protectorate ... We ask that the Government inquire into this matter accordingly while considering the wish of the Bamangwato. We want our Chief and his wife.' What did Noel-Baker (described by his Permanent Under-Secretary as an 'intellectual mosquito') do? He caved in to Baring's demands and set up a judicial enquiry. His successor as Secretary of State subsequently lied about the matter to the House of Commons.[7]

In the meantime Ruth travelled to Serowe to join her husband (advised not to do so by the obvious route from Johannesburg, she went by a round about journey through Northern Rhodesia, so as not to upset the good [white] folk of South Africa and Southern Rhodesia). What she saw on arrival did not deter her: 'I am convinced that I, as the chief's wife, could do much more for the women ... There is no compulsory education. Hygiene and health are practically unknown subjects. There are no welfare centres or clinics worth mentioning. There is a terrific need of these things among the Bamangwatos. ... At the Residency there is a magnificent flower garden – but there are no proper roads in Serowe.'[8] She had little chance of fulfilling any of this. She and Seretse were banished from Serowe, and instead had to make do in a shack in Lobatse, outside traditional Bamangwato territory, where she managed to give birth to a daughter, Jacqueline. Uncle Tshekedi was banished for good measure, and Rasebolai Kgamane, next in royal seniority, was appointed Head of the Native Authority; the British government wanted him to be *kgosi*, but the people refused to recognise anyone other than Seretse. For him and Ruth, worse was to come.

In March of 1950 Seretse was called to London for a meeting with Jim Griffiths, Secretary of State for the Colonies. Afterwards Seretse called a press conference to reveal that he had just been offered £1,100 tax free to renounce the Chieftaincy and live in Britain, an offer that he had refused.[9] The Cabinet now met to consider the removal of the couple entirely from Bechuanaland. Although the Attorney General, Sir Hartley Shawcross, had expressed the view that 'I do not like the idea that an Order deporting a British subject from his home territory could be made on the ground that the Governor or High Commissioner does not like his moral character', the Cabinet decided to exile the couple to London for five years. Sir Evelyn Baring was delighted: 'A major disaster' (recognition of a mixed marriage) 'has been avoided and the effect on relations with Union Government has been admirable', he cabled to London. The following year the incoming Conservative government amended the order, but not along the lines that a senior chief, who had written to Winston Churchill welcoming him back as Prime Minister and expecting for a reprieve for Seretse, had hoped. The order was extended to exile for life. However, recognising Seretse's talents, he was offered an administrative post in Jamaica ('Why Jamaica?' asked a Labour parliamentarian, 'Is there no suitable opening at St Helena?').[10] Seretse politely declined.

Back in Bechuanaland the people were unhappy. They stopped cooperating with their colonial masters, morale sank to a new low, and agriculture declined. Elsewhere in Africa, things looked brighter. The 'Wind of change' (as Prime Minister Harold Macmillan would describe it in 1960) was beginning to blow across all of Africa. The Gold Coast was moving towards independence, which it would acquire, as the new country of Ghana, in 1957. In 1956 the Secretary of State for Commonwealth Relations, Lord Home, decided to lift the banishment order, provided Seretse renounced his claim to be *kgosi* of the Bamangwato. Since this is precisely what Seretse had been offering to do since his banishment, he was soon on his way. Ruth and the children would follow shortly. At the airport in Francistown Seretse was mobbed by a crowd of 3,000. Double that number of cheering followers awaited him in Serowe. Three weeks later the welcomes were repeated as Ruth and the children arrived. The people – tribesmen, women and children – were happy: they had their *Mohumagadi* (Mother of the people) back. The Bangwato (those of the Bamangwato tribe) could now settle down in peace. Cooperation with the authorities resumed. Not a single white woman, though, deigned to greet Ruth on her return.

Events began to move inexorably towards independence. In 1963 elections to a Legislative Council were held. Seretse secured twice as many votes as any other candidate and was accordingly appointed to the Executive Council. He now represented not just the Bangwato, but the entire Bechuanaland Protectorate. 'Democratic development is much better than being a Chief', he said.[11] Two years later elections to a National Assembly, that would take the nation to independence, took place. Seretse, standing for the liberal-leaning Bechuanaland Democratic Party (BDP) that he had set up earlier, won his constituency with 5,904 votes. The candidates of the rival Bechuanaland People's Party and Bechuanaland Independence Party gained 53 and 39 votes respectively. Overall, the BDP won 28 of the 31 available seats. It was a resounding victory for Seretse and he was promptly appointed Prime Minister. On Independence Day (29 September 1966) Sir Seretse Khama (the Queen had conferred a knighthood on him a few days before) moved up to become the nation's first President. Seretse had accepted the barriers that the British

Government had been putting in front of him with dignity, patience and calm. At the same time he had not wavered in his determination to serve the people of his country. They were lucky to have secured his leadership. Seretse Khama was unique in steering his country seamlessly from colonial rule and African feudalism into a modern democracy.

But economic progress would not be easy. As mentioned in the opening paragraph, conditions in the country were dire. Ruth's appraisal 18 years earlier still held true. According to the United Nations, Botswana was the least developed nation in the whole of Africa. 'Few Independence ceremonies may have taken place under dustier, bleaker economic circumstances.'[12] Yet Seretse's skills gradually changed the outlook. He introduced innovative Food for Work programmes that rewarded people's agricultural efforts in regard to the conservation of water and soil. And, as is so often the case in respect of successful politicians, luck was on his side. First, the rains came. Second, diamonds were discovered at Orapa in the east of the country: this would become the world's largest diamond mine. The third piece of luck was that the mine had not been discovered eight months earlier. Had that been the case, it is unlikely that Britain – especially with pressure from South Africa and Southern Rhodesia – would have acceded so readily to independence for Botswana.

Seretse's authority assured the Botswana Democratic Party of victory in the elections of 1969, 1974 and 1979. Continuity was good for the country, as the necessary reforms could be enacted without political setbacks. But Seretse's health, that had never been perfect, was suffering. In 1980 Ruth took him to London for a check-up. The verdict was grim. His malady was diagnosed as abdominal cancer: he had but months to live. Ruth immediately brought him back to the country of his forefathers, where he died on 13 July. He was just 59 years of age. World leaders mourned him. From his prison cell on Robben Island, Nelson Mandela wrote a letter of condolence to President Quett Ketumile Masire (who had taken over when Seretse died). Masire astutely summed up Seretse's legacy: 'I think we were lucky in that the combination of traditional respect for Seretse and his personality really made him the ideal person to have started this country on the course in which it is going. His marriage to Ruth … made Seretse the Mandela of Botswana… It is remarkable how they were able to put the past behind them and act in exactly the opposite way in which a human being would usually act.'[13] Julius Nyerere, President of Tanzania, also hit the nail on the head when he wrote that so-called African experts had expected Botswana to become 'a puppet of South Africa's apartheid Government', but 'Time has proved that the pessimists left out of account two vital factors; the steadiness and determination of the people of Botswana; and the leadership of Seretse Khama and the Botswana Democratic Party … who was completely honest and who brings honour to our continent.'[14]

Botswana today

The country has continued to prosper since 1980. The Botswana Democratic Party has remained in power through successive fair and democratic elections, and as a result the lurches towards Marxist socialism or military dictatorships that have prevailed elsewhere have been avoided. Because of good management under successive Presidents (Quett Masire from 1980, followed in 1998 by Festus Mogae), the economy has grown, as a result of which the average annual income has increased ten-fold. The government had relied heavily on international aid during the 1960s, but in contrast to most other African nations, the money was not salted away by corrupt politicians or used to buy expensive military hardware. Instead it was used to boost a growing market economy. By 2000 the GDP per capita ($8,170) was more than four times the sub-Saharan average ($1,780).

Nevertheless the Gini index,[15] that measures the gap between family income of the richest and poorest in a country, was 63 in 1993 – one of the highest in the world (that of Sweden, at 23 in 2005, is the lowest). Moreover the average life expectancy in 2012 was only 56 years, similar to many other sub-Saharan countries, but more than 20 years less than in most countries of the northern hemisphere or South America.[16] So there's a long way to go in regard to the health of the country. Yet the profits from diamond mining have not been salted away in Swiss bank accounts by Botswana's leaders but have been used for the benefit of the people by improving education, health and infrastructure. The country's current problems are high rates of HIV infection leading to AIDS (despite President Festus Mogae's valiant efforts in 2001), refugees pouring in from neighbouring Zimbabwe, and international pressure to halt the sale of 'blood diamonds'. The last is a myth. Unlike Sierra Leone or Côte d'Ivoire, Botswana does not use the profits to fund wars: as mentioned, the money is invested in projects to improve the well-being of its citizens. In 2009, 9.5% of its GDP was spent on education – the fifth highest in the world. A model country, atypical of the rest of Africa south of the Sahara? Yes.

Today Botswana is fortunate in having as its President the eldest son of Seretse, Lieutenant General (he was educated at the Royal Military Academy Sandhurst in the UK) Seretse Khama Ian Khama, to give him his full title. He has maintained his father's flair for politics and his involvement with the BDP, becoming its Chairman in 2003. He was Vice-President of Botswana from 1998 to 2006 and President since 2008. Like his great-grandfather Khama III, Ian Khama is concerned at the level of drunkenness that has returned to his country. But instead of prohibition, he has introduced an alcohol levy – originally proposed at 70%, subsequently reduced to 30%. However unpopular with the populace and the brewing industry, Ian Khama's first priority is the good of the country.[17] The vision of his parents, and their ability to implement it, is in his bones. A model son, atypical of other outstanding leaders' offspring (Pericles, Akbar the Great, Mahatma Ghandi and Winston Churchill come to mind)? Yes.

After independence, refugees from South Africa's apartheid regime were seeking shelter in neighbouring Botswana, knowing that its government abhorred the policy of its southerly neighbour. At the same time South African patrols were crossing the border into Botswana illegally to try to capture and return them. Diplomatic relations between the two nations were zero. Yet as I write today, President Ian Khama and six ministers are in South Africa to attend the inaugural session of the Bi-National Commission (BNC), which was signed a year earlier, between Botswana and South Africa. President Khama is discussing with President Jacob Zuma areas of mutual interest and collaboration that include trade, energy, transport, defence, security, agriculture, home affairs and science and technology. For the people of the nation termed a 'basket case' in 1966, such efforts bode well for the future. The title of this chapter is no exaggeration.

End Notes

[1] see Table 1 and
   http://data.worldbank.org/indicator/NY.GDP.PCAP.CD

[2] see https://www.transparency.org/cpi2014/results

[3] see http://hdr.undp.org/en/media/HDR_2010_EN_Table2.pdf

[4] Morton *et al* (2008), p 2

[5] Mockford (1931), p 146

[6] Williams (2006), pp 48 and 49.

[7] *ibid*, pp 71, 77 and 132

[8] *ibid*, p 82

[9] Segal (1963), p 49

[10] Williams (2006), pp 134, 177 and p 219

[11] *ibid*, p 306

[12] *ibid*, p 322

[13] *ibid*, p 329

[14] *ibid*, p 326

[15] an index of 0 represents complete equality; an index of 100 complete inequality; see
   http://en.wikipedia.org/wiki/Gini_coefficient

[16] see http://www.photius.com/rankings/population/
   life_expectancy_at_birth_total_2013_0.html

[17] apart from his attitude towards the Bushmen of the Kalahari, whose rights to live and hunt in their tribal lands – they were the first humans in southern Africa – have been woefully

ignored. They are being denied access to their ancient water holes, which now service tourist lodges built with financial support from the European Union. See http://www.survivalinternational.org/tribes/bushmen]. On the other hand President Khama is one of only three African Heads of State who seriously and effectively supports the protection of the African elephant and other endangered large animals.

Chapter Ten
GREAT EXPECTATIONS: GHANA

In contrast to Botswana, Ghana typifies the fate of most sub-Saharan countries during the colonial era and the aftermath of independence: within little more than two decades of freedom from colonial rule the country suffered four military coups and the collapse of three republics. During this time the GDP per capita declined by some 5%. But it has picked up since then. Although, as indicated in Table 1, it's not spectacular by any means, in 2011 Ghana's GDP grew faster than that of any other African nation, and world-wide its growth is eclipsed only by Qatar. In 2013 Ghana received the Africa Peace Award, for promoting democracy, good governance, peace and security, from the African Centre for Constructive Resolution of Disputes (ACCORD) based in South Africa.

Visiting the British High Commissioner in his Accra office a few years ago, I was surprised to see on the wall opposite his desk a photograph of him presenting his letters of credence to the Ghanaian president. For standing next to the president in his suit was another man in highly decorative traditional wear. This was Osei Tutu II, the current *Asantehene*, or king of Ashanti within the Republic of Ghana. The Asantehene has no official role in the government but occupies a position of honour in the country, somewhat akin to that of the traditional royal heads of the nine states in Malaysia (though in their case, one of their number is elected every five years as head of state). Why has the status of Asantehene endured? The obvious answer is that the Ashanti people are Akan, and this ethnic grouping is by far the largest in Ghana, making up almost half the population. Their votes matter.

But I believe there is another reason and that is the pride that Ghanaians, including politicians of all stripes, take in their history, which is essentially that of the Ashanti Empire. It reminds me of a remark made by a Soviet Intourist guide in the 1980s, who when asked why the Soviet government spent so much money on renovating former royal palaces after the end of the Second World War, replied, 'It is our heritage'.

Asante (Ashanti) Empire

As the empires centred on the Niger Delta gradually fell to Berber invaders from the north (chapter 4), so a new nation arose in the rain forest to the south. From around the seventeenth century onwards, the Asante Empire grew to become one of the largest independent kingdoms in the whole of Africa, encompassing all of present-day Ghana and much of Côte d'Ivoire to the west and Togo to the east. Its people, the Akan, had developed a nation state already several centuries earlier. The rituals observed by them have tantalising similarities with those of ancient Egypt, suggesting some form of contact in bygone days.[1] The success of Asante centred on trade: kola nuts [2] and gold were carried (literally: the tsetse fly prevented the use of wheeled traffic pulled by quadrupeds) northwards into the nations of the Sahel and eastwards into Hausa territory. All exports and imports (chiefly slaves, cattle, and shea butter from the nuts of the shea tree) were controlled by the Asantehene. Foreign traders could venture only as far as the boundaries of the kingdom, where goods were exchanged. They were carried between Kumasi and border towns by officials appointed by the Asantehene. From the port of Elmina, cocoa (after the introduction of *Theobroma cacao* from South America into West Africa) for Europe and slaves for the Caribbean were dispatched. Gold had been long been a major export, both to Europe by sea and across the Sahara to eastern markets. Between 1651 and 1700, 1,500,000 ounces were exported to Europe; a further 500,000 ounces went north by caravans. As the slave trade increased, the export to Europe fell dramatically: slaves for the Caribbean were more profitable. Between 1751 and 1800, only

800,000 ounces were exported to Europe, with the land trade virtually unchanged, at 400,000 ounces. The abolition of the slave trade saw the export of gold to Europe restored: between 1801 and 1850, 1,400,000 ounces went to Europe, with the land trade down to 200,000 ounces.[3]

Another ingredient of success was a 40,000-strong army serving the Asantehene, sitting on his symbolically important Golden Stool in the capital of Kumasi (Coomassie). Control from the centre was important because the empire included several vassal states that were permitted a certain amount of independence, rather as had occurred in the Roman Empire. Kumasi, according to English visitors in 1817, was surprisingly modern and sanitary. 'Four of the principal streets are half a mile long, and from fifty to a hundred yards wide. The streets are all named. ... Every household burns its rubbish every morning at the back of the street, and the people are as clean and careful about the appearance of their houses as they are about their own appearance.'[4] But 'Akan kings had no right to make peace or war, make laws, or be directly involved in important negotiations such as treaties without the consent of their elders and/or elected representatives.'[5]

The Portuguese, who in the late fifteenth century were the first Europeans to arrive on the coast, were not the only ones to appreciate the potential of the region's gold. British, Danish and Dutch traders were soon on the scene. The Asante traded with the Dutch through Elmina, while the Fante population further east around Cape Coast – no friends of the Akan of Asante – favoured the British. It did them little good. By 1873 the confederacy they had established among themselves was absorbed by Britain as a colony. The Asante did not give up so easily. They fought off the British in 1823 and again forty years later. In 1873, however, a British force under the command of General Wolseley, with British, West Indian and African troops, fought its way through the marshes into the capital, Kumasi. Henry Morton Stanley, prior to his expedition to rescue Livingstone, covered the campaign as a journalist.

'We saw some thirty or forty decapitated bodies in the last stages of corruption, and countless skulls which lay piled in heaps and scattered over a wide extent.' A European who had been imprisoned in Kumasi but subsequently released, 'says he has seen some two or three hundred slaves slain at one time, as customary after the death of the king's sister'. This was done so that the deceased would have servants in after-life.[6] Stanley continues: 'If it be true that about a thousand slaves, offenders, rebels, and others are executed annually …. At the rate of a thousand victims a year, it would be no exaggeration to say that over 120,000 people must have been slain for "custom" since Ashantee became a kingdom!'[7] A less macabre side of king Kofi Karikari is revealed by his collection of gifts: 'we found the interior court and the rooms opening upon it filled with curious but intrinsically valueless articles, while the upper storey contained much valuable plunder … (that included) a breakfast and dinner service of silver, with English cutlery, Bohemian vases, … gold nugget, and bead bracelets and necklaces, piles of faded Kidderminster carpets, Persian rugs, … leopard skins, European regimental drums, swords, European and native, scimitars of Arabic make, gold and silver-headed canes, … royal stools, beautifully carved and ornamented with gold and silver, … golden toys, damask bed-curtains and counterpanes, … enormous silken umbrellas, … English engravings, … silver tankards and cups … a sword – a gift from Queen Victoria, … porcelain and china ware, a copy of the London 'Times' October 17, 1843, … An old curiosity shop could not exhibit a more miscellaneous variety of things than the interior of the king's bed-chambers, his private apartments, and store-rooms contained.'[8]

The campaign against Asante was successful. The king fled and Kumasi was burnt to the ground. The empire of Asante, together with the Fante-dominated coastal region to the east, was annexed by the British. The new colony was called the Gold Coast – a name that had been appropriately used by the Portuguese four hundred years earlier. But the bold Akan of

Asante were not done yet. A fourth Anglo-Ashanti War, led by the Asante Queen Mother erupted in 1900: her resistance lasted just six months. Not until 1957 would Britain give up one of its favoured African colonies. A particularly beneficial consequence of colonial rule was the founding of a prestigious co-educational boarding school at Achimota in Accra. Its motto of *Ut Omnes Unum Sint* ('That all may be one') is reflected in its crest: an octave of black and white notes. 'You can play a tune of sorts on the black keys only; and you can play a tune of sorts on the white keys only; but for perfect harmony, you must use both the black and the white keys'. These are the words of J E K Aggrey,[9] a notable scholar born near Cape Coast Castle in 1875, who was invited to take a top position when the school was established in 1924. Alumni of the school include five presidents of Ghana (as well as Robert Mugabe). The first of these was the man who led the Gold Coast to independence.

Kwame Nkrumah

He was born in 1909 in the village of Nkroful, situated in the west of the coastal region. Here Kwame went to elementary school, where most African children stayed just a few years. Kwame was exceptional in that he completed all seven stages of the curriculum. This enabled him, at seventeen, to enter Achimota School shortly after its foundation, as a pupil-teacher. He left four years later to teach in a Roman Catholic junior school. A Gold Coast Inspector of Schools recalled watching Nkrumah in action: 'I have never forgotten our meeting … since I was suddenly made aware that here was no ordinary teacher.'[10] Instead of embarking on a career in politics, law or the army via a stint at Oxford or Sandhurst as other Achimota graduates were doing, Nkrumah decided to read theology at Lincoln University in Pennsylvania, USA. He obtained his degree at the head of his class and was soon teaching Negro history at the University of Philadelphia. In 1945 he went to London to study economics and philosophy, at exactly the same time that Seretse Khama was enrolling at the Inner Temple to read law. Whether they ever met is not recorded.

That year the Pan-African Congress, a forty-five year old institution established to co-ordinate the struggle of Africans throughout the world, met in Manchester. Its founder, the American William E B Du Bois, presided. Nkrumah was one of the organisers of the meeting. Pan Africanism,[11] first promoted by Edward Blyden a hundred years before, would remain part of Nkrumah's ideology for the rest of his life. Among the participants in Manchester were two other future African presidents, Dr Hastings Banda (Malawi) and Jomo Kenyatta (Kenya). The congress ended with the following resolution: 'We are not ashamed to have been an age-long patient people. We continue willingly to sacrifice and strive. But we are unwilling to starve any longer while doing the world's drudgery, in order to support by our poverty and ignorance a false aristocracy and a discarded imperialism. We are determined to be free.'[12] Two years later Dr J B Danquah, one of the 'false aristocrats', persuaded Nkrumah to return to the Gold Coast, as general secretary of a new nationalist party, the United Gold Coast Convention (UGCC).

Nkrumah had been in the country barely a year when a boycott of European shops by ex-servicemen, exasperated by the increasingly high prices being demanded for goods, led to violence. Many of the veterans were from the 81st West Africa Division that had been sent to Burma in 1943 in order to halt the advancing Japanese before they reached Assam and India. The rationale behind using West African troops was that they were considered to have a certain amount of resistance against malaria and were familiar with life in the jungle. The first assumption was correct, the second not (there was little jungle in West Africa by this time). The West Africans fought bravely, and together with the rest of General William Slim's 'forgotten' army, drove the Japanese back south out of Burma. Having been promised a better life on return home at the end of the war, they were naturally disappointed when this proved elusive.

Shops were attacked and burnt. The governor asked the police who was behind the fracas. It was a communist plot, he was told.

Knowing of Nkrumah's left-wing views, he was promptly arrested, together with other leading lights of the UGCC that included Dr Danquah himself. For their part, the UGCC sent a note to the Secretary of State in London protesting at the failure of the police to quell the riots. The matter was eventually resolved, but Dr Danquah began to wonder whether Nkrumah might be more trouble than he was worth. So the leaders of the UGCC suspended him from duty. The ousted general secretary responded swiftly. Disillusioned with the rather conservative views of the UGCC, Nkrumah set up his own party, the Convention People's Party (CPP). Its manifesto was to campaign for swift progress towards self-government. Most of the chiefs, as well as the staid members of the UGCC, regarded the CPP as no more than a coalition of 'verandah boys, hooligans, flotsam and jetsam, town rabble.'[13]

Derogatory statements did not deter Nkrumah. In 1950 he launched a movement dubbed Positive Action (for independence). The trade unions called a national strike in support. The recently arrived governor, Sir Charles Arden-Clarke, promptly declared a state of emergency and put Nkrumah behind bars. After a period of cooling down, Arden-Clarke decided to test the mood of the public by calling for municipal elections in the Gold Coast's main cities, Accra, Kumasi and Cape Coast. The contest was essentially between the moderate UGCC and the radical CPP. The latter won hands down. Nkrumah, though still in prison, had been allowed to stand as CPP candidate for Accra Central: he was elected by a landslide. The governor now decided to hold a general election for the legislature in order to satisfy himself that the CPP really represented the majority view. The results left him in no doubt that they did. He accordingly released Nkrumah and asked him to form a government that would prepare the country (under Arden-Clarke's governorship) for eventual independence. The two men respected each other and worked together for a common goal, just as F W De Klerk and Nelson Mandela would do forty years later in South Africa (see chapter 12).

Nkrumah was now in a position to implement real change. Fees for primary education were abolished, as a result of which the number of children in school doubled within two years. If the country was to prosper it needed to train its own scientists, engineers and technicians, rather than sending them abroad. Not only was this expensive, it also encouraged the best brains to remain outside the country. So the university college at Legon in Accra was expanded and a new college of technology inaugurated in Kumasi. They are now the University of Ghana and the Kwame Nkrumah University of Science and Technology (KNUST), respectively. Between 1951 and 1957 the CPP government built nine new hospitals and modernised fifteen more. So far as the main commercial activity of the Gold Coast was concerned, a Cocoa Purchasing Company was established in order to enable farmers to expand their business: in 1953 alone, £1 million was lent to cocoa planters at very low rates of interest.

Arden-Clarke was impressed by Nkrumah's achievements and recommended to the British Government that the Gold Coast be granted independence. The Colonial Office agreed, but with one proviso. The CPP needed to show that it, not the National Liberation Movement (NLM) opposition party that was strongly supported by the Akan population, represented the views of the majority. A general election was accordingly called for 1956. The NLM won in the Ashanti region, but in the country overall the CPP secured 57% of the vote and 71 of the 104 seats up for election. The result was not overwhelming, but decisive enough. Independence, under a CPP government led by Nkrumah, would be granted on 6 March 1957. It was the first sub-Saharan country to break free of colonial rule. Nkrumah felt that 'Gold Coast' smacked too much of the country's history as a trading nation under the British. Instead he adopted the name of 'Ghana', by which the empire to the north that expired in the thirteenth century had been known (see chapter 4). Three years later Nkrumah decided to push for complete independence of Britain. Currently he was merely prime minister of a country under the British crown, as represented by a Governor-General. He proposed to make Ghana a republic and to put himself up for President. The country voted overwhelmingly in favour of a republic. In a run-off for president against Dr Danquah he won 89% of the votes. Nkrumah now had the power to run the country more or less as he pleased.

Nkrumah summarised his achievements as follows: 'Within the short span of eight years of independence, we have built some of the finest roads in the world; we have provided medical and health services for the large majority of our people; we have built universities, secondary schools, training colleges and provided opportunities for free education for the great mass of the population.'[14] He also completed the Volta Dam for the supply of cheap electricity that had been on the drawing board since the 1930s. Electricity from the dam also powers a bauxite processing plant. The USA was the major funder and unsurprisingly US firms were the main beneficiaries. As elsewhere, the flooding of such a huge area of farmland (that created Lake Volta, the largest man-made lake in the world) displaced thousands of people. But the dam does supply a significant proportion of Ghana's energy demand. During the early 1960s the EEC [15] proposed a partnership with various African countries. Nkrumah had the good sense not to participate. He criticised the proposals since they would 'doom the economy of Africa to a state of perpetual subjection to the economy of Western Europe.'[16]

But worse was to come. His trade-and-aid agreements with the Soviet Union were denounced by the opposition. The country was incurring a huge deficit which Nkrumah attempted to redress by cutting wages by 5% and taxing other income by 10%. Strikes broke out. As luck would have it, the world price of cocoa collapsed to an all-time low in 1965. The country was relying on foreign aid to see it through. Nkrumah's solution to all this was political, not economic. In 1964 he proposed turning Ghana into a one-party (the CPP, of course) state, as his friend the Senegalese president Léopold Senghor had done in 1962: 'The multi-party system which exists in Western countries is in fact a reflection of social cleavage and the kind of class system which does not exist in African countries.'[17] Although this assertion has been disputed,[18] 93% of the electorate – a far larger margin than had ever supported the CPP in its heyday – appeared to be in favour. Electoral fraud was now added to Nkrumah's successes. For good measure he pronounced himself president for life.

The greatest error Nkrumah made was to go abroad in 1966. He intended going to Hanoi, to protest against the American military action in Vietnam. He only got as far as Peking. As soon as he was out of the country, his opponents struck. A military coup, abetted by Britain and the CIA,[19] deposed him, and confirmed Lt. Colonel (later General) Joseph A. Ankrah as Head of State. If Nkrumah 'had been remotely like the monster of self-indulgence described by his enemies, duly possessed of great funds abroad, he would have retired to a villa in Switzerland … He did nothing of the kind. He went straight back to Africa. His old friend President Touré of Guinea welcomed him and … appointed him to be co-President with himself.'[20] Nkrumah died in a Romanian hospital in 1972. Col Ignatius K Acheampong, who had taken over as head of state in another military government, following three years of parliamentary government (1969-72), considered Nkrumah to have been 'a great man' and ordered a state funeral.

According to a Ghanaian administrator 'Ghana succeeded in mobilising Africa's efforts towards the emancipation of the dependent territories. Ghana succeeded against formidable obstacles of inertia and opposition in making the idea and ideals of African unity accepted all over Africa as the ultimate objective for all African states … Ghana succeeded in making Africans everywhere feel proud of their Africanness … Most of these successes are due to the sense of dedication, of purpose, of single-mindedness, and the inspired leadership of Dr Nkrumah.'[21] These achievements were set in motion largely between 1950 and 1957, before independence and Nkrumah's presidency. They were his most fruitful years. One is reminded of another leader whose most significant contribution was made in the years *prior* to his reaching the highest office. The abandonment by Tony Blair of Clause IV – by which the Trade Unions in the UK were holding Labour to account – was accomplished in the period between being elected leader of the Labour Party in 1994 and winning the general election in 1997.

From Nkrumah to Rawlings

The coup that deposed Nkrumah in 1966 led to military rule under a government of National Liberation Council for the next three years. In 1969 Brigadier Akwasi Afrifa, who had succeeded to the presidency, re-initiated parliamentary rule. Dr Kofi Busia, a long-time adversary of Nkrumah who had fled abroad in fear of his life in 1959 and had returned in 1966, was elected prime minister three years later. He was moving the country gradually to the right, when in 1972 he made the same mistake as his erstwhile opponent: he went abroad (for a medical check-up in Britain). He was promptly deposed in a coup led by Col Ignatius K Acheampong. Thus ended a brief period of parliamentary government, Ghana's Second Republic. Acheampong, now a general, ruled with an iron fist for more than six years, but was himself deposed in a coup. Lieutenant-General Fred Akuffo succeeded as head of state only to be deposed – you guessed it – by another military coup. This time it was the air force: Flight Lt Jerry Rawlings would lead Ghana, with a brief interlude, for the next twenty-two years.

Jerry John Rawlings was born in Accra in 1947 to a Ghanaian mother and a Scottish father. He studied at the prestigious Achimota School, after which he joined the air force as a flight cadet. During his training he was named best cadet in flying and airmanship. He was commissioned in 1969. As a young officer Rawlings proved to be something of a fire-brand (a role he continues to this day). His sympathy for men in the ranks led to him, together with others, to be charged by a court martial, on 28 May 1979, for leading a mutiny of junior officers and men of the Ghana Armed Forces. A week later Rawlings escaped custody and, with the help of civilians and members of the armed forces, managed to overthrow the governing Supreme Military Council. In its place, the Armed Forces Revolutionary Council (AFRC), with Rawlings at its head, took over. But Ghanaians were not too happy with the new regime. Less than five months later, political parties which had been banned under Acheampong, were again allowed to campaign for government. A People's National Party, modelled on Nkrumah's Convention People's Party, won the election and its leader Dr Hilla Limann, an economist of moderate views, entered the presidency. But not for long.

Ghana's Third Republic, under Limann, endured just two years. Then Rawlings' thirst for military action got the better of him. Accusing Limann of economic failures, Rawlings and his AFRC supporters deposed the president. The country was once more under military rule. The Provisional National Defence Council, as it was called, was anything but provisional: it lasted eleven years, the longest period of continuous government in Ghana's history. Yet under Rawlings the country began to recover. The currency was finally devalued, more than ten-fold, to reflect the true nature of the economy. Inflation fell from 120% to 10.4% in a single year, during which GNP growth increased eight-fold. Cocoa production picked up, rising from 160,000 tons in 1983-84 to 300,000 tons seven years later. Western investors returned, especially as the demise of the Soviet Union, to whom it had been indebted, allowed Ghana to move towards a market economy. But financial recovery was accompanied by unemployment and rising costs of education, health and public utilities. 'The government', it was said, 'saved the country at the expense of the people' [22] (they said the same in the UK about the 2010-15 coalition government).

In 1993 Rawlings, under pressure from the Ghana Bar Association and others, felt sufficiently secure to return the country to parliamentary democracy. He founded a new party – the National Democratic Congress (NDC) – with him at its head. An election was called, which the NDC duly won. Under new rules, the president would serve a four-year term; two terms would be the maximum. Rawlings' first term was marked by a reversal of the previous economic boom. It failed in its obligation towards its lenders (the International Monetary Fund and the World Bank) and confidence sank. The country was rated a 'heavily indebted poor country'. On the other hand the poverty rate began to fall from a high of 51% in 1991-2; by 2006 it had dropped to 28%. So Rawlings' popularity enabled the NDC to triumph in its second election and the president was re-elected to serve for another four years, after which he properly stood down. There are those [23] who view Rawlings as a ruthless despot. It is true that he ordered the execution of three former Ghanaian heads of state and several generals following his coup in 1979, but he is not in the same league as men like Idi Amin or Mengistu Haile Mariam. Rawlings is surely more maverick than murderous dictator.

Democracy Continued

The election following Rawlings' second term of office as president was won by the New Patriotic Party (NPP), led by John Kufuor who became president. The contrast with Rawlings could not be starker. Kufuor is a mild-mannered Asante, educated in London (Lincoln's Inn) and Oxford (Exeter College), with liberal views. He served the country well, and was re-elected for a second term. In 2002 he had summed up the country's economic woes as follows: '… the average per capita income of my people is lower now than in the 1960s, four decades after independence. Some of the blame for this we Ghanaians must accept. My country must acknowledge that corruption has been a canker on our public and economic life and must be contained.'[24] The election at the end of 2008 (Ghanaian elections are held in December, with the elected party forming the government early in January) went to the NDC under John Atta Mills. Mills had attended Achimota followed by the University of Ghana. In England Mills obtained a Master in Law at the London School of Economics and Political Science and a PhD at the School of Oriental and African Studies, all by the age of 27. He returned to teach at the University of Ghana for the next 25 years, interrupted only by visiting appointments at Stanford Law School, Temple University (Pennsylvania) and Leiden University. No wonder he was called *The Prof* when he finally turned to politics. He died unexpectedly in 2012, during the third year of his presidency. The country, and many outside it, held their breath. Would the appointment of the vice-president to the presidency, as stipulated in the constitution, or be marred by violence and another coup? They need not have worried. John Dramani Mahama (another Achimota alumnus), Mills' vice-president, was sworn in without a murmur. On the other hand when the NDC with Mahama at its head narrowly won the election later that year, the opposition NPP did challenge the outcome. The issue rumbled on with considerable ill will between the two parties until the Supreme Court gave its verdict eight months later: the win by the NDC was upheld.

Stable and democratic government has now endured for more than two decades (the Fourth Republic), and there is every likelihood that it will continue to do so. Agriculture grew faster than the overall GDP between 2001 and 2005, due to increased land use and productivity by smallholders. As a result, Ghana is the only African country to reduce its Global Hunger Index by more than 50%.[25] The discovery of offshore oil in the west of the country in 2007 has given the nation a welcome boost. The people complain – like everywhere else – that the profits from the oil industry are not improving their lives, and all political parties are constantly at each other's throats. The NPP, whose support comes mainly from ethnic Akan around Kumasi, in contrast to the NDC who rely on Ga speakers from the Accra region, seem to consider the remarks of Edward Blyden (1887) to resonate to this day: 'Everybody now knows that the tribes of the Gold Coast are no match in intelligence, enterprise and energy for the Ashantees.'[26] The Chinese are trying (illegally) to get their fingers on the mining industry and there is considerable petty crime in the major cities. But there is no violence – ethnic, religious or political – and Ghana can be said to typify a sub-

Saharan nation that has overcome the teething problems of independence and now has an encouraging future.

End Notes

[1] Meyerowitz (1960)

[2] Kola is a medicinal agent that was first introduced as such by Coca-Cola in the late nineteenth century. Coca-Cola and Pepsi Cola stopped adding kola to its fizzy drinks almost a hundred years ago, but the psychoactive properties of the nut have made it a favourite to chew on by followers of Islam who are denied other stimulants. See Abaka (2005) p ix

[3] Gareth Austin: *Between abolition and* Jihad: *the Asante response to the ending of the Atlantic slave trade, 1807-1896* in Law (2002) p 97

[4] Davidson (1998) p 220

[5] Daniel Boamah-Wiafe: *Africa: The Land, People, and Cultural Institutions* (Wisdom Publications, Omaha, 1993) p 169; quoted by Ayittey (2005) p 21

[6] Gareth Austin: *Between abolition and* Jihad: *the Asante response to the ending of the Atlantic slave trade, 1807-1896* in Law (2002), p 101 *et seq*

[7] Stanley (1896) p 185

[8] *ibid* p 188 *et seq*

[9] Niven (1964) pp149-166

[10] quoted in Davidson (1973) p 23

[11] see, for example, George B N Ayittey: The United States of Africa: A Revisit, *Annals of the American Academy of Political and Social Science* **632**: 86-102 (2010); also published by Sage Publications Inc; see http://www.jstor.org/stable/27895950 for a summary

[12] Davidson (1973) p 49

[13] *ibid* p 70

[14] *ibid* p 200

[15] European Economic Community, the precursor of the European Union

[16] Segal (1963) p 273

[17] Davidson (1973) p 199

[18] Ayittey (1992) p 66

[19] James (2016) p 296

[20] Davidson (1973) p 204

[21] *ibid* p 218

[22] Gocking (2005) p 194 *et seq*

[23] for example Daniel K Pryce: *The Unsavory Legacy of Jerry Rawlings* (GhanaWeb 4 February, 2014)

[24] Ayittey (2005) p 1

[25] Juma (2011) p 16

[26] Blyden (1967) p 54

Chapter Eleven
GREAT EXPECTATIONS: RWANDA

R wanda is one of the smallest countries in Africa – no more than a blob in the middle of a map of the continent. It has little history prior to the seventeenth century: no archaeological ruins, few artefacts. Huddled in mountainous territory between its giant neighbour the Democratic Republic of Congo (510,000,000 sq km) to the west, Tanzania (900,000 sq km) to the east and Uganda (242,000 sq km) to the north, it appears no more noteworthy than neighbouring Burundi (28,000 sq km) to the south. Burundi is the same size as Rwanda (26,000 sq km), with a comparable ethnic mix and recent history. Yet there is a difference. Burundi lacks the impressive advances in education, health and the economy that have given Rwanda international fame. The man behind this is Paul Kagame, whom we met briefly in chapter 1. It is Kagame's vision for his country that justifies its inclusion in this chapter. Yet Rwanda's recent history is beset by an incident of catastrophic dimensions: the civil war of 1990-94 and its ensuing genocide.

Before Civil War

The original occupants of the region that includes present-day Rwanda were hunter-gatherer pygmies known as Twa. They probably became settled through interaction with farming Hutu people who migrated into the area subsequently, as did the distantly-related Tutsi who are cattle breeders and herders. All three speak a Bantu type of language. No part of Rwanda is below 1,000 metres, which makes for a very equable climate: the temperature, which is too low for tropical pests like the tsetse fly, varies little throughout the year. With good grazing and fertile soil, the population has grown continuously to become one of the most densely populated regions in the world, similar to that of the Netherlands today. It increased nearly five-fold in just 50 years, between 1934 and 1989.[1] And therein lies one of Rwanda's major problems. Competition for land means that the less favoured lose out, and it's clear to see who these are. The pastoral way of Tutsi life has caused them to have greater wealth and to feel superior to the Hutu farmers. So Tutsi look down on Hutu, and both look down (literally) on the shorter statured Twa. The situation is not unlike the caste system in India (based on similarly dubious ethnic differences), that has an equally high population density.

We know little about the chiefs and rulers who inhabited this land. Some time during the seventeenth century a rather mythical figure known as Ndori founded the kingdom of Nyiginya. The ruling class was essentially Tutsi. As they were also the owners of cattle and land, the latter were brought under the control of the king and his courtiers.[2] The Hutu farmed the land for their masters, growing sorghum, finger millet, water yam, African yams, gourds, calabashes and at a later date, bananas. The Twa became court dancers and menial workers. A strong army was built up under the kings of Nyiginya, with the entire population being conscripted. Throughout the nineteenth century, with local rivalries constantly bubbling up at court but little to fear from their neighbours, the Nyiginya lived in relative amity. And ignorance. The decisions taken in Berlin in 1885 (see chapter 7) in regard to the future of the Nyiginya and their land were totally unknown to them. So the court was not at all put out when in 1897 a young German officer, Hans von Ramsay, visited. Exchanging the usual pleasantries, von Ramsay casually proposed an alliance between Nyiginya and the German colonial office. The mother of the thirteen year-old king Musinga promptly agreed. How was she to know that her entire land, plus that of Burundi and much of present-day

Tanzania, had been acquired by Germany ten years earlier and was now a country named German East Africa?

In fact Berlin left the Nyiginya much to their own devices. German 'residents' merely acted as advisors to the ruler. The monarchy continued and its representatives even expanded their territory while under nominal control by Germany. All the imperialists wanted was to use the extensive reserves of labour in this densely populated land in order to work on plantations controlled by themselves. This resulted in a lucrative trade not with Germany but with Zanzibar, and through it, with India. In 1916, during World War 1, Belgium wrested the country from Germany. This was ratified at the end of the war and Rwanda, together with Burundi, was allocated to Belgium. Britain took the rest of German East Africa. The Belgians ruled Ruanda-Urundi, as it was now called, as a League of Nations Mandate. The social distinction between Tutsi and Hutu was not only maintained, it was exacerbated. For previously some cattle-owning Hutu had been granted chiefdoms by their Tutsi superiors, giving them the possibility of some upward social mobility. Under Belgian jurisdiction this was stopped, and existing Hutu chiefs were stripped of their rights. 'By the end of the Belgian presence in Rwanda in 1959, forty-three chiefs out of forty-five were Tutsi as well as 549 sub-chiefs out of 559.'[3] Part of the reason for Belgian favouritism was their conviction (unsullied by evidence) that the Tutsi represented an exotic tribe from ancient Egypt and beyond who, if not exactly white, had little in common with the sub-Saharan Negro.

The Belgians meddled in Rwandan life in other ways. King Yuhi V Musinga, who had supported Germany in 1916, was deposed in favour of his son (Mutara III Rudahigwa). This meant a shift towards Christianity, which the Belgians encouraged by appointing Catholic priests (one of the most influential of whom was actually a Rwandan Tutsi, Father Alexis Kagame) to positions of authority, including education, throughout the country. Considering the high illiteracy rates, this was no bad thing. But schooling was neither compulsory nor free. It therefore favoured the wealthier Tutsi over the Hutu. More than twice as many of the former became enrolled at Astrida College – the Rwandan version of Ghana's Achimota College, named after Belgian Queen Astrid – in the southern province of Butare. Thus were the seeds of Hutu-Tutsi conflict nurtured.

Belgium continued to have jurisdiction over Ruanda-Urundi, now as a UN Trust Territory, after World War 2. Soon Tutsi and Hutu began to form political parties. In 1957 the Mouvement Social Usutu (MSM) and the Association pour la Promotion Sociale de la Masse (APROSOMA) were formed by Hutu supporters. Two years later the Tutsi responded with the Union Nationale Rwandaise (UNAR), which supported the monarchy (Rwandan, not Belgian) and campaigned for immediate independence. Unsurprisingly the government began to change its position. By the mid-1950s the inequality in wealth between an average Tutsi and Hutu household had disappeared (the family income of a typical Twa household, needless to say, was just a third that of the other two). When fighting between the political parties broke out in 1959 with the Hutu burning Tutsi houses, the authorities chose not to intervene in what they termed a 'social revolution'. The Tutsi community saw the writing on the wall and began to emigrate in large numbers to neighbouring Burundi, to Uganda (the next favourite destination), to Tanganyika and to the Belgian Congo. The UN, influenced by the Soviet bloc which was opposed to capitalist Belgium, supported the Tutsis and pressed the Belgian government to hold legislative elections in 1961. It was too late. PARMEHUTU (Parti du Mouvement de l'Emancipation Hutu), that had replaced MSM and APROSOMA, won 78% of the vote, with the Tutsi UNAR on 17%, which translated into 35 and 7 seats respectively, out of a total of 44. A UN Trusteeship Commission Report on the outcome of the election was prophetic: 'An oppressive system has been replaced by another one … It is quite possible that some day we will witness violent reactions on the part of the Tutsis.'[4]

Belgium granted independence to Rwanda in July of 1962. King Mutara III Rudahigwa had fortuitously died without issue three years earlier (though doubts have been raised about the circumstances of his death [5]) so a Hutu controlled republican government under the presidency of former journalist Grégoire Kayibanda posed no problems (apart from opposition by the Tutsi minority). A more serious threat came from Tutsi refugees in Burundi. In December 1963 a group of them launched a half-baked invasion into Rwanda. They were swiftly repulsed. The resident Tutsi population was made to suffer for their compatriots' audacity: some 10,000 were massacred. President Kayibanda, acting as though he were king, exerted total control over the oppressed Rwandan people. For their part they welcomed a bloodless coup by Major-General Juvénal Habyarimana in 1973. He was head of the army (its officers trained largely by Belgians) and minister of defence. Even the Tutsi minority embraced the new leader because he seemed to guarantee their security. And it was true: provided they kept their heads down and left politics to the Hutu, they would not be harassed.

Habyarimana continued his predecessor's autocratic rule. All political parties save his own Mouvement Révolutionnaire National pour le Développement (MRND) were banned. So no one was surprised when Habyarimana was overwhelmingly re-elected in 1983 and 1988. Under his presidency the economy (the third lowest in the world in 1962) slowly began to recover. Medical care and education (still not free) improved somewhat. But by 1989 matters were deteriorating once again. The country was relying more and more on foreign aid. In order to reduce the budget, social services were curtailed at the same time as taxes were increased. Rwanda's perpetual problem of high population density, coupled with a drought, was causing famine. Voices raised in opposition to the regime were mysteriously snuffed out by 'road accidents'. When in April 1990 the president visited France – that was gradually replacing Belgium as a dominant force in Rwandan affairs – he was advised by François Mitterrand to restore multi-party politics. But it was too late. The Tutsi insurgency from Burundi in 1963 may have come to nothing, but their counterparts in Uganda were better organised. A Rwandan Patriotic Front (RPF) that aimed one day to restore Tutsi authority had been established some years earlier; with Major Paul Kagame as one of its leaders. On the first day of October 1990, some 2,500 men of the RPF, led by senior officers (Kagame was in the United States, receiving specialist training at Fort Leavenworth) entered Rwanda. The civil war had begun.

War

The first phase did not last long. The RPF penetrated 60 km into Rwanda until they were stopped. The invaders lost only one man on the first day, but it happened to be their commander, Major-General Fred Rwigyema. Morale in the RPF fell dramatically, and the 5,000 strong Rwandan army (Forces Armées Rwandaises; FAR), equipped with French armoured cars, heavy artillery and helicopters, was able to see the invaders off within the month. The French also sent a small force of 150 men, not to fight but to guard the airport in the capital Kigali. The decision to do this was taken by President Mitterrand's son Jean-Christophe, who was head of the Africa Office at the Elysée Palace in Paris (the President himself was on a state visit to Oman). Jean-Christophe Mitterrand remarked 'We are going to bail him [President Habyarimana, who had asked for help] out. In any case, the whole thing will be over in two or three months.'[6] This is precisely what was said in Europe in 1914. And just as the Great War would last four years, so did the Rwandan conflict. The difference was that most of the dead in the Great War were soldiers (over 38 million of them); in the civil war, most of the dead were civilians (at least 800,000) with only 10,000 of the militia killed.

Once the invasion started, reprisals against Tutsi – with no connection to the RPF – were swift. Within weeks some 350 were massacred and 500 homes burned in one commune alone. The disheartened RPF did not leave the country entirely. They regrouped and holed down in the Virunga mountains in the north west of the country. At well over 4,000 metres, several men froze to death as autumn turned to winter. Paul Kagame had returned from the USA and slipped unnoticed into his home country. He now led the RPF in guerrilla raids on suitable targets. The insurgents were joined by Tutsi sympathisers from neighbouring Burundi, Zaire (today D R Congo) and Tanzania, as well as from more distant Republic of Congo (formerly French Congo). Their numbers quickly doubled and by the end of 1992 had reached 12,000. To establish his authority, Kagame promoted himself from major to major-general (leaping four ranks in one). On the defenders' side there were grumblings at the increasing cost as the army grew, even though much of the cost was paid by France. The FAR numbered 30,000 by the end of 1992 and 50,000 a year later. But a well-trained guerrilla force, even if out-numbered 4 to 1, is not easily subdued. So the civil war dragged on. To appease disgruntled, mainly Hutu, opponents of the government, Habyarimana finally allowed the existence of political parties other than his MRND, and proclaimed a new constitution in June 1991. But in effect little changed. All that happened was that the president resigned as head of the armed forces.

Habyarimana's idea of democracy was to incite illiterate peasantry to kill RPF 'sympathisers' in so-called 'bush clearing' operations. The fact that the RPF itself was nowhere to be seen was beside the point. Well over 300 innocent victims were massacred in 1991 and again in 1992. The opposition parties had had enough. They decided to talk directly to the RPF who, while not winning the war, were not losing it either. The latter agreed to a cease-fire and announced that the armed struggle would now be a political one. Preliminary peace talks began in Brussels, then moved to Paris. In July 1992 formal negotiations between the Rwandan government and the RPF started in Arusha, Tanzania, hosted by its president, Ali Hassan Mwinyi. In addition to members of President Habyarimana's MRND(D) ('et la Démocratie' had been added to MRND in 1991), opposition parties like the Coalition pour la Défense de la République (CDR), some of whose members now had positions in cabinet, participated on the government side. The CDR was a particularly strong supporter of France's intervention in Rwandan affairs that was intensifying year by year. It is not difficult to see why. President Mitterrand was a staunch supporter of Francophone nations such as Rwanda. 'Anglo-Saxon' countries like Uganda (a member of the Commonwealth, where the RPF was formed) he viewed with the same distaste he felt for Margaret Thatcher's Britain.

Violence against Tutsi stirred up by renegades in both MRND(D) and CDR continued, even while negotiators were trying to find a peace settlement. At an MRND(D) rally one of its leaders told his supporters that 'The opposition parties have plotted with the enemy … to undermine our armed forces. … The law is quite clear on this point: "Any person who is guilty of acts aiming at sapping the morale of the armed forces will be condemned to death." What are we waiting for? … We have to take responsibility into our own hands and wipe out these hoodlums. … We have to act. Wipe them all out!'[7] Remind you of anything? The abuse and false allegations stirred up against the Tutsi, that would result in genocide does indeed have similarities with events in Germany during the 1930s that led to the 'Final solution' (a phrase heard increasingly in Rwanda during this time). An estimated 300 unfortunate Tutsi were tortured, massacred and their homes burnt down in January 1993. The peace talks in Arusha were broken off and the RPF resumed its offensive within Rwanda. A demoralised FAR was no match for the well-trained guerrillas. Additional French troops were flown in to defend the capital. This forced the RPF to stop 30 km north of Kigali and to announce a unilateral cease fire. Instead of persuading the FAR to do the same, the French Minister for Cooperation, recently arrived in Kigali, urged the various opposition parties to join the government in making 'a common front' against the RPF.[8] The seeds of conflict had grown into healthy saplings.

Despite opposition to the 'common front' by moderate Hutu opposition parties who were ready to resume peace talks with the RPF, President Habyarimana persisted in his aims. With two sides of the so-called government now at each other's throats, the RPF were happy to wait and sit things out. They were right to do so. By August 1993 the pro- and anti- 'united front' had resolved their differences sufficiently for a new peace agreement with the RPF to be placed on the table in Arusha. A Broad Based Transitional Government (BBTG) would be set up, followed within two years by democratic elections. The men making up the new Rwandan army would be 60% from FAR (Hutu), 40% from RPF (Tutsi), with the officer corps split 50-50. French troops would depart and be replaced by a UN military monitoring force (United Nations Assistance Mission to Rwanda; UNAMIR) to ensure that the terms of the agreement were kept. The document was signed not only by President Habyarimana but for good measure by his opposite numbers in Burundi, Tanzania, Uganda and Zaire as well.

Yet discord between the various parties, as well as murders and revenge killings, continued. It is doubtful that President Habyarimana and the MRND(D) ever wished the Arusha Accord to succeed. In Burundi, the assassination of President Melchior Ndadaye (a mild, idealistic Hutu engineer) in October by Tutsi extremists caused local bloodshed (some 50,000 – mainly Tutsi – deaths) and a huge influx of refugees (mainly Hutu) to Rwanda. The RPF condemned the killing of President Ndadaye and the ensuing violence, but by February 1994 the transfer of power in Rwanda according to the Arusha agreement had still not taken place. More than a thousand UN troops, under the command of Canadian General Roméo Dallaire, as well as the UN Secretary-General's special envoy, the aptly-named Cameroonian Jacques-Roger Booh-Booh, were on the ground to ensure calm, but procrastination on the government side delayed fulfilment of the accord. And then on 6 April the long fuse of Rwandan power struggles was lit by an incident that destroyed every hope of the Arusha agreement being fulfilled and plunged the country into an inferno from which it has yet to recover.

Massacre

On 6 April 1994 President Habyarimana flew to Dar-es-Salaam for a meeting with other African leaders (representing Burundi, Kenya, Tanzania and Uganda), The main topic of discussion was the plight of Burundi following President Ndadaye's murder, but it soon turned to the situation in Rwanda. Habyarimana was urged by all to implement the Arusha agreement without delay. Reluctantly he acquiesced and boarded the presidential Mystère Falcon 50 jet, a recent present from François Mitterrand. On board were the three-man French crew, Habyarimana's senior advisors and Burundian President Cyprien Ntaryamira who was hitching a lift to Kigali, whence he would fly on to his capital Bujumbura. As the plane was coming in to land at Kigali airport it was hit by a missile and crashed (into the president's garden). There were no survivors. Who fired the rockets (three were said to have been launched; two missed) and why? They were French soldiers, left behind after the departure of the rest in 1993. They were Belgian members of UNAMIR. Both suggestions are extremely unlikely, as neither France nor Belgium had much to gain by the president's death. The only reason for suspicion is that white soldiers are said to have been seen at Masaka Hill, from where the missiles seem to have been launched. It was the work of the RPF. More plausible, perhaps, yet what had they to gain? The Arusha accord was acceptable to them, and they must have realised that the consequences of the murder would be catastrophic for the Tutsi population. The attack was perpetrated by associates of President Habyarimana who might have seen him as a liability (he had plenty of enemies in the various political parties), and so on. As with US President Kennedy's assassination in 1963, conspiracy theories abound to this day.

What is not in doubt is that the murder set off one of the most violent and extensive massacres of the second half of the twentieth century. Within an hour of the crash, the Presidential Guard erected road blocks throughout the capital to prevent any movement of government officials (the prime minister, a pro-democracy opposition politician and her family were soon massacred), of UNAMIR trying to halt atrocities, or of Tutsi families fleeing in terror. Day after day the slaughter by rampaging gendarmes and militia continued. In Kigali, the perpetrators were members of the 1,500-strong Presidential Guard and low-ranking 'militiamen', some of whom were little more than drunken bandits and peasants looking for a fight against innocent Tutsi, or being dragooned to do so by government officials. They numbered around 50,000 throughout Rwanda and took the massacre into the countryside. In the capital, members of UNAMIR were not spared. The autopsies of ten Belgian peace-keepers caught inside Camp Kigali, whose corpses were subsequently repatriated, 'showed that four of them died from weapons fire, three of them from blows to the head with a machete, one was stabbed with a bayonet, one died from a fractured spine due to a severe blow with a blunt object and one from injuries to his throat.[9] On 9 April, five hundred Tutsi were found hiding in a Catholic church. '"The militia began slashing away with machetes", a witness remembered. "They were hacking at the arms, legs, genitals, breasts, faces and necks." Some people were dragged outside and beaten to death. The killing lasted two hours. Then the killers walked slowly among the bodies, looting and finishing off the wounded.'[10]

That the atrocities were condoned and even encouraged by those who could have stopped them is clear. 'Colonel Théoneste Bagosora, a senior official in the Ministry of Defence … was watching from his car. These army officers were coordinating and controlling the situation.'[11] In 2008 Bagosora and two others were found guilty of genocide, crimes against humanity and war crimes by a UN- sponsored international court, and sentenced to life imprisonment. But what of the UNAMIR? Could they have prevented the situation from getting out of hand? I have already mentioned the road blocks that prevented their movement, and that they themselves became victims. The force was far too small and ill-equipped to have been effective and it was eventually pulled out. It was the perpetrators of the massacre who had stock-piled in excess of $100 million worth (some given as aid) of military hardware: hundreds of thousands of hand grenades, bombs and AK47 rifles, as well as mortars, light artillery, armoured cars and helicopters, not to mention half a million machetes and other 'agricultural' equipment. The UN troops could do little to prevent the ensuing blood-shed. Nevertheless the situation is reminiscent of that in Bosnia in 1995, during which in 'UN-declared "safe areas" of Srebrenica … massacres (were) conducted by Serbian forces in the presence of UN peacekeepers.'[12]

Where debate is justified is in relation to the role of the international community in events leading up to 1994. I referred earlier to Belgian influence from 1916 onwards. It now appears that a 'Zero Network', aimed at eradicating the entire Tutsi population, had been clandestinely established a few years earlier. Its members were politicians, army officers, financiers, and others. President Habyarimana's administration was aware of it: the members included his inner circle and his close relatives. Foreign governments were aware of it. In 1992 the Belgian ambassador in Kigali reported to his government that 'This secret group is planning the extermination of the Tutsi of Rwanda to resolve once and for all, in their own way, the ethnic problem and to crush the internal Hutu opposition.'[13] So far as the French government is concerned, it had only to read the papers. 'A French journalist, Jean-François Dupaquier, writing for a weekly magazine, described a "fanatical Hutu" group supporting a "final solution". … Dupaquier tried to interest members of the French parliament in questioning their government as to why support was provided to such a terrible regime, but to no avail.'[14] On 9 February 1993 *Libération* ran an article in Paris pointing out that: 'In the far hills of Rwanda … France is supporting a regime which for two years, with a militia and death squads, has been trying to organize the extermination of the minority Tutsi … the death squads, organized in a Réseau Zéro by the President's clan, are operating a genocide against the Tutsi, as though it were a public service.'[15] For a balanced assessment of who knew what and when, I recommend reading more of Gérard Prunier's *The*

Rwanda Crisis. History of a Genocide [16] and Linda Melvern's *A People Betrayed. The role of the West in Rwanda's genocide*,[17] as well as 'A lesson on Rwanda', which gives a good synopsis of Rwanda's history up to 1994.[18]

The genocide, which at its height lasted until the end of May, had cost the lives of 800,000 victims – possibly more – in just six weeks. That's more than 10% of the entire population. At the same time the RPF, having commenced military action 48 hours after President Habyarimana's murder, started to advance towards the capital. They were at the outskirts within three days. The FAR fled from their better trained and disciplined adversaries, but it took another three months before the RPF gained control of Kigali. In the meantime the French, spurred on by Nelson Mandela's remark that 'The Rwandese situation is a rebuke to Africa ... We must change all that; we must in action assert our will to do so,'[19] decided to send peace-keeping troops (well armoured just in case) as a humanitarian gesture. The mission, named *Opération Turquoise*, arrived a month after the genocide had subsided. The troops set up a humanitarian safe zone to the south of Kigali, in which refugees fleeing the RPF (mainly Hutu, but also some Tutsi who didn't trust their liberators) might find safety. One and a half million did so. Another million and a half fled north west towards the border with Zaire. This means that nearly half the country's 7 million inhabitants had become refugees.

On 13 July the RPF took Ruhengeri and 5 days later Gisenyi, both border provinces with Zaire in the north west of the country. Most of Rwanda was now under control of the RPF. Its success had not been without incidents of violence (in excess of 5,000 Hutu are said to have been murdered in revenge killings). In Kigali a new government, with Pasteur Bizimungo (an RPF Hutu) as president, was sworn in. Paul Kagame was named vice-president. The cabinet was carefully chosen to give it legitimacy: sixteen out of twenty-two ministers were Hutu. The agreements reached in Arusha began to be realised. As the situation started to stabilise, Tutsi refugees who had fled abroad began to trickle back. By November a likely 400,000 had returned to Rwanda. Gradually many of the Hutu refugees who had fled to Zaire, Burundi and Tanzania also started to make their way back. But the economy was dire, with foreign governments – especially France – now reluctant to give any immediate support. The other problem was that of justice. The government thought that as many as 30,000 people might have participated in the massacres, but it was obviously impossible to prosecute such numbers. So in conjunction with the International Criminal Tribunal for Rwanda (ICTR), it was decided to bring to justice those suspected of having ordered or condoned the genocide, as was done in the Nuremberg Trials at the end of World War 2. Around a hundred were identified as being in this category, but the prosecutions linger on to this day: few have been indicted.

Recovery from War

Although many Hutu are still afraid to come home, the last two decades have seen a return to some sort of normality. The population shrank by 1 – 2 million during 1994 as a result of massacre and emigration, but had recovered by 1997. It has grown by a further 5 million, to 12 million, since then. The composition now is 84% Hutu, 15% Tutsi and 1% Twa. At the end of the nineteenth century it was 75% Hutu, 24% Tutsi and 1% Twa. The ratio of Hutu over Tutsi, that was 3-fold in 1900, appears stuck at more then 5-fold today. But the minority Tutsi are once more in control. Rwanda may claim to have democratic rule but the facts are otherwise. With many of the opposition in prison or self-imposed exile, so that the president repeatedly receives more than 90% of the vote, the word democratic hardly applies. It is therefore not an inclusive economy as defined by Acemoglu and Robinson.[20] That does not mean it can't prosper: look at one-party China, or South Africa under *apartheid*.

Rwanda is making good progress in education. The literacy rate (average of males and females over 15 years of age) is increasing steadily: from 38% in 1978, 58% in 1991 to 71% in 2009. The government spends 15% of its budget on education, 9.5% of which goes on universities. It has established a strong Information and Communications Technology (ICT) programme which benefits teachers, primary and secondary school pupils and those going on to university. Primary school children are taught in Kinyarwanda for the first three years, followed by French or English for the last three. All teaching in secondary school is in French or English. Attendance at primary school and the first three years of secondary school is mandatory and free. Nevertheless the average length of time spent in school is only just over three years – poor in comparison with developed countries (10 years) and even with other sub-Saharan countries (4.5 years). There is a long way to go. In two other areas, however, there have been striking advances: health and business friendliness.

The health of the nation has improved dramatically in recent years. The incidence of malaria, for example, fell by 70% between 2005 and 2010. HIV/AIDS is still high, but Rwanda is embarking on a novel programme of male circumcision that is said to reduce the transmission of HIV.[21] At the same time vaccination programmes against childhood diseases have burgeoned. Much of this is due to the efforts of Dr Richard Sezibera, Minister of Health from 2008 to 2011 (he then became Secretary-General of the East African Community – they were lucky to get him). When I met Sezibera on a visit to Rwanda in 2010, he proudly showed me some of the statistics. Coverage, by a single vaccine against diphtheria, pertussis, hepatitis B and *Haemophilus influenzae* b (that causes severe bacterial infections in infants) was 80%. The same was being achieved by an oral polio vaccine, by BCG (against tuberculosis; however the world is still waiting for a more effective vaccine) and by a vaccine – introduced only during the previous year – against *Streptococcus pneumoniae* (that causes pneumonia in the lungs and meningitis in the central nervous system). Since then coverage for most of these vaccines has increased to over 90%. And this in a country in which over 80% of the people live in rural areas. An even more remarkable achievement has been the introduction of a vaccine against human papilloma virus, the main cause of cervical cancer. More than 90% of girls were vaccinated in 2011 according to the World Health Organization.[22] In 2010 the comparable figure for the USA was less than 50%.[23]

The economy, as mentioned in chapter 1, is still poor. But it is improving, albeit slowly. Since 2000 GDP per capita has grown year on year, despite the increase in population. The outlook compares favourably with Ghana, despite the latter's almost 3-fold higher GDP per capita. According to Standard & Poor, in 2012 Ghana's rating was B (highly speculative): outlook STABLE, whereas Rwanda's was also B, but outlook POSITIVE. It is marginally less corrupt than Ghana, and considerably less so than Senegal or South Africa, according to Transparency International's figures for 2014.[24] In one sphere, the country is doing splendidly. The World Bank has devised an index to show how easy it is to do business in a country.[25] The nation with the highest index is Singapore (89.80 in 2006, 92.39 in 2014). Rwanda was 37.36 in 2006, similar to low-ranking countries like Côte d'Ivoire (36.52) or Sierra Leone (37.38). Both those countries improved considerably over the following 8 years, reaching 50.24 and 54.10 respectively by 2014. Such a rise is typical of many sub-Saharan countries, showing that they *are* finally improving. But Rwanda leapt ahead – the fastest rate of growth anywhere in the world – to 70.46 in 2014. The ease of doing business in Rwanda is now similar to that in countries like France (71.31) or Spain (70.84). They say that you can launch a new business in Kigali within an hour.

So the future is potentially bright, provided today's essentially one-party state is eventually replaced by a democratic one. Whether this is achievable under Paul Kagame's presidency (he's not yet 60) is the big unknown that hangs over Rwanda.

End Notes
[1] Prunier (1998) p 4
[2] Vansina (2004) p 67
[3] Prunier (1998) p 27

[4] *ibid* p 53

[5] Melvern (2009) p 16

[6] Prunier (1998) p 101

[7] *ibid* p 171

[8] *ibid* p 178

[9] Melvern (2009) p 148

[10] *ibid* p 156

[11] *ibid* p 5

[12] Bobbitt (2003) p 416

[13] Melvern (2009) p 49

[14] *ibid* p 49, cont

[15] *ibid* p 51

[16] Prunier (1998)

[17] Melvern (2009)

[18] Kapuscinki (1998) pp 165-182

[19] Prunier (1998) p 281

[20] Acemoglu and Robinson (2012) p 435

[21] Vincent Mutabazi, Jamie I Forrest, Nathan Ford and Edward J Mills: How do you circumcise a nation? The Rwandan case study. *BMC Medicine* **12**:184 (2014)

[22] see http://www.who.int/bulletin/volumes/90/8/11-097253/en/

[23] *Nature* **499**: 253-4 (2013); the low rate reflects the fear that the vaccine is not safe; but it is: Heidi Larson: The world must accept that the HPV vaccine is safe *Nature* **528**: 9 (2015)

[24] see https://www.transparency.org/cpi2014/results

[25] see http://www.doingbusiness.org/data/distance-to-frontier

Chapter Twelve
DIMINISHING EXPECTATIONS:
SOUTH AFRICA

In 1912, only three regions within Africa were free of European control. They were Liberia in the west, Ethiopia in the east, and the newly created, nominally independent, Union of South Africa in the south.

What the Boers Brought, and What They Took Away

Europeans have been taking over other people's lands since the sixteenth century. First it was Spanish missionaries, sent out to convert the indigenous population of Mexico to Catholicism. At least that was the story. The truth, as Hernan Cortéz admitted to Moctezuma, was rather different: 'I and my colleagues have a disease of the heart which can be cured only by gold.'[1] Next, it was the English, settling in North America to *escape* religious dogma. French Huguenots followed their example, mostly by way of the Netherlands, and sought a new life at the Cape of Good Hope in South Africa. Towards the end of the eighteenth century, a different batch of immigrants started to arrive at Botany Bay in Australia: undesirables transported by the British government. The previous destination used by the authorities came to an end when Britain lost the war against the American colonies; sending them to Senegambia or to other destinations in Africa had been considered, but was rejected.[2] In the Americas the indigenous people were driven off their land. In Central and South America the Iberian newcomers mated with them. In North America the Anglo Saxons corralled them into reservations. In Australia the settlers simply ignored them (though the natives had been there for thousands of years before *Homo sapiens* ever set foot in Europe). In South Africa the immigrant farmers – *Boers* in their Dutch language – followed a different course.

The Cape of Good Hope was so named to indicate the riches that awaited Portuguese sailors (the first European explorers on the scene) on their way to India and the Spice Islands. The Dutch soon followed. In 1652 the Dutch East Indies Company founded Cape Town and built a hospital where seamen could recover from the scurvy that afflicted them during their long sea journeys: not until a hundred years later were citrus fruits recognised to be the missing nutrient that prevents this disease (animals don't suffer from scurvy because they can synthesise their own ascorbic acid – vitamin C). The natives whom successive Dutch settlers met were Khoisan speakers: Khoi pastoralists, called Hottentot by the Boers, and San hunter-gatherers, also known as Bushmen (whom we met at the beginning of chapter 9). The Boers took their cattle, and – as the English had done in North America – drove their owners away from the best lands while infecting them with smallpox in the process.

Napoleon's rise in Europe caused the British to occupy the Cape Colony when the Dutch became vassals of France. They built a naval base at Simonstown and promoted trade through the export of wool The British had a different view to that of the Boers about race: a colour bar was not tolerated (officially; privately was another matter). So in 1828 Ordinance 50 was put into effect. It 'freed the Coloured' meaning the Hottentot population 'from the pass system' whereby their movement was restricted 'and the risk of being flogged for offences against the labour laws.'[3] This was the irritant that caused Boer farmers to set out on their Great Trek northwards. They occupied the lands that became known as Orange Free State to the north, Transvaal even further north and Natal to the east. Here they met the Zulus, a fierce Bantu-speaking people (who would, as mentioned earlier, in 1879 under the inspired leadership of their king Cetshwayo, inflict one of the greatest defeats in its history upon the British army). Friction between the British in Cape Colony and the Afrikaners (as the Boers referred to themselves) in the rest of the country flared up towards the end of the century in the two Boer Wars. That of 1880-1881 was won by the Afrikaners' South African Republic. That of 1899-1902 reversed the situation, and led to the founding in 1910 of the Union of South Africa as a dominion of Great Britain, but with promises of eventual self-government for the Afrikaners.

What the Boers had brought were efficient farming practices and Roman-Dutch Law (replaced after 1910 by a version of the British legal system). They inherited from the British a sound economy based on the exploitation of precious metals and diamonds that had been initiated by men like Cecil Rhodes. By 1948 there were eight thriving universities in the country, hospitals in every major city with roads and airports to connect them. It was the most developed country in sub-Saharan Africa – no, in the whole of Africa. I recall a conversation with a senior executive of the Wellcome Trust, Britain's – if not the world's – largest biomedical funding agency, some years ago. 'In which countries within Africa would the Trust consider supporting university-based research?' I asked. 'There is really only one country that has universities of sufficient calibre' he replied 'and that is South Africa'. All had been set up under successive Afrikaner regimes. Few of the benefits were available to the majority of the population.

The nation had been ruled until then by the United Party, led by the charismatic General Jan Smuts.[4] Under Smuts the economy boomed: income from steel and electrical industries, as well as from light manufacturing, exceeded that from mining and agriculture. The general election of 1948 was won by the Afrikaner-dominated National Party led by D F Malan. He and his party represented what the Boers had taken away from South Africa: freedom and a sense of justice that applies to all, irrespective of colour. Strict *apartheid* (separateness) was introduced: the blacks of South Africa had virtually no rights, the coloured (those of mixed ancestry plus the Indian community) some rights (conceded, though not until the mid-1980s, by P W Botha), and the white population ruled the country. This situation continued for the next forty years, during which South Africa seceded from the British Commonwealth and declared itself a republic. In 1983 a journalist familiar with Africa wrote 'The Afrikaner is not going to change voluntarily for the sake of being a humanitarian.'[5] He was wrong. For in 1989 the National Party elected a leader who would become president of South Africa later in the year. Everything changed from then on, because of the qualities that the new head had exhibited: the courage of a warrior and the patience of a saint. He was F W de Klerk.

F W de Klerk

De Klerk needed courage in order to abolish apartheid and bring about majority rule in defiance of the views of fellow Afrikaners. He needed patience in his dealings with both the African National Congress (ANC) and their bitter enemy the Inkatha Freedom Party (IFP). When back in 1959 Prime Minister H F Verwoerd formally introduced complete racial segregation for the black community, the twenty-three year-old de Klerk was fully in agreement. 'Together with many young Afrikaners, I welcomed Dr Verwoerd's announcement. He had established the principle that all South Africa's black peoples were entitled to progress to full independence and self-determination within the homelands they had traditionally occupied. … it would assure the rights of all South Africa's peoples – including our own – to self-determination and full political rights within their own areas. Xhosas from the Transkei and Ciskei, Tswanas from their homeland of Bophuthatswana, Zulus in KwaZulu and all our other black people would be able to exercise their political rights in their own areas, but would still be able to work in the white areas if they chose to do so. The states of southern Africa would form a common market, or a commonwealth, in which we would recognize our economic independence while continuing to live as good neighbours. Dr Verwoerd's vision of a multinational commonwealth was an ideal with which many young Afrikaner leaders, including myself, could identify.'[6]

This opinion was voiced despite the fact that Verwoerd spelled out his educational policy very clearly: natives would be taught from childhood that equality with Europeans was not for them. 'Our motto,' he declared in 1963, by which time Libya, Egypt, Sudan, Tunisia and Morocco, followed by Ghana, Guinea, Cameroon, Togo, Mali, Senegal, Madagascar, Congo, Somalia, Benin, Niger, Burkina Faso, Côte d'Ivoire, Chad, Central African Republic, Gabon, Nigeria, Mauretania, Sierra Leone, Tanzania, Rwanda, Burundi, Algeria and Uganda, had gained independence, 'is to maintain white supremacy for all time to come over our own people and our own country, by force if necessary.'[7] The young starry-eyed de Klerk seems to have missed that pronouncement. If he *was* aware of it, we shouldn't perhaps be too surprised. Such views had been commonplace at the beginning of the twentieth century. Had not the Governor of the Cape Colony and High Commissioner for Southern Africa, Lord Milner, opined that 'A political equality of white and black is impossible. The white man must rule because he is elevated by many, many steps above the black man.'[8] And Milner was no fool: a brilliant scholar at Balliol College, Oxford, where he scooped every available university prize, and a man known for his liberal views. Another Balliol man, British prime minister Harold Macmillan, on a visit to South Africa in 1960 tried to reason with Verwoerd (a former professor of Applied Psychology) but without success: 'It was only during these days that I began to realize to the full extent the degree of obstinacy, amounting really to fanaticism, which Dr Verwoerd brought to the consideration of his policies … I had the unusual experience of soon noticing that nothing one could say or put forward would have the smallest effect upon the views of this determined man.'[9]

The trouble with Verwoerd's apartheid policy was that when black South Africans chose to work in the white areas where all the jobs were, they were subjected to stringent pass laws, could not enter a white restaurant, hotel, hospital, school or university, and were harassed at every turn. As a South African writer commented at the time, 'It became increasingly difficult to escape the conclusion that apartheid as propounded by Verwoerd, the whole concept of a divided South Africa with independent African homelands, was either a fantasy or a deliberate fraud.'[10] So far as the Africans' land rights were concerned, de Klerk did feel unease. 'Some of us had long been concerned about the geographic division of the country in terms of which black South Africans, who made up 80% of the population, 'had been allocated only 13.7 % of the total territory.'[11] By 1985, when de Klerk was Minister of Home Affairs, he realised that 'In many respects the [Population Registration] Act', which classified all South Africans according to their racial group 'was the cornerstone of apartheid … Every year there were several hundred applications for racial reclassification – particularly from the coloured community. Many of these cases were tragic and quite often involved decisions that split members of the same family into different racial groups. More than any other task that I ever had to carry out in government, these cases brought home to me the vast difference between the Verwoerdian theory of separate development and its often devastating impact on the lives of ordinary people.'[12]

So in 1990, at the State Opening of Parliament, de Klerk embarked on the most controversial aspect of his career. He announced the release of Nelson Mandela, the unbanning of the ANC, the SACP (South African Communist Party) and the PAC (Pan African Congress) and the lifting of the State of Emergency regulations that affected the media as well as education. The Separate Amenities Act would be repealed. De Klerk committed himself to establishing an internationally acceptable culture of human rights. As a result, 'We had achieved our objective of convincing our friends and foes alike that the National Party had made a paradigm shift.'[13] But his contentious reforms needed legitimacy before the right wing of his party, the apartheid hardliners, would accept defeat. Two years later he succeeded. In 1992 he called for a referendum among the House of Assembly, the whites-only parliament. The question was 'Do you support the continuation of the reform process that the state president started on 2 February 1990 and which is aimed at a new constitution through negotiations?' The results were clear-cut: 69% voted 'Yes', and there was a majority for the 'Yes' vote in every region except the Northern Transvaal (a right wing stronghold). Even here, however, 43% voted 'Yes'.

The stage was set for national elections at the end of April 1994 and the formation of a Government of National Unity. Up until the last moment, de Klerk had to work hard to ensure that all parties were represented. With only a week to go before the election, the IFP were still not on board. Indeed, Nelson Mandela, who since his release from prison had been leading the discussions on behalf of the ANC with de Klerk, demanded that Chief Buthelezi, leader of the IFP, should be deposed. The situation was defused, and the IFP duly participated. Only the Conservative Party, that represented the pro-apartheid opposition, abstained. All things considered, the election passed off peacefully, with relatively few irregularities. The result reflected the composition of South Africa's citizens. The ANC won with 62.6 % of the votes, the National Party received 20.6%, the IFP 10.5%, the Freedom Front (made up of less bigoted Afrikaners than those in the Conservative Party) 2.2%, with other minor parties making up the rest. Nelson Mandela became President, with de Klerk and Thabo Mbeki (Mandela's eventual successor) as Deputy Presidents. Three hundred years after the arrival of the first Boers, majority rule had finally come to South Africa.

Nevertheless, the world awaited the outcome anxiously. Had not South Africa's neighbour Zimbabwe erupted in bloodshed around this stage of reform? Its leader, Robert Mugabe, was condoning – no, encouraging – his ZANU-PF 'war veterans' (paid thugs) to terrorise (murder, rape and evict) white farmers and their African employees and take over the farms. Ignorant of any kind of agricultural practice, the new owners allowed the farms to deteriorate: instead of producing food (Zimbabwe had been the bread basket of Africa), the war veterans provoked poverty. Would the same now happen, in manifold greater numbers, in South Africa under the ANC? Mayhem was avoided because of the new president's three outstanding characteristics: steely determination, the ability to forgive, and immense charisma.

Nelson Mandela

Nelson Mandela was born into a Xhosa chief's family in the Transkei in 1918. He was a direct descendant of King Ngubengcuka, a dominant figure among the Thembu during the 1830s, who had donated land for the erection of the first Wesleyan (Methodist) church in the area. Like his counterpart Seretse Khama in Bechuanaland, Mandela became a ward of the current regent, and like Seretse he thereby received a good (Christian) education at an English boarding school. At Healdtown he distinguished himself by winning a prize for the best Xhosa essay. Here he witnessed at first hand racial tensions between black and white that would occupy him for the rest of his life. For at the school the native and colonial teachers were segregated during such Christian activities as sitting down to a meal together.[14] The similarity with Seretse Khama goes further. Mandela also attended Fort Hare University College, but due to a falling-out with the principal, Dr Kerr, he left after only two years; he would subsequently gain his degree by correspondence course, and returned to Fort Hare only to graduate. And then, like Seretse, he quarrelled with his guardian over marriage. In Mandela's case, it was because he had no intention of marrying the girl chosen by the regent. It was time for him to quit the regent's residence that had been his home for the past twelve years.

Mandela decided to make for Johannesburg where his ambition was to study for the law – like Seretse Khama, though this is hardly a coincidence: most politicians the world over start off as lawyers. He managed to get there – just – on 'borrowed' money. In Johannesburg in 1941 the impecunious Mandela was without a job and had nowhere to stay. It was only after meeting Walter Sisulu, his elder by six years, a strong supporter of African rights and a member of the ANC, that Mandela's luck changed. His 'royal connections, his dignified bearing, his evident ambition all seemed promising material. Sisulu quickly recognised his potential.'[15] The quiet, soft-spoken Sisulu was the perfect foil for the assertive Mandela. They would remain firm friends – in and out of prison together – for the rest of their lives. Sisulu introduced him to Lazar Sidelsky, a partner in the law firm of Witken, Sidelsky and Eidelman. Like Sisulu, Sidelsky was impressed by the tall youngster, and offered to take him on as an articled clerk, a remarkable favour since white law firms did not generally employ Africans. Sidelsky even paid Mandela's fees to enable him to complete his degree. He qualified as an attorney, and in 1952, together with his friend Oliver Tambo, established the law firm of Mandela and Tambo. Mandela's sharp intellect and ready repartee made him an effective and much sought-after attorney by the African population of Johannesburg.

In the meantime Sisulu had introduced Mandela to the ANC. Soon he was playing an active part in its Youth League. He worked all day, studied at night, and somehow managed to combine his legal work with increasing involvement in politics. From 1948 onwards the ANC had to consider its response to the apartheid regulations imposed by the Nationalist government on oppressed Africans with increasing viciousness. Mandela, elected president of the Youth League in 1950, was clear that opposition had to be stepped up – but without resorting to violence. Mandela's stance for non-violence has been compared to that of Mahatma Gandhi. But let us not forget that while Gandhi was campaigning on behalf of the Indian community in South Africa as the nineteenth century turned into the twentieth, he argued that 'Indians are entitled to equal privileges with Europeans in this British Colony, on the ground, firstly that they are British subjects, and secondly ... desirable citizens ... industrious, frugal and sober.'[16] So far as the black community was concerned, Gandhi ignored it with Jeffersonian indifference.

Mandela was gaining confidence as a politician. At an ANC dinner in 1952 he brashly told the guests that he was 'looking forward to becoming the first president of a free republic of South Africa.'[17] But with increasing exposure came greater risks. He was leaving a rally in aid of the Defiance Campaign (a civil disobedience movement organised by ANC and the Indian Congress to protest new laws directed against Indians and Africans) when he suddenly found himself arrested. He spent two days in prison before being released on bail. The protests continued – some 8,000 people were arrested over the next five months – and the offices and homes of protestors were raided. Mandela was arrested yet again. Subsequently found guilty of 'statutory communism', he was confined to Johannesburg for six months and banned from attending further meetings. At the same time his stock as a political leader rose. Walter Sisulu and his wife Albertina were concerned about his haughty attitude in public, 'But he was a Xhosa aristocrat and his training from childhood had made him the way he was, aloof and sometimes a bit arrogant. It didn't matter, because the people liked to look up to a leader who was regal and maybe even a bit distant.'[18] A common enough reaction throughout the world.

Protest continued. In 1960 the PAC organised a peaceful resistance movement in Sharpeville, in southern Transvaal, that culminated in 67 Africans being shot (mainly in the back) and 186 wounded. The unwarranted response of the police caused indignation across the world. The government's response was to introduce the Unlawful Organizations Act that banned the ANC and PAC, making membership illegal. Mandela's house was raided and he was – with many of his colleagues – once more in prison, charged with inciting violence against the state. The hearing that became known as the Treason Trial would last four years. Mandela performed effectively in cross examination of himself, as well as attorney on behalf of the accused when their defence lawyers quit the court. The verdict stunned everyone: all the accused were found not guilty. The government's response was swift: a warrant was issued for Mandela's arrest on a new charge: organising a national strike. But by this time Mandela had decided to go underground.

The reason for this was two-fold. First, he had become president of the ANC Youth League, and needed to attend secret meetings across South Africa. Second, he had decided that nonviolent protest was no longer effective: an armed struggle against the government – but without killing individuals – had become necessary. The movement was called *Umkhonto we Sizwe*, or simply *MK*, and it set out to commit acts of non-lethal sabotage. This, he presciently realised, 'offered the best hope of reconciliation afterwards.'[19] The problem was that neither Mandela nor his colleagues had much knowledge of how to go about it. Moreover they needed funds to support the activities of MK. Mandela therefore secretly left South Africa for military training in Ethiopia and Morocco. He also lobbied widely for financial support: from governments in Africa (Tanzania, Sudan, Nigeria, Ethiopia, Egypt, Tunisia, Ghana, Senegal and Guinea) and from individuals in Britain. In London he met David Astor, editor of the *Observer*, leaders of the Labour and Liberal parties, as well as Canon John Collins, whom he persuaded to continue support through the International Defence and Aid Fund. After six months he returned to South Africa to continue his activities as 'black pimpernel' – the African version of Baroness Emma Orczy's *The Scarlet Pimpernel*. Mandela's underground activities lasted just nine days before he was recognised and arrested. He would spend the next thirty years behind bars.

To begin with he was convicted of inciting workers in essential occupations to act illegally and of leaving the country without a valid travel permit. For this he was sentenced to five years' imprisonment on Robben Island. Six weeks after his arrival his implication in MK activities that were being organised from a farm in Rivonia near Johannesburg was revealed. He was returned to the mainland to stand trial, together with Walter Sisulu and other conspirators, for sabotage. Mandela spent four hours defending himself in the dock, but to no avail. This time the verdict was life imprisonment (he was lucky not to receive the death penalty), and he found himself back on Robben Island for good. His treatment gradually became more humane. He was able to keep both body and mind in good shape. The first through daily exercise – whether in solitary confinement or in the prison yard – the second by borrowing books from the surprisingly well-stocked prison library (like that in the German prisoner-of-war camp in which Léopold Sédar Senghor found himself in 1940 – see the following chapter) and by discourse with other inmates. He read Marx's *Das Kapital* and Nadine Gordimer's novels, as well as Tolstoy's *War and Peace*.[20] With his fellow prisoners he discussed philosophy and the merits of William Shakespeare versus George Bernard Shaw. Like Louis Dega in *Papillon*, he was also able to tend a small patch of garden that, after his transfer to Pollsmoor prison outside Cape Town, supplied warders as well as other prisoners with onions, aubergines, cabbages, cauliflowers, beans, spinach, carrots, cucumbers, broccoli, beetroots, lettuces, tomatoes, peppers, strawberries and a variety of herbs.[21]

After his release from prison in 1990 and the ending of apartheid in 1992, he worked alongside de Klerk – despite increasingly vitriolic disagreements – to prepare a constitution that would precede free elections in 1994. Mandela recognised the disquiet that Afrikaners felt at the prospect of being dominated by a black African majority: 'We understand that fear. The whites are fellow South Africans. We want them to feel safe.'[22] One of his first actions on being elected president in 1994 was to invite the wives and widows of former ANC activists like Steve Biko and Moses Katene, and Afrikaner politicians like John Vorster and Hans Strijdom, to meet over a 'reconciliation lunch'. Percy Yutar, the prosecutor in the Rivonia trial who had demanded the death sentence for Mandela, was another guest. Hendrik Verwoerd's widow, at 94, could not attend, so Mandela made a special visit to her in the whites-only colony at Oriana in the Northern Cape Province.[23] A journalist described all this as 'super-human forgiveness.'[24] Mandela was determined not to let recriminations over past acts of injustice – on either side – fester within the new South Africa. So in 1992 he set up a Truth and Reconciliation Commission under the chairmanship of Archbishop Desmond Tutu. Although some of its findings were repudiated by former ANC officials as well as by de Klerk, it did prevent an outbreak of open hostility against whites such as had occurred in Mugabe's Zimbabwe.

The economy proved a bigger obstacle. International sanctions against trade with South Africa had begun to bite really hard during the 1980s, and the rand had dropped through the roof. Mandela appointed previous members of de Klerk's administration to key financial posts. Stringent controls on public expenditure eradicated a 250 billion rand debt – despite the fact that a million low-cost homes were built, clean water supplied to millions in the countryside, health care and education provided in black areas. A poll in 1998 revealed that 59% of white South Africans believed that Mandela 'was doing his job well.'[25] Yet the assumption by Africans still living in squalor, that the end of apartheid would signal the beginning of prosperity, proved elusive. Unemployment – expected to fall as Africans were admitted to jobs previously restricted to whites – actually rose.

Mandela married three times. His first wife Evelyn, and his third wife Graca, supported him consistently: Evelyn during the late 1940s and early 50s by keeping an open house for ANC colleagues in order to foster his political ambitions and Graca during the last fifteen years of his life by providing undemanding companionship (as Colette had done for Léopold Senghor). His relationship with second wife Winnie – more Messalina than Mandela – was different. Though he loved her dearly (as Roman emperor Claudius loved his errant Messalina), she used his name shamelessly in order to further her own political aims. But even when Winnie was convicted on four counts of kidnap and being accessory to murderous assaults, Mandela stood by her side. He even appointed her as deputy minister for arts, culture, science and technology when he became president. Staunch support against all odds was one of Mandela's defining characteristics.

The decisions taken by leaders at key points in history are sometimes difficult to appraise until a later date. The particular constitution envisaged by the Founding Fathers of the United States has been shown time and again to have been the right one. The desire by Napoleon to dominate Europe by force turned out to have been folly, but his establishment of the Code Napoleon has benefitted the inhabitants of Europe to this day. Lincoln's decision to make war on his own people in 1861 was vindicated only a hundred years later. (I remember from my first visit to the United States in the late 1950s that there were then still three separate lavatories at Greyhound bus stations in the American south: *men, women, colored*). Stalin's enslavement of Russians through communism – and after 1945 also of Eastern Europe – was a disaster; but his drive for heavy engineering projects, including military ware, during the 1930s saved his country from defeat in 1943. Churchill's decision in 1940, after the fall of Poland, Denmark, Norway, Belgium, the Netherlands and France, to counter all advice to deal with Hitler and instead to continue the war alone, eventually rescued Europe from Nazi tyranny. Mandela's conviction that the aim of the ANC should be a multiracial democracy (one man one vote) – rather than African domination through the total overthrow of the Afrikaner government advocated by the PAC – gave South Africa the democratic stability it now enjoys. Many nations on the continent are rightly envious.

To summarise. It was Mandela's humanity, coupled to forceful leadership that prevented a conflagration in 1994. But it was de Klerk's determined support that laid the groundwork. No two individuals in recent memory have been more worthy of the Nobel Peace Prize: their award in 1993 eclipses in appropriateness even those of their predecessors, Chief Albert Luthuli (1960) and Archbishop Desmond Tutu (1984). It is events such as the orderly transition from apartheid to majority rule in South Africa that leads me to use the words 'delayed success' in the title to this book.

After Mandela

Mandela stepped down from the presidency in June of 1999, to be replaced by his Deputy-President, Thabo Mbeki. He is the son of Govan Mbeki, an active ANC leader who was arrested and charged with treason following the Rivonia raid, and subsequently spent 23 years in prison, most on Robben Island. A brief sketch of Thabo Mbeki – especially in relation to his disastrous role in the HIV-AIDS controversy – can be found in a recent publication.[26] His presidency was not a success. 'As disillusionment with Mbeki's leadership gathered momentum – over AIDS, Zimbabwe, economic policy and his dictatorial habits – there was growing talk in ANC circles about the possibility of replacing Mbeki with Jacob Zuma … For a period of five years, South Africa was dragged through a morass of intrigue and infighting that threatened to undermine its young democracy.'[27] Mbeki's relationship with the ANC – that continued to win over 60% of the vote at national elections – soured to the point that he was considered by its National Executive Committee to be no longer fit to lead the nation. Reluctantly he stepped down in 2008, to be replaced, after a 7–month interregnum under Kgalema Motlanthe, by Jacob Zuma.

Zuma won the election of 2009 for the ANC. His past troubles (he is still facing 700 unsettled counts of corruption, fraud, money-laundering and racketeering, not to mention spending hundreds of millions of public money on his private residence) were set aside at this point. But his presidency has continued to be colourful, to say the least. He has also expressed worrisome opinions about such issues as the meaning of democracy. In 2012 he told the South African National Assembly that minority groups had fewer rights than the majority – a betrayal of all that Mandela fought for. He has failed to reverse the prevalence of HIV / AIDS. Four years after Mbeki stepped down, the incidence among adults (aged 15 – 49) remains – at 18% – the fourth highest in the world. Yet the number of people receiving (free) anti-HIV drugs has risen from 50,000 in 2004 to 3 million in 2016.[28] Moreover in 2010 South Africa spent 6% of its GDP on education, just above that of Austria, France and Netherlands. Jacob Zuma won re-election in 2014, but he has not given South Africa the leadership it deserves. The ANC, of which he is president, is leading the country on a downward path.

South Africa Today

In scientific achievement, South Africa is streets ahead of any other African country. In 2015 the five top African scientific institutions, according to the respected international journal *Nature*, were still all in South Africa (University of Cape Town, University of the Witwatersrand, Stellenbosch University, University of KwaZulu-Natal, and University of Pretoria). Having elite universities is fine, but education for the majority has gradually been deteriorating. Improving lives takes time, and self-government and democracy are not enough. South Africa has had two decades of it. India, which achieved independence and democracy at about the same time that serious *apartheid* began in South Africa (1947 vs 1948), still has, after more than half a century of development, one of the highest rates of poverty in the world; its GDP per capita is just a fifth that of South Africa (which at $13,225 is pretty good by African standards). Yet poverty and unemployment in South Africa remain high (the Gini index [29] was 63 in 2005), and the difference in living standard between whites and blacks is stark. The former had a life expectancy in 2009 of 71 years, the latter of just 48 years. On average, though, South Africans are the most optimistic people in the world. An Ipsos MORI poll in 2013 found that 75 percent of South Africans were positive about their prospects – the highest percentage across 20 countries.[30]

A realistic assessment of South Africa today notes that 'As a rule of thumb, anything controlled or touched by the ANC – "the liberation movement" – works very poorly or doesn't work at all. On top of that, abuses of democracy pile one upon the other. Crime and insecurity rack the land, the economy fails, unemployment and inequality grow. The very integrity of the nation state is increasingly at stake.'[31] Yet the author of this doom-laden scenario continues with the observation that 'Somewhere out ahead of us lies a regime change towards a form of government which is closer to South Africa's underlying sociological realities. My own hope – supported by a certain optimism – is that … this will ultimately see the consolidation of liberal democracy here in South Africa.'[32] Given the poor leadership of Mbeki and Zuma, the reader might reasonably consider this chapter to reflect 'declining' rather than 'delayed' success, which is why it is entitled 'diminishing expectations'. South Africa may well have a bright future once more, but this depends on a crucial change of leadership. This happened in 2018, just as this book was going to press. South Africans – and the rest of the world – eagerly await the outcome of Cyril Ramaphosa's presidency.

End Notes

[1] quoted, for good reason, by Sterling Seagrave in *The Marcos Dynasty* (Macmillan, London, 1989) p 15

[2] Curtin (1965) p 89 *et seq*

[3] see http://www.nelsonmandela.org/omalley/index.php/site/q/03lv01538/04lv01646/05lv01658.htm

[4] for a brief biography of this man, see Pasternak (2012) pp 130-131

[5] Lamb (1983) p 337

[6] de Klerk (1998) p 30

[7] Meredith (2010) p 228

[8] *ibid* p 38

[9] *ibid* p 171

[10] Segal (1963) p 17

[11] de Klerk (1998) p 53

[12] *ibid* p 74

[13] *ibid* p 166

[14] Lodge (2006) p 4

[15] Meredith (2010) p 30

[16] Wolpert (2001) p 51

[17] Lodge (2006) p 57

[18] Meredith (2010) p 103

[19] Lodge (2006) p 90

[20] *ibid* p 140

[21] Meredith (2010) p 347

[22] *ibid* p 402

[23] *ibid* p 524

[24] Lodge (2006) p 200

[25] *ibid* p 219

[26] Pasternak (2012) pp 54-56

[27] Meredith (2010) p 594

[28] Linda Nordling. A new era for HIV. South Africa has developed the biggest programme of antiretroviral therapy in the world … *Nature* **535**: 214-217 (2016)

[29] an index of 0 represents complete equality; an index of 100 complete inequality; see http://en.wikipedia.org/wiki/Gini_coefficient

[30] see:http://www.telegraph.co.uk/finance/personalfinance/10513756/Britons-emerge-from-recession-less-materialistic-but-more-stressed.html

[31] Johnson (2015) p 239

[32] *ibid* p 246

Chapter Thirteen
LESSER EXPECTATIONS: SENEGAL

The reader may wonder why I have chosen Senegal and Nigeria as illustrative of countries with lesser expectations. Why not oil-rich nations like Angola or Gabon? Why not Kenya or Tanzania? The answer is that quite a number of countries might be included in this category, and I have to be selective. Nigeria (chapter 14) is the most populous nation, and the largest oil producer, on the continent: it merits a chapter on its own. As regards Kenya and Tanzania, each nation and its leaders were mentioned several times in chapter 8. I selected Senegal because I consider that at least *one* of the countries in this book should be an Islamic one (the most obvious of these, like Algeria or Egypt, being outside the scope of 'Africa South of the Sahara').

Geography

At the most westerly point of Africa (indeed of the entire Old World) three rivers empty into the Atlantic. They are more or less parallel to each other at their mouths, flowing east to west. To the north is the Sénégal, to the south is the Casamance and in between is the Gambia. The region known as Senegal (just under 200,000 sq km or 76,000 sq miles) lies just south of the Sahara and stretches from the Sénégal River in the north to the Casamance in the south. It forms a kind of horse shoe around the independent country of The Gambia (just over 10,000 sq km or 4,000 sq miles) through which the Gambia flows. Various kingdoms have emerged here over the centuries and the easternmost of these had become part of the Ghana Empire by the end of the first millennium (chapter 4). As Ghana was replaced by the empire of

Mali and then by that of Songhay, the area under imperial control gradually expanded westwards as far as the Atlantic shore. Here one of its vassal states, situated in the north-western part of present-day Senegal, was that of Jolof which itself included the kingdom of Cayor (mentioned in chapter 6). The people of Jolof were (and are) largely Wolof, who make up the majority of present-day Senegalese. The remainder are Fula and Serer. Following the Almoravid incursions from North Africa in the eleventh century, the whole area became Islamized, as it is to this day.

Colonial Period

Early during the seventeenth century the Dutch West India Company occupied the western tip of Senegal around the island town of Gorée to form the Dutch colony of Senegambia. The French wrested this trading post (an important harbour for the export of slaves) from the Dutch in 1677 and gradually subjugated the entire region, except for the land to either side of the Gambia River which became a British colony. The first capital, dating back to the seventeenth century, was Saint Louis, at the mouth of the Sénégal River. Over the next two centuries French influence extended eastwards into the present nations of Mali, Burkina Faso and Niger, as well as northwards (present-day Mauretania) and southwards (present-day Guinea, Côte d'Ivoire and Benin). The whole region became known as French West Africa (*Afrique occidentale française*), with its administrative centre at Saint Louis. By the middle of the nineteenth century Senegal was the largest European colony in West Africa. The capital was moved to Dakar, inland of Gorée, early in the twentieth century. The origin of the word Dakar (that continued as the capital of Senegal after the break up of French West Africa) is obscure, but may be the result of a misunderstanding, like the origin of Nyasa, mentioned in chapter 7. A French colonial officer is said to have pointed at the site of the new capital, expecting the locals to tell him the name of the Wolof settlement in this area. They, on the other hand, thought he was asking about the trees in the foreground and replied '*daxar*', the Wolof term for the tamarind tree.[1]

Senegal was fortunate in having as governor between 1854 and 1864 an outstanding administrator. He was General Louis Faidherbe and it was he who was responsible for the establishment of colonies beyond Senegal. The settling of French farmers and business men in Algeria at this time led Faidherbe to consider encouraging similar immigration into Senegal and other parts of French West Africa. However he felt that the climate in West Africa would deter Europeans. And he was right. The region sits within the tropical rain belt, where infectious diseases like malaria (against which the native population has developed some resistance) are endemic, as described in chapter 5. For good reason has West Africa been termed 'the white man's grave'. The climate in North Africa where the French arrived in large numbers during the nineteenth century is relatively benign, as it is in Southern Africa where the Dutch and British have been settling since the seventeenth century. So instead of encouraging Frenchmen to work in Senegal, Faidherbe decided to improve the educational opportunities for locals, in order eventually to be able to run their own affairs (in a French manner). He established schools, not only for those who had been converted to Christianity, but for Muslims as well. Schools within the four communes that had been established around the main towns of Dakar, Gorée, Rufisque and Saint Louis provided an education identical to that in France. Schools in the rest of the country, known as the protectorate, taught subjects more suitable for the African population – farmers rather than administrators. Much of the organisational structure that Faidherbe established endured right up to independence in 1960.

France granted rights to some of those living in its colonies more generously than any other nation. Anyone born in one of the four communes of Senegal was automatically granted French citizenship, irrespective of whether they were European, mixed (mulatto) or African. Those born in the protectorate enjoyed few civil or political rights under the code of *indigénat*, which was not repealed until after the Second World War. Not only could anyone born in one of the communes vote in local (Senegalese) and national (French) elections, they could themselves stand as a candidate. In 1914, Blaise Diagne became the first African to be elected to serve as a deputy in the French National Assembly (black deputies from the Caribbean had won election to France's parliament already a century earlier). Diagne was re-elected without break over the next twenty years, became a member of eight cabinets and was twice appointed as undersecretary of state for the colonies, a position that gave him authority over the governor general himself. Another African, who would not only become a deputy but would serve as Senegal's first president for twenty years, was a quiet intellectual of the Serer clan. His name was Léopold Sédar Senghor.

Léopold Sédar Senghor

The son of a wealthy and influential businessman, Sédar was born in the coastal town of Joal, south of Dakar, on 9 October 1906. His family were Christian, and when the six-year old Sédar received his First Communion, most of Joal – including its Muslims – joined in the procession. At the age of eight Sédar was accepted as a boarder at the nearest mission school. From here he hoped to proceed to a seminary in France to study for the priesthood. It was not to be. When, at eighteen, he was due to graduate, Father Lalouse, one of the Fathers of the Holy Spirit who ran the school, told Sédar that he was not cut out for the priesthood. Instead he recommended him for acceptance at a recently-opened lycée in Dakar. Sédar was devastated and extremely angry. Lalouse, he felt, had discriminated against him because of his colour (which was not the case), and he bore a grudge against the teacher for the rest of his life. In fact, Lalouse's decision had two beneficial consequences: one for Sédar and one for Senegal. For Sédar it meant that he would spend the rest of his life proving, to advantage, that he was as good as any Frenchman. For Senegal it meant that the country lost a potential priest, but gained a future president. The situation reminds one somewhat of the American James McNeill Whistler seventy-five years earlier. Whistler had been admitted to the military academy at West Point, but failed his chemistry exam (he had written 'silicon is a gas') and was consequently expelled. The United States lost a potential general but gained one of the most innovative artists of the nineteenth century.

Most of the students at the Lycée Van Vollenhoven (later Lycée Lamine-Guèye) were the children of French businessmen and administrators whose parents wanted them to have an education identical to that in France. When Sédar graduated at the age of twenty-one, he was one of fifteen Africans in a school of more than a hundred pupils. But he made friends with a number of French students, one of whom was the son of the director, Aristide Prat. Sédar also worked extremely hard in order to prove himself equal to the best of the Europeans. This paid off. Director Aristide Prat recognized Sédar's potential and was determined that this most gifted pupil should have the opportunity to continue his education in France. To obtain a scholarship required the recommendation of the governor-general of the French West African Federation. Prat offered to resign if this was withheld. In the event Sédar was offered a half scholarship to study literature in Paris. His brother and sister-in-law, René and Hélène Senghor, were happy to provide the rest. On arrival, Sédar enrolled at the Sorbonne, but found the freedom to attend lectures whenever he pleased, confusing. He had been used to a strict curriculum. It was on the advice of a sympathetic professor that he switched to a more disciplined and exacting environment: he entered the Lycée Louis-le-grand as a boarding pupil.

The lycée, situated near the Sorbonne, was one of the most prestigious institutions of secondary education in the country. It was founded by the Jesuits in the sixteenth century and has educated many of the country's leading writers, artists and politicians over the years: Molière in the seventeenth century, Diderot and Voltaire, Robespierre and St Just in the eighteenth, Baudelaire and Victor Hugo, Degas and Delacroix, and Emile Durkheim in the nineteenth, Jacques Derrida and Jean-Paul

Sartre, as well as Jacques Chirac, Valéry Giscard d'Estaing and Georges Pompidou in the twentieth. Sédar flourished in the environment. He enjoyed the discipline and the work. He also made new acquaintances. Georges Pompidou shared a desk with him and remained a friend for life. Week-ends would be spent with the Pompidou family or with that of his fellow Senegalese, the deputy Blaise Diagne, who arranged for Sédar to be granted French citizenship (he was not automatically eligible since he was born outside one of the four communes in Senegal). And yet the next goal on which he had set his heart, entry into the prestigious École Normale Supérieure, was denied to him: he failed the entrance exam.

The young scholar was undeterred. He would return to the Sorbonne and study for a teaching diploma. Within a year he succeeded in obtaining the Diplôme d'Etudes Supérieures. He continued his studies (that included a dissertation on Baudelaire) and in 1935 received (admittedly at his third attempt) the *agrégation* – the highest teaching qualification for school teachers – in Grammar. Needless to say he was the first African to have achieved this. He was now well qualified to become a schoolteacher, and he was appointed to teach classics and French at a lycée in Tours, a few hours' train ride (in those days) south of Paris. The students may have been surprised to be taught their language by an African, but they were well served. 'His intellectual qualities are truly French … he has a methodical mind, serious rather than brilliant. I have the impression that he will be a professor rather than an orator … I can easily see M Senghor a professor of oriental languages,'[2] according to a report by the Inspector General of Education for French West Africa. The report was sent to the governor-general, who was still supporting Sédar financially. The funds were used to pay for a *pied a terre* in Paris that allowed the new teacher to maintain access to the facilities of the Sorbonne. These enabled him to become a professor of African languages and civilization at the École Nationale de la France d'Outre-Mer.

During his sojourns in Paris, Senghor continued his friendship with fellow students whom he had met at the Sorbonne. Two, both from the Caribbean, had become close friends. One was Aimé Césaire from Martinique, the other was Léon Damas from Guyana. A constant topic for discussion was this: how to reconcile being black with being French? To men like Blaise Diagne (as well as to most colonial administrators) assimilation was the only answer. Senghor felt differently: assimilate French culture but do not become assimilated. Together the three students proposed to make black ethnicity as acceptable as white ethnicity. They coined the word *negritude* to imply a cultural heritage that was not inferior to that of the European, though their use of the word differed. 'For Senghor it meant "the manner of self-expression of the black character, the black world, black civilisation." Césaire used the word somewhat differently. He wrote that "Negritude is simply recognition that of the fact of being black and the acceptance of that fact, of our destiny of black, of our history and our culture."'[3] Either way, they were not the first to suggest that European (and American) derision of the ability and culture of black people was unjustified. As mentioned in an earlier chapter, the late nineteenth century German anthropologist Frobenius clearly thought that cultures such as those of Europe and Africa each have merit, and to place them into some kind of hierarchy with Europe at the top was unfounded. Senghor adapted Frobenius' views to himself and to other Africans. As his biographer Janet Vaillant put it, 'Senghor was determined to integrate in himself the best of both worlds and to be comfortable in both. He understood that this would be impossible without the re-evaluation and acceptance of the core values of the Africa of his childhood. ... It would require the creation of a new person with a new voice. The voice would be neither French nor African, for the man was neither French nor African. It would be that of a new historical personage, the French Negro.'[4] Out of this, the concept of *negritude* [5] was born. It is different from Pan Africanism,[6] espoused by leaders such as W E B Du Bois in the USA and Kwame Nkrumah in Ghana. *Negritude* is a concept that recognises the innate ability of black people world-wide; Pan Africanism is a political movement designed to unite the people of continental Africa.

These were profitable years for Senghor. His thoughts on *negritude* were published in a sympathetic journal entitled *L'Etudiant Noir* (The Black Student) and he began to write poetry, which would occupy him for the rest of his life. Things changed dramatically after the invasion of France by Germany in 1940. He had been conscripted into the army and was serving as an infantryman south of Paris when his unit was captured. The Africans were separated from the rest and were about to be shot. They escaped death only because their French officer convinced their captors that such an outcome would stain Aryan honour. In a prisoner-of-war camp Senghor wrote poetry in earnest. His first anthology, *Chants d'ombre* (Songs of the Shadow, a title that can be interpreted in different ways) would be published after the war ended in 1945. Many of the poems that made up his second collection, *Hosties noires* (Black Offerings) published in 1948, were composed at this time. Being Senghor, this was not enough to satisfy him intellectually. So he read some of the works of Plato and Virgil, as well as those of the seventeenth century polymath Blaise Pascal. Goethe's works he could follow in the original German (the camp appears to have had an exceptionally good library). Released in 1942 on medical grounds, Senghor spent the rest of the war in the French resistance.

Back in Senegal in the summer of 1945, Senghor was persuaded by his friend Lamine Guèye to stand for election (as a socialist) to the National Assembly. Guèye would contest the seat allocated to the communes, and Senghor that allocated to the rest of the country. Both were elected with handsome majorities. By the end of the year Senghor was back in Paris. His political life, that would run alongside his poetry and championing of negritude for the next 35 years, had begun. Senghor was appointed a member of the constitutional committee that would advise the new president, Charles de Gaulle, on necessary reforms. He was soon asked to rewrite some of the badly expressed phrases in the proposed declaration of rights: the grammatical style of the Senegalese deputy was preferred to that of fellow Frenchmen. In his maiden speech to the National Assembly, Senghor 'showed his characteristic talents: a mastery of French rhetorical technique, a sense of humour, a knowledge of detail, and the ability to appeal to French history and tradition to argue for the African cause.'[7] The lack of interest in African affairs shown by the party (SFIO: Section Française de l'Internationale Ouvrière) to which he was attached in the National Assembly, led Senghor to found a new faction in Senegal: the Bloc Démocratique Sénégalais (BDS). This would promote socialism in an African setting (as Kwame Nkrumah would do in Ghana), it would champion the interests of French West Africa, and it would respect Christianity and Islam equally. The BDS contested the elections to the French National Assembly in 1951 and won both seats, ousting the SFIO. In France BDS was no more than a fringe party, but in Senegal the BDS became the dominant force, winning 41 out of 50 seats in local elections the following year.

Throughout the 1950s Senghor's standing as a politician grew steadily. In France he was appointed a secretary of state by Prime Minister Edgar Faure with a brief to assess the future of the overseas territories. In Senegal he created a new party, the Union Progressiste Sénégalaise (UPS). The BDS that he had launched ten years earlier with Amadou Dia, had merged with other parties, and no longer represented the founders' outlook. Dia, another socialist, and Senghor complemented each other admirably. Dia was a Wolof and a Muslim, Senghor a Serer and a Catholic (both minority groups in Senegal). More important, Dia was a brilliant lawyer who commanded votes in the communes, Senghor a romantic poet who could engage with the people in the countryside. By the time Senegal was granted independence in 1960, Senghor was the obvious choice for president with Dia as prime minister. Two years later amity between the two broke down. Dia was accused of fomenting a coup against the president, Senghor, of trying to oust the prime minister. To what extent one or other – or both – of these suppositions was correct, remains uncertain. What is clear is that Dia was tried, found guilty and imprisoned.

Senghor now stood alone. His leadership did not thrive. He relied heavily on French advice which was not always consonant with Senegal's best interests. The economy faltered. Student riots broke out. Yet Senghor kept his nerve, the country remained at peace, and he was re-elected with large majorities throughout his presidency. By the end of 1980, now past the age of seventy-five, Senghor decided to step down. He was the first African leader to do so voluntarily, a rare occurrence and one that would be repeated two decades later by another president of outstanding integrity, Nelson Mandela. Senghor retired to France where he lived for another twenty-one years in the happy company of his second wife, a Frenchwoman named Colette Hubert whom he had married after the break-up of his first marriage in the 1950s. Senghor was revered not just in Senegal, but in France as well. He had been elected to the French Academy of Moral and Political Sciences to fill the vacancy left by the death of German Chancellor Konrad Adenauer in 1967 and in 1984 an even greater honour fell to him. He was elected to the exalted Académie Française. At his installation, academician and former politician Edgar Faure told him: 'You are among those who think that poets, because they are visionaries, are qualified to lead the destinies of peoples during periods of change, when the movement of history is so rapid that one can only keep up with it by preceding it.'[8] Senegal was lucky to have had Léopold Sédar Senghor to lead it to independence.

After Senghor

Abdou Diouf, the prime minister, succeeded Senghor as president. Diouf had been appointed prime minister by Senghor in 1970, after reinstating the office that had been unfilled since Amadou Dia's fall in 1962. Diouf came from the countryside like Senghor, and like him he studied at the Sorbonne. His connection to France was strong. After serving as Senegal's president for twenty years, he was appointed secretary-general of La Francophonie, the international organisation that promotes cooperation among the French-speaking countries across the world. The 1980s continued to be as difficult for the country as the 1970s had been. Its foreign debt soared, which squeezed expenditure on domestic items like education and health. The government had received a moral boost in 1981 when Amnesty International rated Senegal among the least corrupt nations – a recognition as much of Senghor's presidency over two decades as of Diouf's first year in office. He was re-elected in 1983, 1988 and 1993, with successively decreasing majorities (83%, 70% and 58%). Diouf tried to revive Senegambia, the federation between Senegal (French) and The Gambia (British) that had existed in the eighteenth century. It didn't work any better during the 1980s than it had two centuries earlier. Continued bickering and disputes between the two countries ended the federation eight years after its second birth. In 1994 Diouf presided over the devaluation of the currency that Senegal shared with other West African countries. This resulted in a slight improvement in the economy. In 2000 (the term of president had been increased from 5 to 7 years) Diouf lost to Abdoulaye Wade, who had contested each previous election, and he stepped down gracefully without rancour or political turmoil.

Abdoulaye Wade had studied economics at the esteemed Lycée Condorcet in Paris, where writers Paul Verlaine and Marcel Proust and philosopher Henri Bergson had been pupils, and had gone on to teach there (like Jean-Paul Sartre before him). Wade's political career began with persuading Senghor to found the Senegalese Democratic Party (*Parti Démocratique Sénégalais*: PDS) in 1974. Though he, like Diouf and Senghor, espoused socialism throughout his life, his party distanced itself from outright left-wing views that emerged during the 1970s. Wade was re-elected in 2007, amidst protest from the losing candidates and was not confirmed in office until the following year (the same thing would happen in Ghana two years later). Accusations of corruption and injustice detracted from his time in office, but he was able to persuade the Constitutional Council to allow him to run for a third term in 2012. He was defeated by Macky Sall and, like Diouf, accepted his defeat without protest. Sall, unlike his three predecessors as president, is an engineer by training.

Senegal Today

The country's economy is still weak in comparison with other sub-Saharan countries. It relies heavily on donor assistance and foreign investment. But its GDP has been growing at an increasing rate over the last four years: not as spectacularly as some Asian economies, but up from an annual increase of 2.6% in 2011 to one of 4% in 2013. Any country within the European Union would be delighted had it been able to achieve such figures. Because of a rising population, however, the GDP per capita remains low (a mere $2,577 in 2016). Senegal's main export is no longer in peanuts, though they continue to be grown for local consumption, but phosphates, fertilisers and fish. If the exploration for iron ore and oil currently under way is successful, it could provide a big boost to the country. At present, though, power supplies are unreliable, the cost of living and unemployment are relatively high, and migration to Europe is on the increase. The nation suffers from having one of the world's highest rates of infant and maternal mortality (35th and 28th respectively). Life expectancy at birth is no higher than 60 years. These are some of the reasons why I consider Senegal to be a nation of lesser expectation.

Yet the soubriquet of 'delayed success' is valid for three reasons. First, because Senegal's record on education, the hallmark of a potentially successful nation, is good. In 2010 the government spent 5.6% of its GDP on education – one of the highest in Africa, if not the world, and above that of Canada or the USA. The literacy rate, however is still only around 50% (60% male, 40% female) which is eclipsed by the four countries (Botswana, Ghana, Rwanda and South Africa) discussed in the previous four chapters.[9] So there is a way to go. The second reason for inclusion of Senegal is its praiseworthy record on curbing HIV/AIDS as a result of Abdou Diouf's successful safe sex campaign in the late 1980s, a time during which countries like South Africa were denying the very link between HIV infection and AIDS.[10]

The third and main reason for including Senegal is the democratic nature of government. No coups, no rule by the military, no Islamic terrorist attacks (fingers crossed). Instead, peaceful elections (every seven years for president, every five years for the national assembly), with more than twenty opposition parties allowed to participate. The result has been a series of stable governments: twenty years under Léopold Senghor, twenty years under Abdou Diouf and twelve years under Abdoulaye Wade. Stability alone does not necessarily presage good government. Togo has had 48 years of the same family as president (following a military coup) and is about to elect the present incumbent for another 5 years. But the country's GDP/capita is no better than that of Rwanda, and its record on education, health and corruption is considerably worse. So far as Senegal is concerned, I confess that it is the character of its first president after independence that leads me to assess its future optimistically. Léopold Sédar Senghor, poet, writer and astute politician gave his nation a legacy that is not easily erased. The country's neighbour, Mali, has a notable past. Senegal has a promising future.

End Notes

[1] Dilley and Eades (1994) p xviii

[2] Vaillant (1990) p 121

[3] *ibid* p 244

[4] *ibid* p 128

[5] Senghor (1977)

[6] see, for example, George B N Ayittey: The United States of Africa: A Revisit, *Annals of the American Academy of Political and Social Science* **632**: 86-102, 2010; also published by Sage Publications Inc; see http://www.jstor.org/stable/27895950 for a summary

[7] Vaillant (1990) p 206

[8] *ibid* p 339

[9] the figures in this section are taken from the current CIA Yearbook: https://www.cia.gov/library/publications/the-world-factbook/geos/sg.html

[10] Pasternak (2012) pp 54-56

Chapter Fourteen
LESSER EXPECTATIONS: NIGERIA

A Visit to Ibadan

Clutching my yellow fever vaccination card I made my way through the teeming (and steaming: this was thirty years ago) airport at Lagos to look for my contact. It was my first visit to sub-Saharan Africa and I was somewhat apprehensive. Eventually we were crawling through the jammed streets: Lagos was well on its way to becoming the largest city on the entire continent. We were heading for Ibadan, where its university – the oldest in Nigeria – had invited me to act as external examiner in biochemistry for medical students in their final pre-clinical year.

Next morning I visited the Professor of Biochemistry in his department. 'Did you sleep well after your long road trip yesterday?', he asked. I replied positively, not wishing to mention the lack of running water or the infrequency of electric lighting in the guest quarters. 'I have bad news for you', the professor continued: 'you will not see any of the candidates, as the university has been closed on account of some student problems. In fact no student has sat the exam, so there are no papers for you to look at either.' Since my expenses had all been paid, I was less put out than he seemed to suppose.

We discussed some research that the professor was planning. He asked me whether I could send him certain biochemical reagents. 'I will be happy to do so, but you understand that their efficacy is lost at ambient temperatures'. 'We will of course store them in the refrigerator', he said pointing proudly. 'But the electricity supply here seems rather erratic' I replied. 'It is true that we have no generator here, but when the electricity goes off I send a boy, with some *naira* in his hand, to ask the Chemistry Department to switch their generator output over to our department'. 'Aha' I said, wondering silently what happened when the electricity went off in the middle of the night over a long week-end.

My host, a kind and sensitive man, was obviously embarrassed by the absence of students. He invited me to dinner at his house and introduced me to the Dean of the Medical School, a brother of the then Bishop of Birmingham in England. Next day the Dean showed me round the university hospital in the centre of nearby bustling Ibadan. The patients whom I saw lying passively on their cots reminded me of the Berber patients in Ouarzazate whom I had encountered thirty years earlier (see Prelude). I tried to be as positive as possible to the Dean concerning the conditions in the hospital that, as in the university, suffered from an inconstancy of running water and electricity.

Next, the professor wondered whether perhaps I would like to visit a research institute not too far from campus. I accepted gladly. Driving into the International Institute of Tropical Agriculture reminded me of entering the National Institutes of Health in Bethesda, Maryland, USA. Gone was the dust and squalor of Ibadan. Instead, neatly trimmed and verdant lawns lined the drive up to the institute. Inside it was pleasant and cool. The laboratories were clean, with machines running smoothly and no shortage of running water. Half the staff was African: most were Nigerians, just like those at the University of Ibadan. The difference was that here water was pumped from the nearby river and purified; electricity was generated from the same source. I had earlier wondered why in the town, on the very edge of the rain forest, rainwater could not be conserved. The reason, I had been told, was inefficiency and corruption.

Such explanations for the lack of infrastructure endure in today's Nigeria. Hence the title of this chapter.

Beginnings

Nigeria is in some ways the Greece of West Africa. Around three thousand years ago, even before Athens was giving birth to European culture, there grew around the village of Nok, in the central region of present-day Nigeria, a people of remarkable ability. Not only had they discovered how to smelt iron in novel ways, they produced the most sophisticated terracotta statues known to man. But just as Athens began to decline over the centuries as a result of wars and foreign occupation (first the Romans, then the Ottoman Turks), so did the populace of Nok. This began around AD 200 for reasons that are still unclear. Within the next thousand years the area had become one of the Hausa states that were under repeated threat from its neighbours. The analogy continues into the twentieth century. A coup d'état by five colonels of the Greek army in 1967 resulted in martial rule for the next seven years. In Nigeria in 1966, just six years after achieving independence, a coup by officers from the Igbo-dominated south of the country toppled the government. One of their number, Colonel Odumegwu Ojukwu, declared the southern province of Biafra a separate state. After four years of bitter fighting (a million died), the government (led by General Yakubu Gowon) defeated the secessionists and Nigeria became a single nation once more. Since then it has had twelve heads of government – six generals and six civilians. Over this time Greece had fifteen different prime ministers. Today Greece is the 'poor man' (there are others) of Western Europe because of dishonesty among the rich. Nigeria is one of many poor states in tropical Africa for exactly the same reason.

Ethnic Diversity

I mentioned earlier that present-day Nigeria is home to 250 different ethnicities, speaking 500 languages. To sketch the histories of these diverse people in a single chapter is impossible. Instead, I will try to summarise. To do this, imagine Nigeria's internal boundaries as a large Y: the left diagonal and vertical below it represent the Niger River, flowing in from the north west (in Niger) and emptying due south into the Gulf of Guinea; the right diagonal – lowered a bit towards the horizontal – represents the Benue River which erupts in the Cameroon Highlands to the east and joins the Niger River at the centre of the Y.

The segment to the north of the two rivers (the upper part of the Y) becomes increasingly arid as one moves northwards. By the time the northern border of Nigeria (with Niger) is reached, the land is virtually desert. At the eastern end of the border lies Lake Chad. The two segments to the south are largely savannah, except near the coast where the land is essentially tropical rain forest.

Northern Nigeria, above the Niger and the Benue, has been populated predominantly by Hausa-speaking tribes in the west and centre of the country and by Kanuri-speakers to the east, with some Fulani-speakers in each area (as well as Arabs). In the south, the main tribes to the west of the Niger are Yoruba; to the east they are Igbo (Ibo). Several of these tribes – the Yoruba in particular – consider themselves as having originated beyond the Sahara, in Egypt or Arabia (like the Tutsis of Rwanda). The Fulani, too, are thought to have migrated from Egypt, though some writers have proposed quite bizarre origins, namely that some are of Indian, Jewish, Malayan, or Phoenician stock.[1] All now have black skin, but as mentioned in chapter 3, this is an acquired feature. The Yoruba have been living in their present areas for at least a thousand years, as have the Hausa; the Fulani arrived somewhat later.

Northern Nigeria probably became islamised during the thirteenth century.[2] Certainly by 1513, when Muhammad I Askia extended his Songhay Empire as far east as Kano in the centre of Hausaland, Islam would have been the predominant religion. Hausaland comprised a number of individual states that sometimes supported, at other times attacked, each other. The severest onslaught, however, came from one of their subject tribes. In 1804 Othman dan Fodio, a Fulani sheikh, initiated a *jihad* against the Hausa rulers that eventually ended their individual hegemony. Hausaland became united as the Sokoto Caliphate, with its capital at Sokoto, an old town at the western extremity of the kingdom. Within exactly a century it lost its independence. The British, having been granted the entire area of present-day Nigeria at Bismarck's West Africa conference of 1885, decided to make good on their newly acquired territories, and invaded the caliphate from the south, over which they already had control. A force of less than a thousand, mainly African soldiers, took Kano in 1903. The caliphate surrendered, and although the sultan was allowed to retain his religious position into recent times, his authority over administrative matters was gone.

To the east of Hausaland, the Kanuri had established themselves in the kingdoms of Kanem and Bornu. Just as the territory occupied by ancient Ghana, Mali and Songhay shifted over the centuries, so did those of Kanem and Bornu. The former, said to have stretched from the Niger to the Nile at one time, eventually contracted into the region around Lake Chad. The latter, initially a province within Kanem, grew into the Bornu Empire at the end of the fourteenth century. Like Sokoto, it became a caliphate in the nineteenth. Warring between the various kingdoms within (as well as without) present-day Nigeria had been continuous over the centuries.

Only after the unification of Sokoto and Bornu, together with Yorubaland and the Igbo territories in the south by the British in 1914, were the divisions between these ethnicities, with their different religions (Islam in the north, Christian, part-animist, in the south), papered over: the colony of Nigeria was born. Just as its boundaries had been drawn pretty much at random by the trader and entrepreneur (Sir) George Goldie, so its very name was chosen not by its people, but was casually suggested by Flora Lugard, wife of Nigeria's first Governor-General.[3] In 1947 the three regions – north, west and east – were amalgamated under a federal government based at Lagos. One of the aims had been to rectify the imbalance between the economies of the south and the north. In 1910, for example, the south (then a single region) exported goods worth £4.3 million, while exports from the north amounted to a mere £200,000. This meant that the north relied on subsidies from the south and, what was worse for the colonial power, a sizeable grant from England.[4] But the central government was weak, and the regional administrative centres strong. 'It was a recipe for disaster,'[5] or as a son of Nigeria put it: 'Nigeria is a crippled state. It was crippled from the beginning by the nature of its colonial creation.'[6]

Independence

The three regions became four (Mid-west was inserted between Western and Eastern) at independence in 1963. During 1976, when Major-General Olusegun Obasanjo became head of state in Nigeria's third coup (he would return in a civilian role to become President from 1999 to 2007), the country was divided into twelve states, then nineteen. The number rose to thirty in 1991, then to thirty-six in 1996. None of this tinkering made any difference. The animosity between Islamic north and Christian south endures. Moving the seat of the federal government from the old capital of Lagos in the south to Abuja in the centre of the country in 1991 has not united the nation either. The transition from mostly military rule to democratically elected presidents after 1999 has been beneficial, but the leaders themselves have been largely ineffectual.

The last military ruler, General Sani Abacha who was in power from 1993 to 1998, was not so much ineffectual as malign. Opposition to his edicts was silenced. Political parties and trade unions were banned. Former president Olusegun Obasanjo was jailed. The wife of Moshood Abiola who won the 1993 election but was denied office, was murdered. The writer and activist Ken Saro-Wiwa, who had campaigned on behalf of the people living in the Niger delta that was being polluted by the oil industry, was executed by hanging. Abacha himself deprived the government of millions of dollars by initiating a fraudulent exchange rate for himself and his cronies. The writer Chinua Achebe has stressed the inadequacy of Nigeria's leaders time and again. In conversation with the Peter Cunliffe-Jones in 1999, Achebe was clear that there is nothing basically wrong with the Nigerian character, with Nigerian land, or with the climate. 'The Nigerian problem' he said, 'is the unwillingness or inability of its leaders to rise to the responsibility, to the challenge of personal example which are the hall marks of true leadership … poor leadership is still the case today.'[7]

You might think that the discovery of oil in the region of the Niger delta during the 1950s would have made Nigeria one of the most successful nations on the continent. Between 1959 and 1960 oil had contributed 1% to the government's revenues. By 1998 – 1990 this had risen to over 97%.[8] In many ways the exploitation of oil has had the reverse effect. First, it was probably in the minds of the Igbo secessionists that led to the disastrous Biafran war of 1967-70. Second, it has had an unequal effect on the population. The powerful have grown richer, the disadvantaged have suffered, largely as a result of pollution: 'The people of the delta are poor; they are less likely to go to a school, see a doctor, than those almost anywhere else in Nigeria. The people cannot farm or fish … the waters are slicked with oil, and the air is choked with fumes. … Next to (a Chevron platform for pumping oil to ships offshore) I saw a row of unadorned huts in the sand: the village (had) no electricity, no school or clinic, no running water, and no bridge to connect it to anywhere. Yet this place made Nigerian soldiers and politicians wealthy….'[9]

Today, the fortunes of the country are slowly being turned around. The election of 2015, in which the opposition leader Muhammadu Buhari defeated the charismatic Goodluck Jonathan, was the most trustworthy in modern times. The new incumbent, a former general, may be just the person to eliminate the villainous Boko Haram insurgents. He is boosting agriculture, telecommunications and services to offset the decline in revenues from oil. Nigeria's resources, mineral as well as agricultural, are among the highest in Africa (chapter 5). Its most valuable resource, of course, is its human population. Yet by current criteria it has some way to go in order to achieve its true potential. As I have indicated in this brief account, it is corruption [10] and poor leadership that have held it back. In terms of GDP per capita, for example, Nigeria is still one of the poorest in sub-Saharan Africa. The life expectancy, at less than 53 years, is one of the lowest, due partly to the fact that the death rate from HIV was the highest in the world in 2014. It is for all these reasons that Nigeria should be viewed as a country of lesser expectations than ones like Botswana, Ghana or Rwanda.

Conclusion

The six countries I have selected in chapters 9 to 14 illustrate the fact that some African nations *do* have a future (with a number of provisos as far the last three are concerned). They have little in common except that all are sub-Saharan. This is deliberate. First because it is black Africa that has received the strongest accusations of past failure and is therefore the focus for this book. Second, because I wanted to explore countries whose paths to potential success have all been different.

Botswana is an example of a nation that has succeeded because of a fortunate blood-line in some of its elected leaders – from Khama III to Seretse Khama to Ian Khama (with intervening presidents of high calibre). This is pretty unique in a democracy. Ghana is more typical. It is one of several nations that found the way to achieve democratic government only within the last quarter of a century, but is now steering to success faster than any other. Despite – more likely because of – Paul Kagame's authoritarian rule, Rwanda is prospering in several regards, and there is a fair chance that it will continue to do so. South Africa is exceptional. Prior to 1994 it was by far the most successful economy on the continent, but 80 percent of its population had no vote. The way that the majority became enfranchised at this point without bloodshed is remarkable. It illustrates the potential for beneficial change in a sub-Saharan country if but two of its leaders have integrity and courage. So far as Senegal and Nigeria are concerned, the first now needs economic growth, the second requires an end to inept and corrupt leadership

End Notes

[1] Burns (1972) p 49

[2] *ibid* p 47

[3] Cunliffe-Jones (2010) p 73

[4] *ibid* p 72

[5] *ibid* p 82

[6] Osaghae (1998) p x

[7] Cunliffe-Jones (2010) p 24

[8] Osaghae (1998) p 20

[9] Cunliffe-Jones (2010) p 35

[10] Transparency International rated Nigeria worse than Ethiopia or Senegal, but not as bad as the worst in sub-Saharan Africa for 2016: https://www.transparency.org/news/feature/corruption_perceptions_index_2016

Chapter Fifteen
SYNTHESIS: LUNCH IN CALABRIA

This narrative began in Kigali, deep in the fields and forests of central Africa. Now I am sitting in one of my favourite spots, in the high Sila plateau of Calabria, where it is cool even in August. We are lunching in the shade of a tall *Pseudotsuga menziesii* (Douglas fir) that my host planted on the birth of his first son forty-six years ago. The pines planted to mark the birth of the host's father, and then of himself, stand nearby. It is an idyllic place. The fare is simple, but delicious. Every item is fresh from his farmlands: from the *caccio caballo* cheese and the salami beforehand, to the homemade *orechiette* with broccoli, the prosciutto with zucchini and gratin potatoes that have been specially cultivated for export to Sicily, followed by a cake made with olive oil, not butter. We eat off plates adorned with the crest of our host's ancient family; his monogram is on our napkins and on the bottles of wine from his estates. The meal is served by a uniformed, white-gloved Filipino. The air is fresh and clean, and everyone has an appetite. The shores of Africa may be no more than 250 miles away, yet we are a world totally removed from the stresses of sub-Saharan Africa that have formed the subject of this book. Nevertheless the conversation turns to that very theme. I explain the African project on which I have been working for a number of years to one of the guests. As we leave, the prince (he is a member of the British royal family) turns to my partner and says to her 'Charles is a brave man'. I know she agrees, because she assumes that he really means 'foolish'.

In the evening we go to stay at 'Old Calabria', an eighteenth century house a few miles away that belonged to a Baron

Barracco and is now a museum with guest accommodation. The name pays homage to the eccentric British writer and traveller Norman Douglas whose *Old Calabria* describes the journeys, mainly on foot, that he made throughout this region in the early years of the twentieth century. In fact the whole area is called a literary park in recognition of writers like Henry Swinburne, Vivant Denon, Alexandre Dumas, François Lenormant, George Gissing and Edward Lear, all of whom visited the Sila. The house is set away from the nearest village. We wake to the sound of cow bells. In the evening a crackling log fire is lit for us in the drawing room: at more than a thousand metres above sea level, the nights begin to turn cold at this time of year. The room is lined with pictures of the previous owner's race horses. The walls in the rest of the mansion are covered with prints and water colours of Calabrian wild life, classical figures and imaginary beasts. A faint scent of pine permeates the house.

On return to the palazzo down on the Tyrrhenian coast where we are spending the summer (and I am writing this book), we are in the music room. Our hostess has invited a few friends to listen to a young American sing Handel and Schubert, accompanied on the piano by our host. Clarissa is a student of music with a beautiful, clear voice: her pitch is perfect. Another pleasant moment and a reminder of the European culture we take for granted. The three occasions I have recounted have been most enjoyable, but I have a sense of *fin de siècle*. Are we witnessing the end of an era similar to that of a hundred years ago, on another sunny August day? I do not mean that the European nations are about to embark on another war, but all is not well.

Unemployment here in Calabria is the highest in Italy: it has nearly doubled in just the last two years, and a fifth of Calabrese are now out of work. Interference by 'Ndrangheta Mafiosi doesn't help. The situation is not much better elsewhere in Italy, and it is even worse in the rest of southern Europe, from Portugal to Greece. The single currency enjoyed by eighteen of the twenty-eight nations that constitute the European Union (EU) is not working. Nor is the EU itself. As long as it was simply the EEC

(European Economic Community), it served its purpose – to encourage free trade between member states – pretty well. The (unelected) bureaucrats of Brussels then had delusions of grandeur: a federal Europe, similar to the United States of America that would out-perform the likes of China. Some European ministers had dreamt of federalism from the very start, but had been careful to conceal their ambitions from the populace until it had voted (positively) on it. As Jean Monnet, one of the architects, said 'Europe's nations should be guided towards a super state without their people understanding what is happening....'[1] Negative votes by countries such as France and the Netherlands were disregarded by their heads of government who – besotted with the idea of a United Europe – were also under immense pressure from the architects of that illusion in Brussels. The Treaty of Lisbon, signed by the leaders of all 28 nations in 2007, effectively established the European Union as a self-governing entity

Comparison with the United States is false. The original thirteen colonies of North America had a common heritage and purpose, whereas the nations of Europe have quite separate histories. As the Irish columnist Fintan O'Toole puts it, 'There's an obvious reason for this difference (between the USA and the European Union): Europe's inherent and distinctive diversity. Europe's identity is that there is no single European identity.'[2] This is because Europe's nations have waxed and waned in a manner unique to each country. Take the four dominant member states of the EU: Italy, Germany, France and Britain. Italy was at its height under early Roman emperors such as Hadrian, but has been declining ever since. German-speaking peoples were united under Charlemagne in 800. Their cultural achievements dominated Europe throughout the eighteenth and nineteenth century. The German chancellor in 1933 promised his people a Reich that would endure a thousand years: it finished up in a heap of rubble just 12 years later. France reached a peak of influence under Louis XIV but was unable to maintain it. A century on, Napoleon restored the nation's predominant position, but that too fizzled out within two decades. Britain was the leading nation in the nineteenth century but has been losing power over the last half century or so. Nation states may be made up of humans, but they are unable to control the destiny of their creations. So the idea by the architects of the European Union, that the sum of the participating nations would be greater than its parts was an illusion. The result has been the exact opposite.

Europe's proud record of democracy is being eroded. According to Croatian philosopher Srecko Horvat, 'If we don't restore democracy in Europe, the consequences could be dire.'[3] And as Acemoglu and Robinson [4] imply, it is democracy that leads to economic success. But instead of becoming more competitive globally, Europe is declining. Its growth rate has been hovering near zero for the last two years – worse than that of Asia, North America, South America or Africa. The economically most successful nation in Europe in 2016 (apart from Luxembourg) was Norway (Table 1) and it is outside the European Union. The leaders of the Eurozone countries, Germany and France, don't even feature in the top ten. The introduction of the euro as common currency was doomed to failure. When Bernard Connolly, head of the European Monetary System, National and Community Monetary Policies Unit at the European Commission, pointed out the folly of its establishment,[5] he was promptly sacked. By 2016 the British people had had enough. They voted by a narrow margin to leave the EU. I urge the EAC [6] ECOWAS,[7] COMESA,[8] SADC [9] and other African economic communities to beware: the European model is not the one to follow.

There is another reason for my unease. When I spent a few weeks in Iraq in 1979, helping to set up a second medical school in Baghdad, one's religion was irrelevant. The curiosity of Islamic researchers, that had advanced science so successfully from the eighth century through to Ottoman domination in the fifteenth, had not then been eroded. Today moderate Muslims fear for their lives at the hands of aggressively militant *jihadists*. In the Middle East the Arab spring has turned into a summer of conflagration.

Africa is particularly at risk. Throughout the formerly peaceful Muslim nations in the Maghreb and the Sahel, fanatics now roam. Their ancestors favoured learning and architecture: the striking fourteenth century Sankore madrassa – its library second only to that of Alexandria – and the beautiful sixteenth century Sidi Mahmoud mausoleum in Timbuktu are examples. Both were destroyed by Ansar Dine zealots in 2012.

What is to be done about this? Individual assassins like Gavrilo Princip in Sarajevo in 1914 – though they can cause considerable loss of life (almost 40 million in this instance) – are easily disposed of. It is when men of evil intent form a group that is able to gain the support – reluctant or not – of the populace in which it operates, that is the problem. The solution is to win over the bystanders and eliminate the perpetrators through military action. None of this is happening in today's hot spots: Isil may be losing its bases in Iraq and Syria, but they are spreading to North Africa and elsewhere instead. Boko Haram in northern Nigeria, Al-Shabaab in Somalia, the Taliban in western Pakistan and Afghanistan, are all able to cause mayhem and murder with impunity because the people are cowed and the military incompetent.

However there is one example at the end of colonialism in south-east Asia, where the proposed solution worked. Not in the north-west of Viet Nam, where the French forces under Marshal de Lattre de Tassigny were too weak to counter the insurgent forces of Ho Chi Min at Dien Ben Phu in 1954. Nor a decade later when the Viet Cong, now occupying the north of the country, attacked the Vietnamese forces to the south. The outcome of that conflict is well known. The Viet Cong were supported by China, the Soviet Union and other communist states. The US, together with more than a dozen other anti-communist countries, came to the aid of the Vietnamese. The ensuing war lasted from 1965 until 1975 when Saigon, the Vietnamese capital in the south, fell to the insurgents. The 500,000-strong US force, under General William Westmoreland, had failed to win over the peasants who gave succour to Ho Chi

Min's Viet Cong bandits: not surprising, as they were bombed with napalm instead.

In another part of south-east Asia following the end of the second world war, the Malayan Communist Party was giving the British Commissioner General, Malcolm MacDonald, a hard time by terrorizing the countryside. By 1951 the British government, once more under the premiership of Winston Churchill, decided that what the country needed was a military figure as both Governor-General and Commander-in-Chief. Bernard Montgomery, then head of the army, recommended General Gerald Templer who had distinguished himself at the evacuation of the British Expeditionary Force from Dunkirk in the summer of 1940 and subsequently as Divisional Commander in Sicily and Italy. Churchill told him that 'You must have power – absolute power – civil power and military power. I will see that you get it. And when you've got it, grasp it – grasp it firmly. And then never use it. Be cunning – very cunning. That's what you've got to be.'[10]

Templer soon proved himself. He saw clearly that winning the shooting war and winning the battle for 'the hearts and minds of the people' (probably the first use of that phrase) were inseparable: 'The shooting side of the business is only 25% of the trouble and the other 75% lies in getting the people of this country behind us.'[11] On arrival Templer imposed emergency regulations that included restriction of movement and food rationing on the whole country (including, to their chagrin, the Europeans). Within two years he was able to lift the regulations for 25% of the population. The insurgency had not ceased, but it had been checked, and it would peter out over the next few years. By 1957 the country had achieved independence, and Singapore would do so in 1965 (from the Malaysian Federation, not from Britain). Singapore (just look at Tables 1, 3 and 4) has fared better than any other Asian nation. Malaysia is not far behind Japan and South Korea. It was Templer's swift and decisive action that laid the groundwork for this outcome. A colleague has pointed out that the general's name was subsequently given to a military barracks in Nairobi. After Kenya gained its independence in 1963 the base was donated to the new nation and is now part of Kenyatta University – a fitting legacy.

Could Templer's approach be applied in regard to Isil, Boko Haram, Al-Shabaab and the Taliban? Winning over the hearts and minds of the populace living under the yoke of Isil is not possible, for the fanatics are in sole charge of their territory. Nor is it likely that the alternative approach of diplomatic rapprochement between the warring parties, such as the one that brought the conflict in Northern Ireland to a reasonably satisfactory conclusion, would work. Defeat of the Isil fanatics by military means is probably the only solution. But in the other cases, Templer's approach might work. The only reason why the conflicts are ongoing is that the respective governments (Nigeria, Somalia, Afghanistan and Pakistan) are weak, and their military commanders inept.

In this book I have analysed several assumptions regarding the so-called failure by African states south of the Sahara. I am conscious that in regard to a quality like self-sufficiency, every country in the world can be said to have failed relative to the few tribes (of whom the Bushmen of the Kalahari used to be one) that have remained isolated from technological development since the Neolithic Age. But I write from the standpoint of the predominant inhabitants of this world. Over the millennia we have exercised our innate curiosity [12] to develop novel technologies on which we then depend.

The first assumption is that tropical Africa's failure – retardation may be a better word – is somehow due to a genetic incompetence of its people. Chapters 3 and 4 have exposed the falsehood of this idea. Outstanding personages in medicine (Africanus Horton) or mathematics (George Saitoti), distinguished writers (Edward Blyden) and poets (Léopold Senghor), as well as politicians with integrity and vision (Seretse Khama and Nelson Mandela – how Europe and the USA could do with such men today!) and effective rulers (Tewodros II and his successor Menilek II), appear from time to time in Africa, just as they do in Asia, the Americas or Europe. In chapter 3 I also mentioned some of the Ethiopian slaves who proved themselves to be highly effective commanders once they had thrown off their fetters. All this should surprise no one: all are members of the same species, *Homo sapiens*. Much the same point has recently been made by Ghanaian-born Kwame Anthony Appiah in his 2016 Reith Lectures.[13] A friend of Appiah's parents told me that when Anthony's father Joe married Peggy, daughter of Sir Stafford Cripps, it invoked controversy similar to that caused by Seretse Khama's marriage to Ruth Williams (chapter 9).

Nevertheless Africa – especially that south of the Sahara – clearly *has* failed in comparison with other continents. Why, for example, did the early nations of West Africa (Ancient Ghana, Mali and Songhay) or East Africa (Nubia and Great Zimbabwe) not prosper into modern times? Internal and external conflicts weakened the ruling order, just as they have done throughout the rest of the world (chapter 2). Indeed one could argue that this book should not be about black Africa's failure, but about Europe's unique success. Yet sub-Saharan Africa has failed also in comparison with Asia or the Americas. Why?

A second supposition is that sub-Saharan Africa's poor record can be explained by geography. This is certainly true so far as agriculture and the health of the people in the tropics are concerned. The countries that lie south of the tropics, like Angola, Botswana, Namibia, South Africa and Swaziland, are all economically better off. Mauritius, a sub-tropical island, is the most successful nation in the whole of Africa (for reasons of democratic government as well as geography). Zimbabwe is the exception, due to the annihilation of its agriculture under Robert Mugabe's disastrous rule for 37 years. The countries north of the tropics have also all fared better.

Famine in the tropics is a recurrent theme that has impeded population growth. A particularly striking example occurred between 1738 and 1756, when 'West Africa's greatest recorded subsistence crisis, due to drought and locusts, reportedly killed half the population of Timbuktu,'[14] a key centre of cultural development. The tropical climate is hardly conducive to rigorous mental or physical exercise. As writer Ryszard Kapuscinski, who spent over forty years living on and off in sub-Saharan Africa, says: 'Nature on this continent strikes such monstrous and aggressive poses, dons such vengeful and fearsome masks, sets such traps and ambushes, that man lives with a constant sense of anxiety about tomorrow, in unabating uncertainty and dread. Everything here appears in an inflated, unbridled, hysterically exaggerated form. ... There is nothing here to temper the relations between man and nature – no compromises, no in-between stages, no gradations. Only ceaseless struggle, battle, a fight to the finish. From birth until death, the African is on the front line, sparring with his continent's exceptionally hostile nature, and the mere fact that he is alive and knows how to endure is his greatest triumph.'[15] Climate indeed remains a major reason for lack of progress in this part of the continent (chapter 5).

What other causes might explain the fact that African advancement was relatively static for centuries, while the nations of Western Europe were developing rapidly from the seventeenth century onwards? On the one hand, Africa never had an industrial revolution (but nor did China), and that of Europe passed it by. Appeals for technological help during the nineteenth and early twentieth century were generally ignored. On the other hand, the Atlantic slave trade was obviously detrimental to the demography of West Africa. The Arab slave trade out of East Africa had an equally negative influence in that part of the continent for over a thousand years. More than 20 million Africans were removed from sub-Saharan Africa, and many more died in the process.

The impact of such losses on indigenous development has surely been significant. It has been suggested that 'without the slave trades, 72% of Africa's income gap with the rest of the world would not exist today.'[16] Yet Europe lost a third of its population as a result of the Black Death in the fourteenth century, 50 million who emigrated to America during the nineteenth century, and more than 20 million over just two decades due to Stalin and Hitler in the twentieth: each time it eventually recovered. Edward Blyden, addressing the American Colonization Society in 1880, agrees: '…notwithstanding the thousands and millions who, by violence and plunder, have been taken from Africa, she is as populous today, as she ever was'. While not exactly defending slavery, he goes on to assert – in a vein typical of nineteenth century bias – 'Africa has never lost the better classes of her people. As a rule, those who were exported … belonged to the servile and criminal classes. Only here and there, by the accidents of war, or the misfortunes of politics, was a leading African brought away.'[17] Perhaps not the 'better classes' (some of whom were doing the enslaving in the first case), but 'millions of youth and young adults who are the human agents from which inventiveness springs' [18] and who are therefore the fount of a country's success. The fear of deportation alone must have dampened any entrepreneurial spirit that enslaved or free Africans might have had. As David Livingstone wrote to the *New York Herald*, 'The strangest disease I have seen in this country (Manyema, the western part of today's Tanzania) seems really to be broken-heartedness, and it attacks free men who have been captured and made slaves.'[19] So a third supposition, that the slave trade contributed to sub-Saharan Africa's failure, is undeniable, even if it is not the primary reason (chapter 6).

The kings and chieftains of West Africa, who were responsible for the success of the Atlantic slave trade by providing the goods to Europeans, sowed the seeds of their own demise. For after the Atlantic slave trade petered out during the early years of the nineteenth century, the foreigners turned first to trade in goods and then to protection of the traders as these moved inland, by forced annexation. In East Africa the slave trade continued undisturbed for another century: abolishing it was one of the reasons for European intervention. So colonialism in West Africa resulted because the slave trade was dwindling, in East Africa because it was not. Either way, this outcome constitutes the fourth assumption: that colonialism during the nineteenth and first half of the twentieth century, at a time when European countries and the USA were forging ahead, prevented African development. As Blyden, in the speech quoted above continues, 'The opening up of Africa is to be the work of Africans … Centuries of effort and centuries of failure demonstrate that white men cannot build up colonies there.'[20] This is certainly true in so far as settling permanently by Europeans in Africa is concerned. Only along its northern and southern coastal regions (Algeria and South Africa respectively) or in the highlands of Kenya, have Europeans been able to settle. Everywhere the climate has been too inhospitable.

This was not the case in North America or Australia. Here the immigrants who arrived during the seventeenth and eighteenth century respectively, were able to subjugate the indigenous people and to occupy the entire land mass. Africa is the only continent where this was attempted but eventually failed. Africans can take pride in the fact that they, and not the Europeans, have been able to withstand the tropical climate for millennia and to improve, albeit at a slower pace, the quality of their lives. From the latter decades of the nineteenth century to the middle of the twentieth century, though, Africans had to endure the soldiers and civilian officials sent out from Europe on temporary appointments to administer their homelands. These were divided by the foreigner into arbitrary regions regardless of ancient tribal boundaries, which created tensions to this day. Moreover the African was deemed a second-class citizen, which denied him the opportunity of developing his lands, and destabilised his very life-style. To what extent more economic progress would have been achieved in the absence of the colonists, however, is a moot point (chapter 7).

The first two decades following independence showed the opposite: GDP per capita actually declined. And it is worth pointing out that Ethiopia and Liberia, neither of which was colonised by Europeans, have remained two of the poorest countries in the whole of Africa, whereas Mauritius, under colonial rule by the Dutch, the French and the British until it gained independence in 1968, is the leading African country in each of Tables 1 to 4. During the first fifty years of the twentieth century under colonial rule, the productivity of many African nations had increased because of the expansion of education and infrastructure, just as it had in India under British rule. But independence did not accelerate the process: in most cases it reversed it. The main reason for this has been the pursuit of economically-flawed policies, as well as greed among some leaders, and an insatiable reliance on foreign aid. A racist might be tempted to refer to South Africa's relative economic success in mid-twentieth century to the fact that it was ruled by Europeans, until he is reminded that 80 percent of the work force was disenfranchised. There, and elsewhere, the extractive nature – as defined by Acemoglou and Robinson – during colonial and post-colonial times has held back the citizenry of virtually every country save Bechuanaland (Botswana) and Mauritius. So a fifth assumption, that the initial decades of independence failed to improve sub-Saharan Africa's performance, is correct (chapter 8).

But don't just take my word for it. Listen to former UN Secretary-General Kofi Annan, himself a Ghanaian, addressing the Organization of African Unity Summit in Togo in 2000: 'UN Secretary-General Kofi Annan told African leaders that they are to blame for most of the continent's problems. Mr Annan said Africans were suffering because the leaders are not doing enough to invest in policies that promote development and preserve peace. He told the OAU Summit that Africa was the only region where the number of conflicts was increasing and pointed out that 33 of the world's 48 least developed countries were African. Mr Annan said African leaders bear much of the responsibility for the deterioration of the continent's security and the withdrawal of foreign aid. "This is not something others have done to us. It is something we have done to ourselves. If Africa is being bypassed, it is because not enough of us are investing in policies which would promote development and peace. We have mismanaged our affairs for decades and we are suffering the accumulated effects".'[21]

The leadership issue is crucial. Countries like Botswana, Ghana, and Rwanda are succeeding because of strong leadership. Most others have suffered from their leaders' poor qualities: 'obsession with power rather than the use of power for good, puffed-up posturing, intolerance to dissent, indifference to the welfare of their citizens, subordination of national interests to personal aggrandizement, super-inflated egos, misplaced priorities, poor judgement, reluctance to take responsibility for personal failures, and total lack of vision and understanding of even such basic and elementary concepts as "democracy", "fairness", "rule of law", "accountability" and "freedom". Some African leaders are given to vituperative utterances, outright buffoonery, stubborn refusal to learn from past mistakes, and complete absence of cognitive pragmatism' (I could of course give examples of similar failed leadership outside Africa) 'The prosperity or poverty of an African country often depends on the essence of good or bad government; it is the political leadership that creates the environment within which development proceeds.'[22] The eminent Nigerian writer Chinua Achebe, whom I mentioned in the preceding chapter, has made the same point. What is the solution?

'1. Africa's human and natural resources are more than sufficient to revive progress if a concerted, determined effort is launched within each society, and coordinated regionally.
2. Such efforts will succeed only if Africans take full charge of them and formulate policies that are geared to meet national needs rather than win international approval.
3. Participatory political structures and "good governance" are essential preconditions for effective policymaking.
4. Only Africa can reverse its decline.'

These are some of the priority propositions expressed by participants at an international conference on 'Africa's Imperative Agenda' held in Nairobi in 1995.[23] The last point is particularly relevant in view of Chinese interests in Africa's potential. It's disappointing, though, that two decades on, most of these fine words have yet to be implemented. Indeed, in several instances the situation seems to be getting worse.[24] Nevertheless they remain a blue print for the future, for the success that has for so long been delayed.

So a sixth assumption that not much will change in the foreseeable future appears to have merit. But I believe this to be wrong, and some examples of potentially successful nations were presented in chapters 9 to 14. Given good governance by leaders of integrity, parts of tropical Africa *can*, and *will*, make it. Not all of sub-Saharan Africa, of course. Just as China and India outperform Bangladesh and Nepal in Asia (and Japan and South Korea have long done so), just as in Europe there are less well performing countries like Bulgaria and Romania, just as in the USA the life of many in states like Alabama or Mississippi is not as agreeable as it is in California or New York, so in Africa nations like DR Congo and Liberia, Somalia and Sudan, are likely to remain poor for a while yet.

In other words, both parts of my title are correct: 'continued failure' applies to countries like those mentioned above, but to others like Botswana, Ghana, Nigeria, Rwanda and Senegal 'delayed success' is the correct description. For South Africa it is at present a case of 'declining success'.

It is time to take stock. China is now overtaking the USA as the major economic power in the world. India and Russia are yapping at its heels. The European Union is haemorrhaging. By the end of the twenty-first century, sub-Saharan Africa, with its huge potential of mineral wealth – provided it hasn't all been bought up by foreigners – may well overtake the northern powers to move centre-stage in world affairs. There is a second proviso. Africans need to keep the *jihadists* at bay. I fancy, though, that these will have over-sold themselves to their adherents by then. Possibly not in North Africa and the incandescent Middle East, but in sub-Saharan Africa, its Muslim citizens may once more be at peace with their non-Muslim neighbours.

Arabs and Europeans, slavers and colonisers, soldiers and commercial entrepreneurs, all secure in their perceived superiority, have strutted across sub-Saharan Africa for a thousand years. No wonder these countries have been considered a failure. Yet just as Europe emerged to world supremacy in the nineteenth century and China regained its sway in the closing decade of the twentieth century, so black Africa is surely set to find its rightful place during the twenty-first century. If culture can flourish in the unmanicured big toe of Italy, with malaria endemic well into the twentieth century, then why not in the sweaty arm-pit of tropical Africa that stretches from the Atlantic to the Indian Ocean? The 'failed' region of the world now looks more likely to be in the Middle East and North Africa. Today the message to Asians, Europeans and Americans who still view sub-Saharan Africa as a failure, is simple: 'stop patronizing, stop exploiting, and start collaborating as equals'. The people of sub-Saharan Africa themselves should take pride in their achievements in former times, and look to the future with optimism.

End Notes

[1] von Maltzahn (2016), p 69

[2] *Irish Times* Sunday Feb 21, 2016

[3] *The Guardian* Monday Feb 8, 2016

[4] Acemoglu and Robinson (2012)

[5] Bernard Connolly: *The Rotten Heart of Europe. The Dirty War for Europe's Money* (faber and faber, London, 1995)

[6] East African Community, comprising Burundi, Kenya, Rwanda, Tanzania, and Uganda

[7] Economic Community of West African States, comprising Benin, Burkina Faso, Côte d'Ivoire, Gambia, Ghana, Guinea,

Guinea-Bissau, Liberia, Mali, Niger, Nigeria, Senegal, Sierra Leone, Togo and Cape Verde

[8] Common Market for Eastern and Southern Africa, comprising Burundi, Comoros, Democratic Republic of Congo, Djibouti, Egypt, Eritrea, Ethiopia, Kenya, Libya, Madagascar, Malawi, Mauritius, Rwanda, Seychelles, Sudan, Swaziland, Uganda, Zambia and Zimbabwe

[9] Southern African Development Community, comprising Angola, D R Congo. Lesotho, Madagascar, Malawi, Mauritius, Mozambique, Namibia, Seychelles, South Africa, Swaziland, Tanzania, Zambia and Zimbabwe

[10] Cloake (1985) p 204

[11] *ibid* p 262

[12] Pasternak (2007)

[13] see http://www.bbc.co.uk/programmes/articles/ 2sM4D6LTTVlFZhbMpmfYmx6/kwame-anthony-appiah

[14] Iliffe (1995) p 69

[15] Kapuscinski (1998) p 317

[16] see https://visionaryfoundation.wordpress.com/2014/11/ 11/the-economics-of-trans-atlantic-slave-trade/

[17] Blyden (1967) p 126

[18] Rodney, p 105

[19] Jeal (2007) p 123

[20] Blyden (1967) p 127

[21] reported in Ghana's *The Daily Graphic* on July 12, 2000, p 5; quoted by Ayittey (2005) p 404

[22] Ayittey (2005) p 407

[23] quoted by Ayittey (2005) p 418

[24] see, for example, Amadou Sy (2016): *Sub-Saharan Africa: Land of Promise or Peril?* https://www.brookings.edu/research/ sub-saharan-africa-land-of-promise-or-of-peril-a-complex-narrative-of-a-continent-in-flux/

BIBLIOGRAPHY

Abaka, Edmund: *'Kola is God's Gift'. Agricultural Production, Export Initiatives & the Kola Industry of Asante & the Gold Coast. c 1820-1950* (Ohio University Press, Athens, Ohio, 2005)

Acemoglu, Daron and Robinson, James A: *Why Nations fail. The Origins of Power, Prosperity, and Poverty* (Profile Books, London, 2012)

Adams, Robert McC: *Heartland of Cities* (Aldine, Chicago, 1981)

Akyeampong, Emmanuel Kwaku (ed): *Themes in West Africa's History* (Ohio University Press, Athens; James Currey, Oxford; Woeli Publishing Services, Accra, 2006)

Allen, Captain William: *A plan for the immediate extinction of the slave trade ... ... and for the diffusion of civilisation and Christianity in Africa, by the cooperation of mammon with philanthropy* (The Athenaeum, 1849; available in Pamphlet 136 of the London Library)

Anstey, Roger: *The Atlantic Slave Trade and British Abolition 1760-1810* (Macmillan Press Ltd, London, 1975)

Armattoe, R E G: *The Golden Age of West African Civilization* (Lomeshie Research Centre, Londonderry, N Ireland, 1946)

Aslan, Reza: *No god but God. The Origins, Evolution, and Future of Islam* (William Heinemann, London, 2005)

Ayittey, George B N: *Africa Betrayed* (St Martin's Press, New York, 1992)

Ayittey, George B N: *Africa Unchained. The Blueprint for Africa's Future* (Palgrave Macmillan, New York, 2005)

Bailey, Catherine: *Black Diamonds. The Rise and Fall of an English Dynasty* (Penguin Books, London, 2008)

Bernal, Martin: *Afrocentrism and Historical Models for the Foundation of Ancient Greece.* In: David O'Connor and Andrew Reid (eds): *Ancient Egypt in Africa* (Left Coast Press, Walnut Creek, CA; publication of the Institute of Archaeology, University College London, 2003)

Blanchard, Pascal, Lemaire, Sandrine, Bancel, Nicolas and Thomas, Dominic (eds): *Colonial Culture in France since the Revolution* (translated Alexis Pernsteiner, Indiana University Press, Bloomington, IN, 2014)

Blyden, Edward W: *Christianity, Islam and the Negro Race* (1887; 2nd edition Edinburgh University Press, 1967)

Bobbitt, Philip: *The Shield of Achilles. War, Peace and the Course of History.* (Penguin Books, London, 2003)

Boucher, Maurice (ed): *Livingstone Letters 1843 1872* (The Brenthurst Press, Johannesburg, 1985)

Brett, Michael and Fentress, Elizabeth: *The Berbers* (Blackwell Publishers, Oxford, 1996)

Budge, E A Wallis: *The A Short History of the Egyptian People* (J M Dent & Sons, London, 1914)

Bulliet, Richard W: *The Camel and the Wheel* (Harvard U Press, Cambridge, MA, 1975)

Burns, Alan: *History of Nigeria* (George Allen and Unwin, 8th ed, London, 1972)

Carey, Nessa: *The Epigenetics Revolution. How modern biology is rewriting our understanding of genetics, disease and inheritance* (Icon Books, London, 2011)

Clarke, Bryan: Berber Village. *The Story of the Oxford University Expedition to the High Atlas Mountains of Morocco* (Longmans, London, 1959)

Cloake, John: *Templer: Tiger of Malaya. The Life of Field Marshal Sir Gerald Templer* (Harrap, London, 1985)

Collins, Robert O and Burns, James M: *A History of Sub-Saharan Africa* (2nd edition, Cambridge University Press, NY, 2014)

Connah, Graham: *African Civilizations. An archaeological perspective* (2nd ed, Cambridge University Press, 2001)

Conrad, Joseph: *Heart of Darkness* (Edited with Introduction and Notes by Owen Knowles; Penguin Classics, London, 2007)

Conway, Gordon, with Wilson, Katy: *One Billion Hungry. Can We Feed the World?* (Cornstock Publishing Associates, a division of Cornell University Press, Ithaca, 2012)

Corballis, Michael C: *The Recursive Mind. The Origins of Human Language, Thought, and Civilization* (Princeton University Press, Princeton, 2011)

Cunliffe-Jones, Peter: *My Nigeria. Five Decades of Independence* (Palgrave Macmillan, New York, NY, 2010)

Curtin, Philip D: *The Image of Africa. British Ideas and Action, 1780-1850* (Macmillan & Co, London, 1965)

Daniels, Anthony: *Monrovia mon amour. A visit to Liberia* (John Murray, London, 1992)

Daniels, Morna: *Côte d'Ivoire* (World Bibliographic Series volume 131, Clio Press, Oxford, England, 1996)

Davidson, Basil: *Black Star. A View of the Life and Times of Kwame Nkrumah* (Allen Lane, London, 1973)

Davidson, Basil: *West Africa before the Colonial Era. A History to 1850* (Longman, London and New York, 1998)

De Fries, Ruth: *The Big Ratchet. How humanity thrives in the face of natural crisis* (Basic Books, NY, 2014)

de Klerk, F W: *The Last Trek – A New Beginning. The Autobiography* (Macmillan, London, 1998)

de Secondat, Charles, baron de Montesquieu: *The Spirit of the Laws* (trans and edited by Anne M Cohler, Basia Carolyn Miller, Harold Samuel Stone, Cambridge University Press, Cambridge, 1989; originally published as *De l'esprit des lois* in 1748),

Derrick, Jonathan: *Africa's 'Agitators'. Militant Anti-Colonialism in Africa and the West, 1918-1939* (Columbia University Press, New York, 2008)

Dilley, R M and Eades, J S. *Senegal* (World Bibliographic Series volume 166, Clio Press, Oxford, England, 1994)

Diop, Sheikh Anta: *Precolonial Black Africa. A Comparative Study of the Political and Social Systems of Europe and Black Africa, from*

Antiquity to the Formation of Modern States (translated from the French by Harold J Salemson. Lawrence Hill Books, Brooklyn, NY, 1987)

Dunbar, Robin: *How Many Friends Does One Person Need? Dunbar's Number and other evolutionary quirks* (faber and faber, London, 2010)

Dunbar, Robin: *Human Evolution. Our Brains and Behaviour* (Oxford University Press, New York, 2016)

Dunn, D Elwood, and Holsoe, Svend E: *Historical Dictionary of LIBERIA* (African Historical Dictionaries, No 38. The Scarecrow Press Inc, Metuchen, New Jersey, 1985)

Dunn, Ross E: *The Adventures of IBN BATTUTA. A Muslim Traveler in the 14th Century* (Croom Helm, Beckenham, Kent, 1986)

Edgerton, Robert B: *Sick Societies. Challenging the Myth of Primitive Harmony* (The Free Press, New York, 1992)

Forde, Daryll (ed): *Ethnographic Survey of Africa* (International African Institute, London, 1953)

Forde-Johnston, J L: *Neolithic Cultures of North Africa. Aspects of one phase in the development of the African Stone Age Cultures* (Liverpool University Press, Liverpool, 1959)

Fuller, Dorian Q: *Pharaonic or Judaic? Models for Meroitic society and change*. In David O'Connor and Andrew Reid (eds): *Ancient Egypt in Africa* (Left Coast Press, Walnut Creek, CA; publication of the Institute of Archaeology, University College London, 2003)

Fyfe, Christopher: *Africanus Horton 1835-1883. West African Scientist and Patriot* (Oxford University Press, New York, 1972)

Gamble, Clive, Gowlett, John and Dunbar, Robin: *Thinking Big. How the Evolution of Social Life Shaped the Human Mind* (Thames & Hudson, London, 2014)

Gardner, Howard: *Frames of Mind. The Theory of Multiple Intelligencies* (Heinemann, London, 1984)

Garlake, Peter: *Early Art and Architecture of Africa* (Oxford University Press, Oxford, 2002)

Glubb, John Bagot: *A Short History of the Arab Peoples* (Hodder and Stoughton, London, 1969)

Gocking, Roger S: *The History of Ghana* (Greenwood Press, Westport CT, USA, 2005)

Greene, Barbara: *Land Benighted* (Geoffrey Bles, London, 1938)

Herrnstein, Richard J and Murray, Charles: *The Bell Curve. Intelligence and Class Structure in American Life* (The Free Press, NY, 1994)

Hobsbawm, E J: *The Age of Revolution in Europe 1789 – 1848* (Abacus, London, 1977)

Hochschild, Adam: *King Leopold's Ghost. A Story of Greed, Terror and Heroism in Colonial Africa* (Macmillan, London, 1999)

Horton, James Africanus B: *West African Countries and Peoples … and a Vindication of the African Race* (W J Johnson, 121 Fleet Street, London, 1868)

Horton, Africanus B: *Political Conditions of the Gold Coast* (1870; second edition introduced by E A Ayandele; Frank Cass & Co, London, 1970)

Huxley, Aldous: *Little Mexican and other stories* (Chatto and Windus, London, 1928)

Iliffe, John: *Africans. The history of a continent* (Cambridge University Press, Cambridge, 1995)

Irele, Abiola: *The African Experience in Literature and Ideology* (Heinemann Educational Books Ltd, London 1981)

James, Lawrence: *Empires in the Sun. The Struggle for the Mastery of Africa: 1830-1990* (Weidenfeld & Nicolson, London, 2016)

Jeal, Tim: *Stanley. The Impossible Life of Africa's Greatest Explorer* (faber and faber, London, 2007)

Jean, Clinton M: *Behind the Eurocentric Veils. The Search for African Realities* (University of Massachusetts Press, Amherst, 1991)

Jerven, Morton: *Poor Numbers. How We Are Misled by African Development Statistics and What to Do about It* (Cornell University Press, Ithaca, 2013)

Johnson, R W: *How Long Will South Africa Survive?* (Hurst and Company, London, 2015)

Juma, Calestous: *The New Harvest. Agricultural Innovation in Africa* (Oxford University Press, Oxford, 2011)

Kapuscinki, Ryszard: *The Shadow of the Sun. My African Life* (trans from Polish by Klara Glowczewska; Allen Lane, The Penguin Press, London, 1998)

Kemp, Barry J: *Ancient Egypt. Anatomy of a Civilization* (Routledge, London, 1989)

Lamb, David: *The Africans* (Bodley Head, London, 1983)

Law, Robin (ed): *From slave trade to 'legitimate' commerce. The commercial transition in nineteenth-century West Africa* (Cambridge University Press, Cambridge, 2002)

Leach, E R: *Social Anthropology* (Oxford University Press, Oxford, 1982)

Leslie, Ian: *Curious. The Desire to Know & Why Your Future Depends on it* (Quercus, London, 2014)

Levtzion, Nehemia: *Ancient Ghana and Mali* (Methuen & Co Ltd, London, 1973)

Levtzion, Nehemia and Pouwels, Randall L (eds): *The History of Islam in Africa* (Ohio University Press, Athens, Ohio, 2000)

Lodge, Tom: *Mandela. A Critical Life* (Oxford University Press, Oxford, 2006)

Lynch, Hollis R: *Edward Wilmot Blyden. Pan-Negro Patriot 1832-1912* (Oxford University Press, London, 1967)

MacKendrick, Paul: *The North African Stones Speak* (Croom Helm, London, 1980)

Mackintosh-Smith, Tim (ed): *The Travels of Ibn Battutah* (Picador: Macmillan, London, 2002)

Mahama, John Dramani: *My First Coup d'Etat. And Other True Stories from the Lost Decades of Africa* (Bloomsbury, New York, 2012)

Marcus, Harold G: *A History of Ethiopia* (University of California Press, Berkeley, 1994)

Melvern, Linda: *A People Betrayed. The role of the west in Rwanda's genocide* (Zed Books, London, 2009)

Meredith, Martin: *Mandela. A Biography* (Public Affairs, New York, 2010)

Meyerowitz, Eva L R: *The Divine Kingship in Ghana and Ancient Egypt* (Faber and Faber, London 1960)

Miele, Frank: *Intelligence, Race and Genetics. Conversations with Arthur R Jensen* (Westview Press, Boulder, Colorado and Oxford, 2002)

Mockford, Julian: *Khama: King of the Bamangwato* (Jonathan Cape, London, 1931)

Montesquieu: see de Secondat

Morton, Fred, Ramsay, Jeff & Mgadla, Part Themba: *Historical Dictionary of Botswana* (4th ed, The Scarecrow Press, Inc, Lanham, Maryland, 2008)

Moyo, Dambisa: *Dead Aid. Why Aid Makes Things Worse and How There is Another Way for Africa.* (Penguin Books, London, 2010)

Moyo, Dambisa F: *Winner Take All. China's Race For Resources and What It Means For Us* (Allen Lane, London, 2012)

Naylor, Phillip C: *North Africa. A History from Antiquity to the Present* (Texas University Press, Austin, 2009)

Niven, Rex: *Nine Great Africans* (G Bell and Sons, London, 1964)

North, John: *Attributing colour to the ancient Egyptians: Reflections on* Black Athena. In: David O'Connor and Andrew Reid (eds): *Ancient Egypt in Africa* (Left Coast Press, Walnut Creek, CA; publication of the Institute of Archaeology, University College London, 2003)

Nussbaum, Martha C: *The New Religious Intolerance. Overcoming the Politics of Fear in an Anxious Age* (Belknap Press of Harvard University, Cambridge, Mass, 2012)

O'Connor, David: *Ancient Nubia: Egypt's rival in Africa* (University of Pennsylvania, Philadelphia, 1993)

O'Connor, David and Reid, Andrew (eds): *Ancient Egypt in Africa* (Left Coast Press, Walnut Creek, CA; publication of the Institute of Archaeology, University College London, 2003)

Oliver, Roland: *The African Experience* (Weidenfeld & Nicolson, London, 1991)

Oliver, Roland and Atmore, Anthony: *Africa since 1800* (third edition, Cambridge University Press, Cambridge, 1981)

Osaghae, Eghosa E: *Crippled Giant. Nigeria since Independence* (Hurst & Co, London, 1998)

Pakenham, Thomas: *The Scramble for Africa 1876-1912* (Weidenfeld and Nicolson, London, 1991)

Pasternak, Charles: *Quest. The Essence of Humanity* (Wiley, Chichester, 2003)

Pasternak, Charles: *Curiosity and Quest*. In Charles Pasternak (ed): *What Makes Us Human?* (Oneworld, Oxford, 2007)

Pasternak, Charles (ed): *Access Not Excess. The search for better nutrition* (Smith-Gordon, St Ives, Cambridgeshire, 2011)

Pasternak, Charles: *Blinkers. Scientific ignorance and evasion* (Smith-Gordon, Huntingdon, Cambridgeshire, 2012)

Pauketat, Timothy R: *Ancient Cahokia and the Mississippians* (Cambridge University Press, Cambridge, 2004)

Plomin, Robert, Defries, John C, Craig, Ian W and McGuffin, Peter (eds): *Behavioral Genetics in the Postgenomic Era* (American Psychological Association, Washington, DC, 2002)

Prunier, Gérard: *The Rwanda Crisis. History of a Genocide* (Hurst and Company, London, 1998)

Ransford, Oliver: *'Bid the Sickness Cease'. Disease in the History of Black Africa* (John Murray, London, 1983)

Rice, Michael: *Egypt's Making. The Origins of Ancient Egypt 5000-2000 BC* (Routledge, London, 1990)

Rodney, Walter: *How Europe Underdeveloped Africa* (Pambazuka Press, Cape Town, 2012; earlier editions: Codesria, Dakar; Bogle-l'Ouverture Publications, London; Howard U Press, Washington, DC)

Sachs, Jeffrey D: *Tropical Underdevelopment* (Working Paper 8119, National Bureau of Economic Research, Cambridge, MA, 2001)

Segal, Ronald: *African Profiles* (Penguin Books, London, 1963)

Segal. Ronald: *The Black Diaspora* (faber and faber, London, 1995)

Segal, Ronald: *Black Slaves. The history of Africa's other black diaspora* (Atlantic Books, London, 2001).

Senghor, Léopold Sédar: *Négritude et Civilisation de L'Universel* (Éditions du Seuil, 27, rue Jacob, Paris VI, 1977)

Shinnie, P L: *Meroë: a civilization of the Sudan* (Thames and Hudson, London 1967)

Skinner, Elliott P: *West African Economic Systems*, in *Economic Transition in Africa* (ed M J Herskovits and M Harvitz, Northwestern University Press, Evanston, Ill, 1964)

Stanley, Henry M: *Coomassie. The story of the campaign in Africa 1873-4* (Sampson Low, Marston and Co, London, 1896)

Stoecker, Helmuth (ed): *German Imperialism in Africa. From the Beginnings until the Second World War* (translated from German by Bernd Zöllner; C Hurst & Co, London, 1986)

Stringer, Chris: *The Origin of Our Species* (Allen Lane, London, 2011)

Suddendorf, Thomas: *The Gap. The science of what separates us from other animals* (Basic Books, New York, 2013)

Tainter, Joseph A: *The Collapse of Complex Societies* (Cambridge University Press, Cambridge, 1988)

Tattersall, Ian: *Masters of the Planet. The Search for Our Human Origins* (Palgrave Macmillan, New York 2012)

Temple, Robert K G: *The Sirius Mystery* (Sidgwick and Jackson, London, 1976; second ed 1998)

Temple, Robert: *The Crystal Sun. Rediscovering a Lost Technology of the Ancient World* (Century, London, 2000)

Toynbee, Arnold J: *A Study of History* (vols I-VI, abridged by D C Somervell, Oxford University Press, New York, 1946)

Vaillant, Janet G: *Black, French and African. A Life of Léopold Sédar Senghor* (Harvard University Press, Cambridge, Massachusetts, 1990)

Vansina, Jan: *Antecedents to Modern Rwanda. The Nyiginya Kingdom* (James Currey, Oxford, 2004)

van Vugt, Mark and Ahuja, Anjana: *Selected. Why some people lead, why others follow, and why it matters* (Profile Books, London, 2010)

von Maltzahn, Imre: *An Austro-German as an Englishman. A Life, Times and Commentaries 1938-2015* (Austin Macauley, London 2016)

Wendorf, Fred and Schild, Romuald (eds): *Prehistory of the Eastern Sahara* (Academic Press, NY, 1980)

Williams, Susan: *Colour Bar. The triumph of Seretse Khama and his nation* (Allen Lane, London, 2006)

Wilson, Edward O: *The Social Conquest of Earth* (Liveright Publishing Corporation, NY, 2012)

Wolpert, Stanley: *Gandhi's Passion. The Life and Legacy of Mahatma Gandhi* (Oxford University Press, 2001)

Yanacopulos, Helen and Hanlon, Joseph (eds): *Civil War, Civil Peace* (Ohio University Press, Athens, Ohio, 2006)

Zewde, Bahru: *A History of Modern Ethiopia 1855-1974* (James Currey, London, 1991)

INDEX

This book was produced by

www.wordsbydesign.co.uk

Words by Design offers a range of services to individual and corporate clients, as well as to the printing and publishing industry.

In a digital age, authors wish to publish their own books; families seek to research and write the history of their ancestors; businesses see the marketing significance of commissioning their corporate history; and publishers use freelance experts in all the many varied stages of publishing.

At Words by Design we have the necessary experience and knowledge to help with these and many other projects. With expertise in research, writing, editing, design, photography, typesetting and print production, we aim to be able to help on any project.

office@wordsbydesign.co.uk
+44 (0)1869 327548